European Conquest and the Rights of Indigenous Peoples

Paul Keal examines the historical role of international law and political theory in justifying the dispossession of indigenous peoples as part of the expansion of international society. He argues that, paradoxically, law and political theory can now underpin the recovery of indigenous rights. At the heart of contemporary struggles is the core right of self-determination, and Keal argues for recognition of indigenous peoples as 'peoples' with the right of self-determination in constitutional and international law, and for adoption of the Draft Declaration on the Rights of Indigenous Peoples by the General Assembly. He asks whether the theory of international society can accommodate indigenous peoples and considers the political arrangements needed for states to satisfy indigenous claims. The book also questions the moral legitimacy of international society and examines notions of collective guilt and responsibility.

PAUL KEAL is a Fellow of the Department of International Relations at the Research School of Pacific and Asian Studies, The Australian National University. He is the author of *Unspoken Rules and Super Power Dominance* (1983), editor of *Ethics and Foreign Policy* (1992), and with Andrew Mack, co-editor of *Security and Arms Control in the North Pacific* (1988).

CAMBRIDGE STUDIES IN INTERNATIONAL RELATIONS: 92

European Conquest and the Rights of Indigenous Peoples

Cambridge Studies in International Relations is a joint initiative of Cambridge University Press and the British International Studies Association (BISA). The series will include a wide range of material, from undergraduate textbooks and surveys to research-based monographs and collaborative volumes. The aim of the series is to publish the best new scholarship in International Studies from Europe, North America and the rest of the world.

CAMBRIDGE STUDIES IN INTERNATIONAL RELATIONS

Series list continues after index

European Conquest and the Rights of Indigenous Peoples

The moral backwardness of international society

Paul Keal

The Australian National University

CAMBRIDGE
UNIVERSITY PRESS

PUBLISHED BY THE PRESS SYNDICATE OF THE UNIVERSITY OF CAMBRIDGE
The Pitt Building, Trumpington Street, Cambridge CB2 1RP, United Kingdom

CAMBRIDGE UNIVERSITY PRESS
The Edinburgh Building, Cambridge, CB2 2RU, UK
40 West 20th Street, New York, NY 10011–4211, USA
477 Williamstown Road, Port Melbourne, VIC 3207, Australia
Ruiz de Alarcón 13, 28014 Madrid, Spain
Dock House, The Waterfront, Cape Town 8001, South Africa

http://www.cambridge.org

First published 2003

Printed in the United Kingdom at the University Press, Cambridge

Typeface Palatino 10/12.5 pt.   *System* LaTeX 2$_\varepsilon$ [TB]

A catalogue record for this book is available from the British Library

Library of Congress cataloguing in publication data
Keal, Paul.
European conquest and the rights of indigenous peoples : the moral
backwardness of international society / Paul Keal.
   p.   cm. – (Cambridge studies in international relations; 92)
Includes bibliographical references and index.
ISBN 0 521 82471 0 (hb) – ISBN 0 521 53179 9 (pb)
1. Indigenous peoples – Legal status, laws, etc.   I. Title.   II. Series.
K3247 K43   2003   323.1 – dc21
2003043946

ISBN 0 521 82471 0 hardback
ISBN 0 521 53179 9 paperback

Contents

Acknowledgements

The intellectual and personal debts I have accrued over the years extend far beyond the time I have spent researching and writing this book. The idea to write it came to me from reading a passage in the Postscript to the second edition of Andrew Linklater's *Men and Citizens in the Theory of International Relations*. I am very grateful to Andrew, not only for this but his friendship and support over many years. An initial draft of the book was written while I was on study leave in the Department of International Relations at Keele University. The welcoming members of that Department helped make it a very productive time and I thank the University of New South Wales for making it possible for me to be there. After returning from Keele I had the good fortune to meet Jim Tully then visiting Canberra. His suggestions and encouragement have been fundamental. Special thanks must also go to Steve Smith who generously gave me his time and guidance.

At the Australian National University, Greg Fry has been my close friend, intellectual companion and trenchant but always constructive critic for almost longer than either of us probably care to remember. Our colleagues in the Department of International Relations and in other parts of the ANU make it a splendid place to work. I am especially thankful to Chris Reus-Smit, Heather Rae and Pete Van Ness for their friendship and support. Barry Hindess and Tim Rowse from the ANU's Research School of Social Sciences both generously read an earlier version of the book and made incisive comments and I thank them for doing so. Among the community of Australian international relations scholars outside Canberra I would like to thank Jacinta O'Hagen, Richard Devatak and Richard Shapcott for their good humoured camaraderie and continuing conversation. From outside Australia I have been privileged by the support and friendship given to me by Nick Wheeler, Tim Dunne, Richard Little and Rob Walker.

I am very grateful to the anonymous readers for Cambridge University Press for their incisive and helpful comments, which have helped make the book better than it would otherwise have been. I wish to also thank John Haslam at the Press for his patience and advice. In preparing the book for publication I have been cheerfully helped by Mary Lou Hickey and Michelle Burgis. My special thanks go to Robin Ward for compiling the index and to Sheila Kane for her meticulous copy editing.

Ever since beginning university studies I have been engaged in a long conversation about many things with Daniel Connell. His unfailing friendship over the years has been inestimable. So also has been the patience, understanding, love and support given to me by Leonie and my daughters Hannah and Onela. Without them I would not have been able to complete the book.

Introduction

This book investigates the representation of indigenous peoples and the denial of their sovereign rights as an important but neglected aspect of the expansion of international society. The expansion of the European society of states to an international society global in scope entailed the progressive dispossession and subordination of non-European peoples. As well as being a society of states international society represents a moral community with shifting boundaries. From its inception these boundaries were drawn in ways that involved the simultaneous inclusion and exclusion of certain categories of non-Europeans. In the early phases of European expansion the first nations encountered by Europeans were granted rights but these were gradually eroded in response to the changing demands of European colonists. These rights are now being reclaimed by indigenous peoples in ongoing struggles with the settler societies in which they are located.

International society assumes the legitimacy of states as a form of political organisation and has as one of its purposes the preservation of the states system. It also sets the standards against which the moral standing of states is measured. Increasingly, the moral standing or legitimacy of particular states is bound up with the extent to which other members of international society perceive them to be protecting the rights of their citizens. In this book I am particularly interested in the ways in which indigenous rights are also fundamental to the moral legitimacy of particular states. This theme was suggested to me by Tim Rowse's discussion of the Australian 'nation's responsibility to indigenous people'. Rowse refers to the version of Australia's colonisation told by Hobbles Danayarri, an aboriginal resident of Australia's Northern Territory and the High Court case initiated by Eddie Mabo that resulted in the recognition of native title. Rowse comments that Mabo's legal argument and Danayarri's story of colonisation, though in different ways, make the same point: ' "Australia" is morally illegitimate to the extent that it is founded on European denial of the continent's prior ownership by indigenous people.'[1]

To my mind this suggested interesting and important questions about what constitutes a morally legitimate state and a morally legitimate international society. I argue that the moral legitimacy of states with unresolved indigenous claims, like those that abuse human rights, is in question, and that it follows from this that the legitimacy of international society as a defender of such states is also questionable. Rather than accept that the expansion of international society, resulting in the establishment of the state as a universal form of political organisation, has been a success story, I argue that the dispossession and destruction of indigenous societies is part of the dark side of the story of expansion which needs correction. I further argue that the moral basis of international society ought to be an obligation to promote and safeguard world order, understood, not just as order between states, but in human society as a whole. The worth of international society would then be measured by the extent to which it furthers world order values, including especially the welfare and rights of individuals and sub-state groups, both of which include indigenous peoples, everywhere.

International society is both an idea and assumed to be an actual historical and evolving association between states. A major reason for thinking that it is more than an idea is that in their mutual relations with one another states behave as if there is a society of states or an international society. Through both direct negotiation and unspoken inter-subjective understandings states establish norms and rules that govern, not only their conduct towards each other, but also increasingly towards groups and individuals within their borders. To 'refer to an international *society*', writes Chris Brown, 'is simply a way of drawing attention to the (posited) norm-governed relations between states, the fact that there are general practices and customs of international law and diplomacy to which states usually adhere.'[2] In this book I am interested in how indigenous peoples have figured in both the theory and practices of international society.

I have chosen to focus on international society for four reasons. First, the story of its origins and expansion is important for understanding

---

[1] Tim Rowse, Mabo and Moral Anxiety, *Meanjin*, 2 (Winter 1993), p. 229.
[2] Chris Brown, 'Moral Agency and International Society,' *Ethics and International Affairs*, 15: 2 (2001), p. 89.

contemporary world politics, but is incomplete. It has been told as one in which, according to Bull, the 'society of Christian or European states [became] . . . global or all-inclusive'.[3] Bull did not mean to suggest by this that there were already existing non-Western states waiting to be admitted to the society of European states. Rather, that the modern states system originated in Europe and expanded from there to become universal. For indigenous peoples the expansion of this society was not all-inclusive. As well as anything else the story of the expansion of international society is one of state formation which often resulted in the decimation of indigenous peoples or, if not that, at least the destruction of their cultures. Indigenous peoples were isolated from state formation and largely excluded from the full rights enjoyed by citizens of the states that are the members of international society. Understanding the reasons for this exclusion and how the rights of indigenous peoples are more recently being incorporated into the norms of international society is necessary to making the story of the expansion of international society more complete than it has been.

Second, early conceptions of international society included individuals and sub-state groups, as well as states. The subsequent inclusion of individuals and groups in the theory and practice of international society has not been consistent or sustained, but is immanent in both and has found expression in human rights. Further inclusion can be achieved by, for instance, giving formal recognition to indigenous rights.

Third, international society occupies the middle ground between the bleak world of realism, in which individuals have no international personality and sovereign states are driven by their own narrow self-interest, and the morally desirable, but possibly unobtainable, cosmopolitan ideal of the great society of humankind. The survival of international society requires states to act sometimes in the interests of the society as a whole and to defend the internationally accepted rights of individuals. Through the adoption and promotion of indigenous rights international society could contribute to the achievement of a more cosmopolitan moral order.

Finally, international society is constituted by rules and norms. New norms regarding indigenous peoples have emerged in the context of international society and been facilitated by it. There is considerable scope for extending the rules and norms of international society to more fully

---

[3] Hedley Bull, 'The Importance of Grotius in the study of International Relations' in H. N. Bull, B. Kingsbury and A. Roberts (eds.), *Hugo Grotius and International Relations* (Oxford: Clarendon Press, 1992), p. 80.

include indigenous peoples. This will mean the adoption of norms, such as self-determination, which states perceive to be against their interests. Self-determination is a particular challenge to states, but I shall argue later that it need not be. Indigenous peoples generally are not seeking secession but, instead, control over the conditions of their existence within already existing state structures.

As an object of study, international society is a central concern of the tradition of theorising about international relations that Martin Wight named 'rationalism'. For Wight, rationalism was one of three such traditions, the other two being 'realism' and 'revolutionism'. Alternative names for each of these traditions come from the major thinker associated with them. Rationalism is consequently also known as the Grotian view of the world, realism as the Hobbesian and revolutionism as the Kantian.[4] By 'rationalism' Wight did not mean philosophical rationalism, which contrasts *a priori* reason with empiricism as sources of knowledge.[5] Nor did he have in mind the rational choice theories that inform neo-realist and neo-liberal theories of international relations.[6] Wight's sense of rationalism is derived from Grotius, who as well as being a highly influential thinker about international society, placed natural law at the centre of his thought. Natural law, discoverable by right reason, is essential to Grotius's conception of international society. Natural law binds not only individuals but also states. The rights of states are the rights that individuals have and indeed states derive their rights from those of individuals. For Grotius, states are the moral equivalents of individuals in a state of nature.[7] In short, rationalism is a reference to the use of reason as the means to discovering the natural law at the core of Grotius's conception of international society. Natural law has long since ceased to have the importance it once had, and as

---

[4] Martin Wight, Gabriele Wight and Brian Porter (eds.), *International Theory: The Three Traditions* (Leicester: Leicester University Press, 1991).

[5] For a discussion of this see John Cottingham, *Rationalism* (London: Paladin, 1984), pp. 6–7, and Lawrence H. Simon, 'Rationalism' in E. Craig (ed.), *The Routledge Encyclopedia of Philosophy*, vol. ix (London: Routledge, 1998), pp. 75–86.

[6] See, for example, Robert Keohane, 'International Institutions: Two Approaches' in R. Keohane, *International Institutions and State Power* (Boulder: Westview Press, 1989), Herbert Simon, 'Human Nature in Politics: The Dialogue with Political Science', *The American Political Science Review*, 79: 2 (June 1985), pp. 293–304, Robert Gilpin, *War and Change in World Politics* (Cambridge University Press, 1981), and Alexander E. Wendt, 'The Agent–Structure Problem in International Relations Theory', *International Organisation*, 41: 3 (Summer 1987), pp. 335–370.

[7] Richard Tuck, *The Rights of War and Peace: Political Thought and the International Order from Grotius to Kant* (Oxford University Press, 1999), p. 82.

4

much as anything else rationalism is now shorthand for conceptions of international life that centre on international society.

The rationalist tradition figures in this book precisely because international society is its central concern. I believe international society is a powerful and important idea with increasing relevance to world politics and regard that as sufficient reason for being interested in rationalism. That said, I want to make it clear that I do not believe it is acceptable to simply carve up thought about international relations into Martin Wight's three traditions. Apart from any other consideration, the identification of Grotius, Hobbes and Kant each with one of the traditions is misleading, especially with regard to the question of natural sociability. Sociability encompasses the important issue of how we should treat 'others' and conceive of proper relations with them. Hobbes is seen typically as having promulgated an 'unsociable' theory of human nature which stands in contrast to the views shared by Grotius and Pufendorf and their successors Locke and Vattel. Kant regarded Hobbes as being right in disparaging the idea of a general society of mankind and dismissed Grotius and Pufendorf as 'sorry comforters'.[8] Contrary to this, Richard Tuck persuasively argues that Grotius, Hobbes and Kant held essentially similar views on sociability. There are thus important continuities as well as differences between the thinkers of Wight's three traditions, but to be fair, he did emphasise that there is an inter-play between them.

My departure point in this book is Bull and Watson's work on the expansion of international society.[9] The book is in some respects a continuation of that project but has drawn from a much more diverse set of writers and concerns, from both within and outside of the discipline of international relations. From within international relations scholarship it has been inspired by Andrew Linklater's work on inclusion, exclusion and community,[10] Chris Brown's insights into human rights, culture and the ethical character of international society,[11] Richard Shapcott's

---

[8] Ibid, pp. 12, 209.
[9] Hedley Bull and Adam Watson (eds.), *The Expansion of International Society* (Oxford University Press, 1985).
[10] Andrew Linklater, *Men and Citizens in the Theory of International Relations*, 2nd edn (London: Macmillan, 1990), and Andrew Linklater, *The Transformation of Political Community: Ethical Foundations of the Post-Westphalian Community* (Cambridge: Polity, 1998).
[11] Chris Brown, 'International Theory And International Society: The Viability of the Middle Way', *Review of International Studies*, 21: 2 (1995), pp. 183–196. Chris Brown, 'Universal human rights: a critique' in Timothy Dunne and Nicholas J. Wheeler (eds.), *Human Rights*

studies of diversity and the need for dialogue between cultures,[12] and Tim Dunn's intellectual history of international society, together with his work on colonial encounters.[13] Beyond international relations Richard Tuck's work on natural rights and *The Rights of War and Peace*,[14] James Tully on Locke's theory of property and his later work on diverse federalism and multinational states,[15] and finally Anthony Pagden's magisterial studies of European Encounters with the New World[16] have all been of fundamental importance.

The principal general questions guiding this inquiry into the consequences of the expansion of international society are these: How did Europeans represent non-Europeans? How were these representations deployed in conceptualising rights and justifying dispossession? How are indigenous rights now being recovered? What political and moral problems resulted from European expansion? What forms of political organisation do states need to adopt in order for international society to be regarded as a legitimate guardian of indigenous rights? Does rationalism have the capacity to conceptualize such a society?

Before beginning to address any of these questions the remainder of this introduction first discusses what is meant by the term 'indigenous peoples'. It then sets some limits to the scope of the examples used in the book and concludes with a statement of the content of the chapters to follow.

Defining indigenous peoples

There is no one fixed or incontrovertible definition of the term 'indigenous peoples'. How the term should be understood has long been and continues to be a controversial question. The most widely cited

in Global Politics (Cambridge University Press, 1999), Chris Brown, 'Cultural diversity and international political theory', *Review of International Studies* 26: 2 (April 2000), pp. 199–213, and Brown, 'Moral Agency and International Society', pp. 87–98.

[12] Richard Shapcott, *Justice, Community and Dialogue in International Relations* (Cambridge University Press, 2001).

[13] Timothy Dunne, 'Colonial Encounters in International Relations: Reading Wight, Writing Australia', *Australian Journal of International Affairs*, 51: 3 (November 1997) and Dunne, *Inventing International Society: A History of the English School* (London: Macmillan, 1998).

[14] Tuck, *Rights of War and Peace* and Richard Tuck, *Natural Rights Theories: Their Origin and Development* (Cambridge University Press, 1979).

[15] James Tully, *An Approach to Political Philosophy: Locke in Contexts* (Cambridge University Press, 1993) and James Tully, *Strange Muliplicity: Constitutionalism in an Age of Diversity* (Cambridge University Press, 1995).

[16] Anthony Pagden, *European Encounters with the New World: From Renaissance to Romanticism* (New Haven: Yale University Press, 1993).

definition has been the one advanced in 1986 by Special Rapporteur José Martinez Cobo:

> Indigenous communities, peoples and nations are those which, having a historical continuity with pre-invasion and pre-colonial societies that developed on their territories, consider themselves distinct from other sectors of the societies now prevailing in those territories or parts of them. They form at present non-dominant sectors of society and are determined to preserve, develop, and transmit to future generations of their ancestral territories, and their ethnic identity, the basis of their continued existence as peoples, in accordance with their cultural patterns, social institutions and legal systems.[17]

This means an indigenous person is 'One who belongs to these Indigenous populations through self-identification as Indigenous (group consciousness) and is recognised and accepted by these populations as one of its members (acceptance by the group).'[18]

Cobo's definition encompasses four key inter-related factors common to most definitions of indigenous peoples: subjection to colonial settlement, historical continuity with pre-invasion or pre-colonial societies, an identity that is distinct from the dominant society in which they are encased, and a concern with the preservation and replication of culture. Of these, continuity with pre-invasion societies and social, cultural and economic conditions are written also into the definitions contained in Article 1 of the International Labour Organisation's Convention 169 and the Draft of the Inter-American Declaration on the Rights of Indigenous Peoples. Additionally, the latter includes, as well as peoples 'who embody historical continuity with societies which existed prior to . . . conquest, – peoples brought involuntarily to the New World'.[19] Belonging to non-dominant sectors of society and being concerned with the preservation of culture are attributes indigenous people share with minorities that might not be indigenous. To more fully appreciate the difficulties involved in defining 'indigenous peoples' it is necessary to enlarge upon the factors just mentioned and the related concepts of self-determination and self-identification.

---

[17] José Martinez Cobo, *Study of the Problem against Indigenous Populations*, vol. v, *Conclusions, Proposals and Recommendations*, UN Doc E/CN 4/Sub 2 1986/7, Add 4, para 379 and 381. Cited by Sarah Pritchard (ed.), *Indigenous Peoples, the United Nations and Human Rights* (London: Zed Books, 1998), p. 43.
[18] Ibid.
[19] Sharon Venne, *Our Elders Understand Our Rights: Evolving International Law Regarding Indigenous Rights* (Penticon, BC: Theytus Books, 1998), p. 219.

Colonial settlement

Indigenous peoples define themselves and are defined by others in terms of a common experience of subjection to colonial settlement. Further, while Europeans have not been the only colonisers, indigenous peoples are typically framed by reference to European settlement. This much is demonstrated by Benedict Kingsbury when he explains that the governments of several 'Asian states argue that the concept of "indigenous peoples" is so integrally a product of the common experience of European colonial settlement as to be fundamentally inapplicable to those parts of Asia that did not experience substantial European settlement.'[20] The position of China, for instance, 'is that the concept . . . is inextricably bound up with, and indeed a function of, European colonialism.' In this way China links the situation and definition of indigenous peoples to 'saltwater settler colonialism'.[21] I will return to the position of Asian states concerning indigenous peoples shortly; for the moment, it is sufficient to note only that the term is, in the broadest sense, 'used nationally and internationally to refer to colonized peoples of the world who are prevented from controlling their own lives, resources, and Cultures',[22] which currently includes West Papuans. The issues that most concern indigenous populations are perceived to be ones that have resulted from a collective history of colonisation.[23]

One consequence of linking the definition of indigenous peoples to colonisation, particularly in the deliberations of the United Nations, was that at the time of decolonisation 'the entire non-settler or non-European population of European colonies' was regarded as "indigenous peoples"'. The failure to distinguish between different peoples contained within the boundaries of new states established by formal decolonisation meant that for many indigenous peoples one set of oppressors had been replaced by another.[24] It is then hardly surprising that many indigenous peoples around the world do not accept that colonialism has

---

[20] Benedict Kingsbury, 'The Applicability of the International Legal Concept of "Indigenous Peoples" in Asia' in J. R. Bauer and D. A. Bell (eds.), *The East Asia Challenge For Human Rights* (Cambridge University Press, 1999), p. 340.
[21] Kingsbury, 'Applicability', p. 350.
[22] Independent Commission on Humanitarian Issues 1987, cited by Andrew Gray, 'The Indigenous Movement in Asia' in R. H. Barnes, A. Gray and B. Kingsbury (eds.), *Indigenous Peoples of Asia* (Ann Arbor, MI: Association for Asian Studies, 1995), Monograph and Occasional Paper Series, 48, p. 35.
[23] Raidza Torres Wick, 'Revisiting the Emerging International Norm on Indigenous Rights: Autonomy as an Option', *Yale Journal of International Law* 16 (Summer 2000), p. 1.
[24] Gray, 'Indigenous Movement', p. 37.

ended. This applies not only to indigenous peoples in states dominated by people of European origin but also those in anti-colonial states now ruled by non-Europeans, such as India, Indonesia and the Philippines.

Historical continuity

For the Cree scholar Sharon Venne the answer to the question 'Who are Indigenous Peoples?', is straightforward. 'They are the descendents of the peoples occupying a territory when the colonizers arrived.'[25] Indigenous peoples are the prior occupants of lands colonised. As the Office of the High Commissioner for Human Rights put it: 'Indigenous or aboriginal peoples are so-called because they were living on their lands before settlers came from elsewhere: they are the descendants . . . of those who inhabited the country or a geographical region at the time when people of different cultures or ethnic origins arrived, the new arrivals later becoming dominant through conquest, occupation, settlement or other means.'[26] Continuity with pre-invasion or pre-colonial societies is therefore an essential element in the definition of indigenous peoples and is, to reiterate an earlier point, inscribed into the definition given in Article 1(b) of the International Labour Organisation's 1989 Convention 169. It also underpins Stavenhagen's definition of 'indigenous populations' as 'the original inhabitants of a territory who, because of historical circumstances (generally conquest and/or colonisation by other people), have lost their sovereignty and have become subordinated to the wider society of and the state over which they exercise no control'.[27] This draws attention to descent from original inhabitants, domination by others and loss of sovereignty as defining factors, but it neglects the central importance of cultural identity.

Identifying indigenous peoples as the occupants of territory at the time of colonisation involves some difficulties. People who clearly are the 'historical descendents of original inhabitants are termed *aboriginal* or *autochthonous*'. Where there are such people 'indigenous' does refer 'to the inhabitants of areas that were overtaken by a settler form of colonisation'. In places where this occurred, such as the Arctic, the Americas,

[25] Venne, *Our Elders*, p. 88.
[26] Office of the High Commissioner for Human Rights, Fact Sheet No. 9 (Rev. 1), The Rights of Indigenous Peoples, http://www.unhchr.ch/html/menu6/2/fs9.htm accessed 14/3/2002.
[27] Rodolfo Stavenhagen cited by Richard Falk, 'The Rights of Peoples (in Particular Indigenous Peoples)' in J. Crawford (ed.), *The Rights of Peoples* (Oxford: Clarendon Press, 1979), p. 18.

Australia, New Zealand and parts of the Pacific, aboriginal and non-aboriginal peoples are clearly distinguishable. Gray points out, however, that 'whereas all aboriginal people are indigenous, not all indigenous people are aboriginal'. To be aboriginal a people must be the original occupants but in a number of cases people regarded as indigenous are not the original inhabitants. Gray cites the example of the Chackma of the Chittagong Hill Tracts in Bangladesh. They 'were by no means the first people to enter the Hill Tracts; – only the Kuki peoples can be considered indigenous to the Hill Tracts'. Regardless of this, Gray argues, 'all the tribal peoples of the Hill Tracts would be considered equally indigenous *vis-à-vis* the later Bengali settlers and the Bangladesh army ...'. For this reason he advocates using the term 'prior' instead of 'original'. 'The concept of "prior" is useful because it avoids speculative history as to who are the "original" peoples of an area and concentrates on current patterns of colonialism.'[28]

Defining indigenous peoples in terms of who came first is one reason why India and China insist that the concept does not apply within their borders. India claims it does not 'because after centuries of migration, absorption, and differentiation it is impossible to say who came first'. China similarly argues 'that all of the nationalities in China have lived there for eons'.[29] Not only this, Kingsbury cites Fiji and Malaysia to make the case that who came first is not always a helpful criteria:

> In effect, if some people are "indigenous" to a place, others are vulnerable to being targeted as non-indigenous, and groups deemed to be migrants or otherwise subject to social stigma may bear the brunt of a nativist "indigenist" policy. Once indigenousness or "sons of the soil" becomes the basis of legitimation for a politically or militarily dominant group, restraints on abuses of power can be difficult to maintain.

His observation about this is that continuity works 'well enough in some regions but is unlikely to be adequate and workable in all regions'.[30]

Kingsbury's arguments concerning the difficulties inherent in applying the term to Asia are reinforced by Owen Lynch who declares that his experiences in Asia and Africa had left him 'studiously avoiding any effort to develop a precise definition of indigenous'.[31] Consequently, he suggests that a two tiered description can be applied to indigenous peoples.

---

[28] Gray, 'Indigenous Movement', pp. 38–39.
[29] Kingsbury, 'Applicability', p. 352.   [30] Ibid., p. 353.
[31] Owen J. Lynch, 'The Sacred and the Profane', *St. Thomas Law Review*, 9 (Fall 1996).

The first tier relates to ethnic groups that are original long-term occupants of a region, such as the great billion-strong Han people in
eastern China: or, the Javanese who live on the densely populated island of Java, in Indonesia. – The second tier is more specific and local,
and more closely fits what we think of as indigenous in the American
context. It refers to people still residing in the ancestral domains of
their fore-bearers.[32]

A further complication associated with the notion of being 'first' or
'original' is that it appears to imply a set of rights against states in
which indigenous peoples are located. As Fleras puts it: indigenous
peoples 'are descendants of the original occupants of land, whose inherent and collective rights to self-determination over the jurisdictions
of land, identity, and political voice have never been extinguished by
conquest, occupation or treaty, but only need to be reactivated as a basis
for redefining their relationship with the State'.[33] The claims to rights
that indigenous peoples have made and might in future make are an important factor in the suspicions and reluctance of some governments to
admit the concept of indigenous. In Kingsbury's words: 'If "indigenous
peoples" are deemed in international practice to have particular entitlements to land, territory, and resources, based on historical connections,
customary practices, and the interdependence of land and culture, the
question whether a particular group is an "indigenous people" may
take on great political and legal importance'.[34] A number of states, particularly in Asia, are simply not willing to admit these entitlements,
connections and interdependencies. In essence, the indigenous movement is for many states an actual or potential challenge, especially as it
extends to the fundamental issue of self-determination.

The search for self-determination

For indigenous people the state should not be allowed to 'take control out of the hands of those who live within its area'.[35] Indigenous
peoples around the world are united by a common concern with control of land, preventing the exploitation of natural resources to the
detriment of indigenous rights and ways of life, and cultural survival or preservation; all of which cohere in the 'overarching theme of

---

[32] Ibid., p. 95.
[33] Augie Fleras, 'Politicising Indigeneity: Ethno-politics in White Settler Dominions',
in P. Havermann (ed.), *Indigenous Peoples' Rights in Australia, Canada and New Zealand*
(Auckland: Oxford University Press, 1999), p. 219.
[34] Kingsbury, 'Applicability', p. 337. [35] Gray, 'Indigenous Movement', p. 41.

self-determination'.[36] Andrew Gray thus explains that 'Indigenous peoples use *self-determination* to express most broadly their aim of controlling their political, cultural, and economic lives.'[37] Self-determination is, he asserts, 'the clinching concept in the definition of *indigenous* . . .'[38] The self-determination sought by indigenous peoples is inescapably linked to the identity they have as peoples who lived in an area prior to conquest or colonisation and the consequent dispossession of their cultural, economic and political rights. Self-determination is discussed at length in Chapter 4 and further discussion of it need not detain us at this juncture. For the moment it need only be noted that the search for self-determination is an identifier of indigenous peoples, but it is not unique to them.

Self-identification

The concepts discussed so far are all ones that enable individuals and groups to identify themselves as indigenous. Self-identification has been widely regarded as the most acceptable means of defining indigenous peoples and formed, as mentioned earlier, part of Cobo's definition. Sharon Venne observes that indigenous representatives on the Working Group have, more than once, argued that 'a definition is not necessary or desirable' and have instead 'stressed the importance of self-identification as an essential component of any definition which might be elaborated by the United Nations . . .'.[39] As well as expressing scepticism about the need for a definition the prevailing view in the Working Group On Indigenous Peoples has been that 'definition is the concern of Indigenous peoples and not states'.[40] This is in part because states can use definitions based on so-called 'objective' criteria to exclude peoples who regard themselves as indigenous.

Equally, indigenous peoples are concerned that self-identification should not be unrestricted. In particular, they object to it being used as a means by which individuals can either falsely claim to be indigenous or

---

[36] Alison Brysk, 'Turning Weakness into Strength: The Internationalisation of Indian Rights', *Latin American Perspectives*, 23: 2 (Spring (1996), p. 41. See also June Nash, 'The Reassertion of Indigenous Identity: Mayan Reponses to State Intervention in Chiapas', *Latin American Research Review*, 30: 3 (1995), p. 33, Wick, 'Revisiting', p. 1 and Kingsbury, 'Applicability', p. 346.
[37] Gray, 'Indigenous Movement', p. 37.   [38] Ibid., p. 46.
[39] Venne, *Our Elders*, p. 118. Note also Article 2 of ILO 169 which stipulates that: 'Self-identification as indigenous or tribal shall be regarded as a fundamental criterion for determining the groups to which the provisions of this convention might apply.'
[40] Pritchard, *Indigenous Peoples*, p. 43.

over-ride the collective rights of indigenous communities to determine who belongs. Taiaiake Alfred argues that a Native person is not constituted by 'pure self-identification and acting the part, however diligent the research or skilful the act'. For Alfred membership of a community of indigenous peoples

> is a matter of blood and belonging determined through the institutions governing a community at a particular time. – The collective right of Native communities to determine their own membership must be recognised as a fundamental right of self-determination, and respected as such. No individual has the right to usurp the identity of a nation simply by claiming it, much less when a collective decision has been made to the contrary. And no nation (or state or organisation) has the right to force an identity on another nation.[41]

Practical difficulties that can result from self-identification include disputes over entitlements. Examples include whether particular individuals qualify to vote in elections open only to indigenous electors or to receive special benefits intended only for indigenous peoples. An instance of contested electoral rights arose in Australia when, in August 2002, the Federal government delayed elections to the Aboriginal and Torres Strait Islander Commission's Regional Council in the state of Tasmania. The purpose of the delay was to give people who had 'been deleted from a trial Indigenous Electors Roll, on the grounds that they were not Aborigines', the opportunity to appeal.[42] Australia serves also to illustrate the nature of the problems related to benefits. Its 2001 census revealed that as a result of increasingly intermixed families there was, between 1986 and 2001, a substantial growth in the number of people identifying themselves as Aboriginal. The inference drawn from this was that children with one Aboriginal parent are more likely than not to identify themselves as Aboriginal. This prompted two researchers to ask whether government programmes for Aborigines should 'extend to all the children of mixed households in the capital cities?' 'Are they', these scholars continued, 'victims of colonialism or part of the wonderful mixing of people that is modern Australia?'[43] This and the broader question of entitlements can surely be asked of a number of other countries with indigenous populations.

---

[41] Taiaiake Alfred, *Peace, Power, Righteousness: An Indigenous Manifesto* (Ontario: Oxford University Press, 1999), pp. 85–86.
[42] Michael Millet, 'Identity Fight Delays Poll', *Sydney Morning Herald*, 14 August 2002.
[43] Bob Birrell and John Hirst, 'In 2002, Just Who Is an Aborigine?' *Sydney Morning Herald*, 15 August 2002.

If nothing else, the discussion so far should have demonstrated the veracity of the assertion by the United Nations Development Program that despite shared common characteristics there is no single accepted definition that captures the diversity of indigenous peoples. Some of the difficulties that crop up when applying the term to Asia were mentioned above. Benedict Kingsbury, who has had a particular interest in 'the applicability of the international legal concept of "indigenous peoples" ' in Asia, argues for a flexible approach to definition. For him what is most important is the 'fundamental values underlying the concept of "indigenous peoples" ',[44] and these are most likely to be promoted by a flexible approach. This, he explains, 'might involve the compilation of a list of indicia, some of which would be requirements, others strongly indicative but not required in special circumstances, others simply relevant factors to be evaluated and applied in cases of doubt or disagreement'. As requirements Kingsbury lists 'self-identification as a distinct ethnic group; historical experience of, or contingent vulnerability to severe disruption, dislocation, or exploitation; long connection with the region; and the wish to retain distinct identity'.[45] There is considerable overlap between these requirements and the identifying characteristics contained in Cobo's definition. The one clear difference is that for Kingsbury historical continuity is a strong indicia rather than an essential requirement for definition. The reason for this should be clear from the earlier discussion of the problems associated with who came first or who were the original inhabitants of particular sites in Asia.

As will be explained presently, this book is mainly concerned with peoples for whom historical continuity is an important aspect of their rights claims and is not an issue in the way that it is in many Asian states. For the purposes of this book I propose to adopt Cobo's definition and the criteria of self-definition as reference points. An important reason for doing so is that they inform and guide the United Nations. The major forums for promoting indigenous rights operate under the auspices of the United Nations and, as well as this, it is regarded as an organisation that codifies and stands for the values of international society.

At the first session of the Working Group on Indigenous Populations (WGIP), set up under the auspices of the Economic and Security Council (ECOSOC) in 1982, the issue of definition was discussed. The WGIP noted 'the importance of both objective criteria, such as historical continuity, and subjective factors including self-identification', but resolved

---

[44] Kingsbury, 'Applicability', p. 373.   [45] Ibid., p. 374.

to defer the matter of definition. The Eleventh Session of the WGIP, held in 1993, agreed to the Draft Declaration on the Rights of Indigenous Peoples. It recognised 'the right of Indigenous peoples to identify themselves as Indigenous and to be recognised as such', but it did not define 'indigenous peoples'.[46] As late as 1998, five years into the United Nations International Decade of the World's Indigenous Peoples, Sharon Venne was obliged to observe that there was still 'no officially recognised UN definition for Indigenous Peoples'.[47] At this juncture that is still the case but United Nations practice is guided by Cobo's definition. It is regarded as the United Nations definition by relevant United Nations bodies including the United Nations Development Program.[48]

Before concluding this already prolonged inquiry into definition it is necessary to briefly mention two other terms used in the book. The first of these is 'non-Europeans', which includes but is not synonymous with indigenous peoples. In the first three chapters I am concerned with European attitudes towards and representations of non-European others in general. While there were clearly non-Europeans that Europeans thought of either as belonging to a different civilisation or as having achieved a higher level of development than others, the concept of 'indigenous' was not part of the debate. Using the term non-European avoids the unnecessary complication of having to decide whether particular peoples were the 'first' or 'original' and were properly speaking 'indigenous'. My preference is instead to think of them as the peoples who occupied territories and regions prior to the arrival of Europeans. In many cases the peoples encountered were 'indigenous', and, equally, representations of non-Europeans either referred to peoples who would now be called indigenous or could be applied to such peoples. In later chapters the focus is contemporary and is more rigorously focused on the narrower category of indigenous peoples rather than the broader one of 'non-Europeans'.

The second and more straightforward term is 'first nations'. This is used principally by the indigenous peoples of North America to describe themselves. As well as indicating that the members of first nations are the descendants of those who occupied land and territory before the arrival of Europeans, it encapsulates the fact that there are many distinct groups of indigenous people in North America. The first nations of

---

[46] Pritchard, *Indigenous Peoples*, pp. 43–44.   [47] Venne, *Our Elders*, p. 116.
[48] See The Earth Council Indigenous And Tribal Peoples http://www.ecouncil.ac.cr/indig/ accessed 22/2/2002 and The United Nations Development Program http://www.undp.org/csopp/CSO/NewFiles/ipaboutdef.html. accessed 9/7/2002.

North America are also referred to as 'Native Americans' but this term is not generally applied to South America.[49] There the once pejorative term 'Indian' has come back into use. A further closely related term is 'first peoples', which extends beyond the Americas and is used to refer to indigenous peoples in general.[50] I will now turn to the restrictions the book imposes on the range of indigenous peoples discussed and cited to illustrate particular points.

Scope of the examples

First it is not the intention of this book to consider the entire panoply of indigenous peoples; that would be an enormous task. There are reckoned to be 250 million or more indigenous peoples spread around the globe. Canada and North America, Central and South America, the Arctic and Europe, East Asia and Russia, Africa, Oceania, South Asia and South-East Asia all have states and regions containing indigenous peoples. Among them are the Inuit and Aleutians of the circumpolar region; the Saami occupying a region that includes parts of Norway, Sweden, Finland and Russia; the Chittagong Hill Tract Peoples, which includes the Chakma, Marma and Tripurs; the Kalinga and others in the Philippines; the Mae-Enga, Dani and Tsembaga peoples of West Papua; the Naga and others in India; the Karen and Kachin in Myanmar; the Ainu of Japan; the Hmong peoples of Thailand and Vietnam; the Aborigines and Torres Strait Islanders of Australia; the Māori of New Zealand, and the indigenous peoples too numerous to name in South America, Central America, North America and Canada. In South America alone there are an estimated 40 million indigenous peoples that include the Awá in Brazil, the Ayoreo in Paraguay and Bolivia, the Enxet in Paraguay, the Guarnani peoples located in Paraguay, Brazil, Bolivia and Argentina, Makuxi in Brazil and Guyana, Yanomami in Brazil and Venezuela, the Yora in south-east Peru and the Wichī in Argentina and Bolivia.[51] There are simply too many distinct groups of indigenous peoples in widely differing contexts to consider all of them. Apart from that, the book is neither a history of indigenous peoples nor a comprehensive study of the politics of their struggles with the states in which they are located.

[49] Brysk, 'Weakness Into Strength', p. 54, footnote 1.
[50] See, for instance, Julian Burger, *The GAIA Atlas of First Peoples: A Future For The Indigenous World* (London: Penguin, 1990).
[51] Survival International, wysiwyg://297/http://www.survival-international.org/ Accessed 3/21/02.

The point of departure for the book, to reiterate, is the neglect of indigenous peoples in the story of the expansion of international society from Europe. It should be abundantly clear from the discussion so far that Europeans are not the only peoples to have colonised and subjugated indigenous peoples. Further, while the indigenous peoples of South and South-East Asia, for example, might once have been under European rule, they are now ruled by ethnically different and dominant groups of non-Europeans. A study of the indigenous peoples of South and South-East Asia would in itself be a complex and potentially vast topic and for the sake of setting some limits to the book I have chosen to discuss neither those regions, nor contemporary cases of non-European rule over indigenous peoples. This omission is not, I believe, one that affects the claims made later in the book.

A further restriction is that the contemporary examples cited in the book relate to English-speaking rule and, in particular, what Haverman calls the Anglo-Commonwealth, comprised by Canada, New Zealand and Australia. Apart from the discussion, in Chapter 2, of the conquest of Mexico 500 years ago, Central America, South America and Mexico do not figure in this book. This does not meant to imply they are unimportant. On the contrary, the struggles of indigenous peoples in those places extend from the time of the Conquest and colonisation by Europeans, down to the present. In colonial and post-colonial times the indigenous peoples of Central and South America have been subjected to genocidal practices and continuing dispossession. Forest peoples including the Yanomami in the Amazon Basin of Brazil have been faced with the dispossession of their traditional lands and, in some cases, extinction. The continual expansion of mining, agriculture and forestry interests is a form of internal colonialism that often has tragic results for the cultures and the survival of indigenous peoples. As Susan Stonich puts it, economic development strategies, 'along with growth in road building, lumbering, agribusiness, hydro-electric projects, mining and oil operations, unregulated and planned colonisation, and the exploitation of genetic materials (and the associated cultural knowledge), pose an augmented threat to indigenous peoples'.[52] Together with indigenous peoples in other places, the indigenous peoples of Latin America thus share common goals related to land rights, maintaining access to natural resources, and relief from human rights abuses. All of these are subsumed

---

[52] Susan Stonich (ed.), *Endangered Peoples of Latin America: Struggles to Survive and Thrive* (Westport, Conn: Greenwood Press, 2001), p. xxi.

by the overarching goal of achieving self-determination which would allow indigenous peoples more control over the 'pace and content' of the development that affects the conditions of their existence.[53]

During the 1980s there was a significant growth of the indigenous movement in Latin America and that movement has had an important role in promoting indigenous rights globally.[54] Alison Brysk characterises indigenous movements in Latin America as relying for their effectiveness on a combination of identity and politics and internationalisation. In a major study of how indigenous movements have successfully sought to establish indigenous rights as international norms, she examines the links between local communities and the wider world community. She argues that 'welfare, human rights, and even survival', of the Indian peoples of Latin America, 'are increasingly dictated by global forces beyond their control'. Even so, they have been able to challenge 'the states, markets and missions that seek to crush them'. They do so by building global networks. 'In the spaces between power and hegemony, the tribal village builds relationships with the global village.'[55]

An example of this is the campaign waged by the Zapatistas in the southern Mexican state of Chiapas. In January 1994 the self-styled Zapatista National Liberation Army led by Subcomandante Marcos initiated armed attacks against the Mexican state, aimed at securing improved conditions and rights for the estimated 10 million indigenous Indian peasants in Mexico. The Zapatistas soon shifted from acts of violence to extensive use of the Internet.

> The Zapatista use of international support and information networks has been conscious and extensive; thousands of academics, journalists, and activists received frequent unsolicited e-mail from the "Zapatistas Intergalactic Network". The transnational network of Zapatista electronic communication is so dense that a separate Web site has been established just to track the proliferation of Zapatista homepages, listservs, [sic] archives, advocacy links and email addresses . . .'[56]

In March 2001 the Zapatista campaign seemed to have achieved success when Subcomandante Marcos led a peaceful march into Mexico City, but journalists and activists alike were quick to point out that many of

[53] Brysk, 'Weakness Into Strength', p. 41.
[54] Hector Diaz-Polanco, 'Indian Communities and the Quincentenary', *Latin American Perspectives*, 19: 3 (Summer 1992), p. 15.
[55] Alison Brysk, *From Tribal Village to Global Village: Indian Rights and International Relations in Latin America* (Stanford University Press, 2000), p. 2.
[56] Brysk, *Tribal Village to Global Village*, p. 160.

the rights and reforms for which the Zapatistas had been fighting were yet to be achieved.[57]

As with the cases of South and South-East Asia, the situation of the indigenous peoples of Latin America is huge in its own right. My purpose in dwelling on Latin America has been, first, to recognise the important place it has had, and continues to have, in the story of the place of indigenous peoples in international society. Second, I wanted to make it quite clear that the use of examples drawn from the Anglo-Commonwealth is not in any way meant to imply that European rule is coterminous with English-speaking rule. Extending the discussion to the contemporary political and legal struggles of the Latin American indigenous movements would, however, have greatly extended the length of the book and been more appropriate to a book with a different purpose. It is once again largely a matter of needing to set limits to the discussion. In any case, the argument in later chapters concerning the legitimacy of both states with indigenous populations, and the implications this has for international society, apply to Latin America. The selection of examples is emphatically not an intentional expression of Anglo-centric values. Nor should it be interpreted as overlooking the differences between the ideologies of empire and the colonial practices of European states.

In his study of Spanish, British and French ideologies of empire from around 1500 to roughly 1800, Anthony Pagden demonstrates that these differences were present from the beginning of European expansion. They were manifested in the divergence of approaches to settlement, contrasting conceptions of legal authority, and attitudes to race relations. In contrast to the Spanish settlers who 'formally styled themselves as *conquerors*' and reduced Indians to servitude, the British and French either excluded 'Native Americans from their colonies, or . . . incorporate[d] them as trading partners.'[58] Whereas the Spanish thought the conquest and subjugation of Indian peoples was legitimate, the French attempted to integrate them and the English to exterminate them.[59] The Spanish had an overwhelming concern with rights over

---

[57] Nash, 'Reassertion', Jason Rodrigues, 'Long Haul', *The Guardian* http://www.guardian.co.uk/Archive/Article/0,4273,41503314,00.html accessed 3/21/2002, Duncan Campbell and Jo Tuckman, 'Zapatistas March into the Heart of Mexico', *The Guardian* http://www.guardian.co.uk/Archive/Article/0,4273,4151908,00.html accessed 3/21/2002, Naomi Klein, 'The Unknown icon', *The Guardian* http://www.guardian.co.uk/Archive/Article/0,4273,4145255.00.html accessed 3/21/2002.
[58] Anthony Pagden, *Lords of all the World: Ideologies of Empire in Spain, Britain and France c.1500–c.1800* (New Haven: Yale University Press, 1995), p. 65.
[59] Ibid., p. 73.

people and the British with rights over property. France and Britain regarded the Spanish justification of conquest as 'unsustainable' and based their own settlements 'upon one or another variant of the *res nullius*, or on purchase and "concession" '.[60] In relation to the crucial matter of race, the Spanish and the French 'established their first colonies with the explicit if loosely understood, intention of creating a single cultural as well as legal, and – uniquely in the French case – racial, community.'[61] France adopted a Roman approach to citizenship, which extended the rights of French citizenship to those colonised. It stood alone also in being the only European power that 'attempted to replicate [its] society in America with a mixed population' by actively encouraging miscegenation.[62] Differences such as these between the ideologies and practices of European powers had important and lasting effects on the peoples colonised and can be traced through to the present. There are elements of this in the chapters that follow, but my purpose has been neither to write a systematic history nor give a comprehensive account of the undeniable differences between European states.

The layout of the book

Chapter 1 introduces a number of themes and concepts essential to the argument. It first discusses the nature of international society, the place of Hugo Grotius in its intellectual origins, and the English School and the rationalist tradition, which have been the main bearers of the idea. It argues that although international society initially included individuals, it became an exclusive society of states. Also, that its expansion from Europe cannot be separated from dispossession, genocide and the destruction of cultural identity. Consequently, particular states that resulted from the expansion of Europe are morally flawed because of unresolved issues related both to the acts that established them and their continuing practices with respect to their indigenous populations. International society is in turn morally flawed to the extent that it legitimates and protects morally reprehensible states among those that constitute it. Next the chapter surveys conquest, imperialism, empire and colonialism as modes of expanding international society that assumed European superiority and resulted in both domination and complex interactions between cultures. It argues that while the relationship between Europeans and non-Europeans was generally one of domination,

---

[60] Ibid., p. 86.   [61] Ibid., p. 149.   [62] Ibid., p. 150.

it was not a simple tale of subjugation and denial. Further, at its apogee European dominated international society was a society of empires. Contemporary international society, in which Europe has become much less important, continues nevertheless, in important cases, to be a society of empires marked by cultural misunderstanding. The chapter closes by defining the principal legal terms used in substantiating claims to sovereign rights over people and territory and then explaining the legal and political significance of using the term 'peoples' rather than the singular 'people'.

Chapter 2 concerns the incommensurability of cultures and the construction of 'otherness' in ways that justified the dispossession of indigenous peoples. It compares three different accounts of European encounters with non-Europeans. Each demonstrates the inability of Europeans to understand people from other cultures in their own terms, with the result that non-Europeans were progressively conceptualised in ways that dehumanised them and enabled their dispossession and subordination. This argument is extended by a survey of concepts that categorised peoples as either 'civilised' or 'uncivilised', thereby making it easier to deny rights to peoples regarded as the latter. It then rehearses the idea of stages of development that provided further justification for denying the rights of those seen as stuck in earlier stages that Europeans had moved beyond. Finally it argues that the state of nature and natural rights theory were also very effectively deployed to justify dispossession.

Chapter 3 advances the argument that international law was, at crucial junctures of its history, a form of cultural imperialism. It marked the boundaries between those who were and were not treated according to the norms the members of international society applied to themselves. Over a period of 400 years following the conquest of Mexico there was a progressive retreat by Europeans from conceding sovereign rights to particular non-European peoples. During this span of time international legal thought progressed from recognizing sovereignty in non-European peoples to recognizing limited or conditional sovereignty to eventually denying it, especially in the case of peoples regarded as 'uncivilised'. Important moments in these developments were the Spanish debate of 1550–51 over the status of Indians as human beings, the adoption by legal theorists of Locke's labour theory of property and the impact of social Darwinism. Also relevant was, first, the displacement of natural law concerned with the rights and duties of humans everywhere by the positive law of states; and second, changing conceptions of 'otherness' that constructed ideas of identity and difference in ways that did not comprehend cultural difference as compatible with equality of legal rights.

Chapter 4 concerns the contemporary claims of indigenous peoples. It first outlines the United Nations system as it pertains to indigenous rights. It next explains the centrality of land to indigenous culture and identity. The argument concerning this is that land rights lead to claims to self-determination which are interpreted by states as secessionist and resisted as conflicting with the fundamental norms of international society and international law. Consequently, a major task is to consider the contemporary meaning of self-determination and how it should be understood in relation to the situation of indigenous peoples. This leads to consideration of the issues to be resolved, from the perspective of international law, before indigenous aspirations to self-determination can be realised. Of particular importance among these is the conflict between human and indigenous rights. The right of self-determination is one held by groups and in some cases this might undermine the essential character of human rights. The chapter closes with a discussion of some indigenous perspectives on self-determination and suggestions that sovereignty needs to be uncoupled from the state if indigenous peoples are ever to recover fully authorship of their identity.

Chapter 5 shifts the focus to three political and moral issues resulting from conquest and the subjugation of indigenous peoples. The first of these is that the construction of others has resulted in a variety of harms being done to them. Second is the argument that 'the West' bears a collective responsibility for historic injustices. This requires giving an account of how collective responsibility should be construed and one argument is that it means engaging in dialogue, premised on others being different but equal, that attempts to understand others in their own terms. Concerning historic injustices, I argue, contrary to Jeremy Waldron,[63] that some injustices are not superseded with the passage of time and special measures are needed if they are to be satisfactorily redressed. Crucial to this argument is the philosophy of history and how the relationship between past, present and future is interpreted. The final issue, already mentioned, is whether the legitimacy of states depends on the treatment of their indigenous populations and in turn the worth of international society depends on the moral standing of the states that constitute it. The position taken in the book is that the

---

[63] Jeremy Waldron, 'Superseding Historic Injustice', *Ethics* 103: 1 (October 1992).

legitimacy of states with indigenous populations depends on the degree to which those states engage in a politics of reconciliation, recognition, difference and cultural rights and that there is a case to answer about the legitimacy of international society.

Chapter 6 takes up the question posed by Timothy Dunne[64] of whether the rationalist tradition of thought about international relations remains a prisoner of its ethnocentric origins or has instead, to use his words, the potential to reinvent itself for our post-colonial times. It first argues that while the intellectual origins of rationalism do contain elements necessary for it to reinvent itself, it is nevertheless not an adequate basis for establishing indigenous rights in the normative framework of international society. Rationalism draws on the very classical theory that was implicated in the denial of indigenous rights and codified difference. Following discussion of this is a review of selected writings located in critical theory and post-modern approaches to international relations that suggest ways of dealing with the barriers to cross-cultural understanding, ending the marginalisation of indigenous peoples and widening their legal rights. Central concerns of this body of writing are accepting and dealing with difference, the meaning of autonomy and what is needed to achieve it, and, extension of the boundaries of moral community. Finally the chapter considers forms of political community most likely to accommodate the claims of indigenous peoples.

The Conclusion first reiterates the theme of legitimacy and then argues for recognition of indigenous peoples as 'peoples' with the right of self-determination in constitutional law and in international or global law. It then revisits the barrier to self-determination posed by the tension between human and indigenous rights. Finally, it addresses the problem of whether setting an international standard for the treatment of indigenous peoples represents an anti-pluralist view of international society.

---

[64] Dunne, 'Colonial Encounters'.

1 Bringing 'peoples' into international society

This book is about the loss of life, land, culture and rights that resulted from the overseas expansion of European people and states following Columbus' voyages to the Americas in the late fifteenth century. At that time the modern state and with it the European states system was beginning to emerge from the social and political structures of medieval Christendom. By the end of the nineteenth century the states system had developed to the point of being known by its mainly European members as the *society of states* or *international society*. The story of the expansion of international society to one that embraced the world as a whole has been written as one of states and the rivalry between them. War and its recurrence has long been assumed to be the central problem of relations between states and a key institution of international society. The loss of life with which this book is concerned is not life lost in war between states or in the numerous post-World War II intrastate wars of the Third World. It is instead the losses that resulted from the arrival of Europeans, from the time of Columbus, in lands inhabited by non-European peoples.[1] The story of the expansion of international society is simultaneously a story of the subjugation and domination of others in historically momentous ways that are frequently overlooked

[1] The ensuing loss of Amerindian life, for example, was enormous. James Tully writes that 'The Aboriginal population of what is now commonly called the United States and Canada was reduced from 8 to 12 million in 1600 to half a million by 1900, when the genocide subsided.' Tully, *Strange Multiplicity*, p. 19. In the case of Mexico, David Stannard estimates that the population was reduced from about 25 million in 1519 to 1,300,000 in 1595; a reduction of 95 per cent. David Stannard, *American Holocaust* (New York: Oxford University Press, 1992), p. 85 cited by James P. Sterba, 'Understanding Evil: American Slavery, the Holocaust, and the Conquest of the American Indians', *Ethics* 106: 2 (1996), 427. It is estimated that for the Americas as a whole 74–94 million Indians lost their lives as a result of conquest compared with 40–60 million Africans captured for slavery who died on the voyage from Africa to America. See Sterba, 'Understanding Evil', 430.

by the emphasis on states and interstate conflict. Consequently while the expansion of international society is the departure point for this study, it is concerned not just with states and the society of states but with the immediate and lasting consequences of European expansion for non-European peoples.

The purpose of this chapter is to clarify various key terms and concepts that inform the discussion in later chapters. First it concerns the idea of international society and the relationship it has with both Grotius and rationalism as a tradition of international theory. It outlines some key points about the expansion of international society and makes the suggestion, which is taken up in Chapter 5, that the moral legitimacy of international society is open to question. The second section discusses conquest, imperialism, empire, colonialism and colonisation as the methods of expansion of international society. It points out that while the relationship between Europeans and non-Europeans was generally one of domination, it is not a simple tale of subjugation and denial. The relationship also involved a complex interaction between cultures that did not necessarily deny the agency of non-Europeans. Next some terms related to the rights of non-Europeans at different junctures of thought about international law are defined. The chapter closes with an explanation of the choice of 'peoples' in the chapter heading in preference to the singular 'people'.

International society and its expansion

International society is a society of states but its intellectual roots allowed the inclusion of individuals. It is the core concept of what Martin Wight called the 'rationalist' tradition of international relations theory. His reason for giving it this name derives from his identification of Hugo Grotius as a seminal thinker about international society, and consequently as a foundational figure of rationalism. In Grotius' writings natural law is an essential element and the content of that law is known by the use of right reason. It represents divine law but is discoverable by rational human beings. 'Reason', Wight explained, 'is a reflection of the divine light in us: "*Ratio est radius divini luminis*". This is the justification for using the word Rationalist in this special sense in connection with international theory.'[2] To call a tradition of thinking about international relations 'rationalist' was then to associate it with the element of reason

[2] Wight, *International Theory*, p. 14.

contained in the conception of natural law. Rationalists were those who maintained the tradition of natural law and because it concerned the 'rights and duties attaching to individual human beings'[3] it meant accepting that individuals as well as states were subjects in international relations. Grotius' vision of international society was one that combined natural law and the positive law of states as essential components of the law of nations.

When assessing Grotius' contribution to thought about international relations, Hedley Bull argued that his work is 'cardinal because it states one of the classic paradigms that have since determined both our understanding of the facts of life of inter-state relations and our ideas as to what constitutes right conduct'.[4] That paradigm was international society and as three of five features standing out in Grotius' conception of it, Bull identifies the centrality of natural law, the universality of international society, and the place of individuals and non-state groups.[5] Grotius thought of international society as containing individuals as well as states and as being universal. It was 'not just the society of states, it is the great society of mankind'.[6] And it 'was not composed merely of Christian or European rulers and peoples but was world-wide'.[7] However, the idea of it being 'world-wide and all-inclusive' gave way in the eighteenth and particularly the nineteenth centuries, 'to the idea that it was a privileged association of Christian, European, or civilised states . . .'[8]

Claire Cutler similarly argues that Grotius' writings reflect 'the absence at the time of a clearly perceived distinction between individual and state personality'. Alongside states, individuals held rights and duties under international law and these were universal.[9] For Cutler '[t]he most profound component of the Grotian world view is the assumption that there is a universal standard against which the actions of states may be judged'.[10] Natural law entailed not only 'the essential identity of the individual and the state' but also 'provided the "element of universalization" necessary to the conception of a universal moral order'.[11]

---

[3] A. Claire Cutler, 'The "Grotian Tradition" in International Relations', *Review of International Studies*, 17: 1 (1991), 46.
[4] Bull, 'Importance of Grotius', in Bull, Kingsbury and Roberts (eds.), *Hugo Grotius*, p. 71.
[5] The other two are 'Solidarism in the Enforcement of Rules' and 'The Absence of International Institutions'.
[6] Bull, 'Importance of Grotius', p. 83.   [7] Ibid., p. 80.
[8] Ibid., p. 82 and see Gerrit W. Gong, *The Standard of 'Civilization' in International Society* (Oxford: Clarendon Press, 1984).
[9] Cutler, 'Grotian Tradition', 45.   [10] Ibid., 48.   [11] Ibid., 46.

Her further argument is that Bull's rejection of natural law in favour of positive international law meant his conception of international order could not accommodate a universal moral order and is necessarily confined to a morality of states.[12]

For Martin Wight international society is not merely an idea but a political and social fact known by inference from the way states and other actors behave.[13] As observers of this behaviour we conclude that there is an international society because states behave as if there is one. International society is, according to Wight, 'the habitual intercourse of independent communities, beginning in the Christendom of Western Europe and gradually extending throughout the world'.[14] For Hedley Bull also, international society is implicit in and revealed by the practice of states; but in particular by the way they identify and articulate rules to guide their relations with one another. In a frequently quoted sentence, he asserts that:

> A *society of states* (or international society) exists when a group of states, conscious of certain interests and common values, form a society in the sense that they conceive themselves to be bound by a common set of rules in their relations with one another, and share in the working of common institutions.[15]

In Bull's version of international society the primary function of these common institutions is to provide a foundation for order between states (international order). According to Wight, '[I]f there is an international society . . . then there is an order of some kind to be maintained, or even developed.'[16] International society necessarily supports a normative order that accepts the legitimacy of states and the society constituted by them. The rules meant to maintain or develop order between states are, for the most part, determined by the great powers of the time, but their aims are not necessarily those of all states. In many ways, international society is never more than an expression of the interests of the great or dominant powers that determine the rules of membership and conduct.

In the lexicon of international society it is by articulating and observing rules and norms that states advance their common interests; but

---

[12] Ibid., 53–8.   [13] Wight, *International Theory*, p. 30.
[14] Martin Wight, 'Western Values in International Relations', in H. Butterfield and M. Wight (eds.), *Diplomatic Investigations: Essays in the Theory of International Politics* (London: George Allen & Unwin, 1966), p. 97.
[15] Hedley Bull, *The Anarchical Society* (London: Macmillan, 1995), p. 13.
[16] Wight, 'Western Values', p. 103.

what exactly is the basis of these common interests? One way of answering this is to situate international society in relation to the distinction between practical and purposive associations.[17] International society is generally seen as a 'practical association' in which states, driven by the need for coexistence and the imperatives of cooperation under anarchy, establish certain rules to govern their relations and participate in the workings of institutions to support those rules.[18] The case for seeing international society as a practical association is that the over-riding common interest of states is simply to coexist without conflict rather than to achieve common values. During the Cold War, for instance, the United States and the former Soviet Union both articulated and agreed upon rules meant to guide their mutual relations, but they had very little common interest apart from the important one of avoiding nuclear war. Consequently, they found rules that would allow them to coexist without direct, armed conflict.[19] Rules of practical association impose restraints that allow states to coexist and they may be expressed in custom, in positive international law, or in unspoken rules. The goal of coexistence is achieved primarily through respecting the so-called basic norms in inter-state behaviour: sovereign equality, independence and the rule of non-intervention.

A major problem in conceiving of international society as a practical association is that it assumes that 'the identities and purposes of states are formed prior to social interaction'. It overlooks the fact that international society is constituted by the inter-subjective understandings of states and other actors. It is through their mutual relations that the identities and interests of states are formed. 'States create institutions not only as functional solutions to cooperation problems, [as in a practical association] but as expressions of prevailing conceptions of legitimate agency and action that serve, in turn, as structuring frameworks for the communicative politics of legitimation.'[20]

---

[17] Terry Nardin, *Law, Morality and Relations of States* (Princeton University Press, 1983). Nardin defines a purposive association as one in which the constituents 'are associated in a cooperative enterprise to promote shared values, beliefs, or interests [and] are united by their convergent desire for the realisation of a certain outcome that constitutes the good they have come together to obtain'. By contrast, the 'values of a practical association are those appropriate to the relations among persons who are not necessarily engaged in any common pursuit but who nevertheless have to get along with one another. They are the very essence of a way of life based on tolerance and diversity,' pp. 9–14.

[18] See Bull, *The Anarchical Society*, Nardin, *Law, Morality*, Robert Keohane, *International Institutions*, and Brown, 'International Theory and International Society'.

[19] Paul Keal, *Unspoken Rules and Superpower Dominance* (London: Macmillan, 1983).

[20] Chris Reus-Smit, 'The Politics of International Law', unpublished manuscript.

While there are certainly elements of practical association in international society it is better regarded as essentially purposive. As well as being a society of states, international society is a moral community. A moral community is one in which the members concede to each other rights and obligations with regard to being treated alike. The members of such a community do not regard themselves as being bound to treat non-members as they would treat fellow members. This is not to say that they never will treat others according to the same rules. Just that they don't see themselves as in any way bound to do so. Implicit in this idea is that moral communities have boundaries that draw the line between who belongs and who does not. Or, to put this another way, between who gets included and who gets excluded. In essence, moral communities have rules; not only about the rights and duties members owe each other, but also rules determining rightful membership.

For example, at the end of the nineteenth century the great powers of Europe proclaimed 'the standard of civilisation' as the criteria for membership of international society. To be counted as members of international society, and consequently as subjects of international law, political entities had first to attain this standard, which stipulated a level of political and social organisation recognised by Europeans. The standard of civilisation was thus a crucial instrument for drawing the boundaries between the 'civilised' and 'uncivilised' worlds, and for determining who did or did not belong to international society. At the present time its place appears to have been taken, as Gerrit Gong rightly suggested in the early 1980s, by the human rights record of states.[21] It is this, above all else, that confers the degree of legitimacy on states necessary for them to be accepted as rightful members of international society. In its constabulary role of determining legitimacy, international society is a purposive association.

Legitimacy is fundamental also to a further sense in which international society is purposive. In an important revision of Bull's understanding of international society, Fred Halliday renders 'society' as inter-societal and inter-state homogeneity.[22] His sense of international society is one that incorporates the links between the internal structures of societies and the international pressures that shape them. The term refers, in essence, to the idea that as a result of international pressures states

[21] Gong, *Standard of 'Civilization'*, and Jack Donnelly, 'Human Rights: A New Standard of Civilization?', *International Affairs* 74: 1 (1998).
[22] Fred Halliday, 'International Society as Homogeneity', in F. Halliday *Rethinking International Relations* (Basingstoke: Macmillan, 1994).

are compelled, increasingly, to conform to each other, in their internal arrangements. An international society is then one in which states in the same vicinity have similar governments and uphold similar, or at least compatible, ideals. Conceived in this way, international society is necessarily limited to states with similar domestic arrangements based on a shared political culture. It is not a pluralistic international society in which, so long as there are rules to guide mutual relations, the internal relations should not matter.

In Bull's account of international society order between states is the central concern. Whether we are talking about the society of states at the beginning of the twentieth century or international society in the 1970s and early 1980s, when Bull was writing about it, the idea of international society focuses attention, in the first instance, on great powers. As an approach to contemporary international politics it is fundamentally state-centric and has been concerned largely with order in relations between states and the role of great powers in either buttressing or undermining it. There is consequently justification for Martin Shaw's criticism that the theory of international society was 'a central ideology of the international system in the Cold War period'.[23] At the same time as promoting an idea of the common good it served as a justification for maintaining the status quo as essential to international order. Nevertheless, against this has to be set Bull's argument that, in their revolt against the West, Third World states adopted and employed fundamental concepts of international society to break the political hold great powers had over them.[24]

Fundamental to the rules underpinning international order is mutual recognition, which Wight identifies as one of the distinguishing characteristics of historical states systems. For there to be a system of states, without which there cannot be either international society or order, states must mutually recognise each others' right to sovereign independence. An international society is for this reason a community of mutual recognition. Unless states do recognise each other as legitimate and sovereign actors there can be no basis for agreement over the practices that are to guide their mutual relations. 'It would be impossible to have a society of sovereign states unless each state, while claiming sovereignty for itself,

---

[23] Martin Shaw, *Global Society and International Relations* (Cambridge: Polity Press, 1994), p. 119.
[24] Bull, 'The Revolt Against the West', in Bull and Watson (eds.), *The Expansion of International Society*.

recognised that every other state had the right to claim and enjoy its own sovereignty as well.'[25]

Coupled to mutual recognition is legitimacy, which, for Wight, meant 'the collective judgement of international society about rightful membership of the family of nations, how sovereignty may be transferred, and how state secession is to be regulated, when large states break up into smaller, or several states combine into one'.[26] More than this, in contemporary world politics the domestic arrangements of states are increasingly important in determining which states are regarded as legitimate. The status and moral authority of states depends, perhaps more than ever before, on factors such as their human rights record, their treatment of indigenous populations, whether they are governed by democratic institutions, and the degree of social justice that obtains in them. In earlier phases of world politics, legitimacy was also important in relations between Christendom and what lay beyond it, especially whether non-Christian rulers could be accepted as legitimate.[27]

The legitimacy or otherwise of including non-Christian or non-European peoples is a vital but often neglected part of the story of international society. Bull and Watson tell this as a success story of states in which the expansion of Europe resulted in both the state becoming a universal form of political organisation and the evolution of a body of rules and institutions based on mutual recognition that constitute international society. But hidden under this success story of the expansion of international society is another story of moral failure with respect to the indigenous peoples of the world, many of whom had to struggle to be accepted as members of international society, and even of the human race.

The state, as a universal form of political organisation, was however not regarded by Bull as the end of the story. States, he pointed out, 'are simply groupings of men, and men may be grouped in such a way that they do not form states at all'. Consequently, there are questions of deeper and 'more enduring importance' than those connected with international order; questions 'about order in the great society of mankind'. In this way he introduced the idea of world order based not on an international society of states, but a world society of individual human beings, with world order cast in terms of a concern with

---

[25] Martin Wight, *Systems of States* (Leicester: Leicester University Press, 1977), p. 135.
[26] Ibid., p. 153.   [27] Ibid., p. 156.

'social life among mankind as a whole'.[28] World order, he thought, was both 'something more fundamental and primordial than [international society]' and morally prior. '[I]t is order among all mankind which we must treat as being of primary value, not order within the society of states. If international order does have value, this can only be because it is instrumental to the goal of order in human society as a whole.'[29] Bull appears to have regarded international society, buttressed by international order, as a step on the long journey to a normatively preferable world society and world order, giving international society the moral purpose of promoting world order.

The importance of this is that contrary to Claire Cutler's argument, that Bull's rejection of natural law meant his conception of international order lacked a basis for a universal moral order, Timothy Dunne argues that Bull's conception of international society is underpinned by moral universalism. In support of this he cites Bull's contention that the 'society of states' is 'an instrument for delivering the moral value of world order', and writes that 'the underlying moral universalism in Bull's thinking concerns his insistence that individuals are the ultimate moral referent. International order is to be valued to the extent which it delivers "world order", which Bull makes the litmus test for the ethical claims of the society of states.'[30]

So far my concern has been to highlight the place of individuals in the intellectual roots of thought about international society, the claim that international order has a moral basis to the extent that it promotes world order centered on individuals, and that it is fundamentally an inter-subjective and purposive society in which mutual recognition founded on legitimacy is a central concern. As well as anything else, international society should be thought of as a moral community. It casts the criteria for membership in terms of legitimacy and what counts as legitimate at any one time is determined by the states that belong to the community. The remainder of this section concerns the historical expansion of international society.

In their introduction to *The Expansion of International Society*, Bull and Watson make it clear that international society was, in its inception, a society of European states. Their concern is then with the expansion of this European society of states 'across the rest of the globe, and its transformation from a society fashioned in Europe and dominated by

---

[28] Bull, *The Anarchical Society*, p. 20.   [29] Ibid., p. 22.
[30] Dunne, *Inventing International Society*, pp. 145–6.

European states into the global international society of today'.[31] As a result of Europeans imposing themselves, in various ways, on the lands of non-Europeans they gradually spread the European state as a form of political organisation. Bull and Watson outline the growing involvement, after 1500, of European states with regional systems that had different cultural bases. There was at first no 'shared outlook' or common interest that is 'presupposed in the membership of a common international society'.[32] Instead the rules and institutions that constitute international society developed in tandem with the expansion of Europe. European international society 'did not first evolve its own rules and institutions and then export them to the rest of the world. The evolution of the European system of interstate relations and the expansion of Europe were simultaneous processes, which influenced and affected each other.'[33] Prior to Europe unifying the globe there was no common legal and moral basis for 'relations between states and rulers that were members of the different regional international systems – there was no single, agreed body of rules and institutions operating across the boundaries of any two regional international systems, let alone throughout the world as a whole, such as we imply when we speak of an international society'.[34] It was only once the 'numerous and extremely diverse political entities' of the world 'had come to resemble one another, at least to the extent that they were all, in some comparable sense, states',[35] that there could be a global international society.

While there was no shared outlook or common interest in the early stages of the formation of international society there was the idea, already mentioned, of natural law. It was 'often invoked in Europe to show that there were rules governing the relationship between Europeans and other peoples'; and it was, as we have seen, a source of 'rights and duties attaching to human beings as such – throughout the world as whole'.[36] Bull depicts it as having had an important role in promoting the idea that relations between Christian or European peoples and between them and Amerindians, Asians and Africans 'formed an international society partly, even if not wholly, upon the moral bonds alleged to bind human beings together by nature'.[37] It supported both the notion of common humanity and consequently of common interests, and the rights of

---

[31] Bull and Watson (eds.), *The Expansion*, p. 1.
[32] Hedley Bull, 'The Emergence of a Universal International Society', in Bull and Watson (eds.), *The Expansion*, p. 191.
[33] Bull and Watson (eds.), *The Expansion*, p. 6.   [34] Ibid.
[35] Bull, 'The Emergence', p. 121.   [36] Ibid., p. 119.   [37] Ibid., p. 119.

non-Europeans, and was invoked 'to defend the rights of Amerindians against Spanish conquerors, of Africans forced into trans-Atlantic slavery, and aboriginal peoples in many parts of the world against dispossession and demoralisation by European settlers'. Equally it provided, for Europeans, 'a rationale for forcing non-European peoples into commercial and diplomatic discourse against their will . . .'.[38]

It is clear from this that Bull is claiming that although 'ideas of a universal law of nations or law of nature were contested by doctrines of a fundamental division of humanity between Greeks and barbarians, Christians and infidels, Europeans and non-Europeans'[39] there was, in the earlier phases of European expansion, a recognition that non-Europeans had rights. In the later phases of expansion this changed. With the passage of time Europeans moved further and further away from conceding rights or acknowledging non-Europeans as equals. With regard to Africa, for instance, Bull observes that as the nineteenth century progressed the distance between Europeans and Africans widened. Whereas 'in earlier centuries [Europeans] had sometimes been able to deal with black Africans as equals, [they] came increasingly to perceive them as objects either of exploitation, or of curiosity and compassion'.[40]

The development of the states system and consequently of international society meant a progressive denial by Europeans to non-Europeans of the rights they accorded themselves. Whereas natural law theories were once a basis for drawing disparate cultures and political entities together, the development of a state-centric international society divided them. The norms of international society became the norms of relations between states that relegate individuals to secondary importance in international life. The common interests that define international society are those of states; not those of individuals with which they may indeed be in conflict. In natural law doctrine there is support for a degree of cosmopolitanism that is missing from the contemporary idea of international society. Natural law doctrine was integral to the medieval order that the society of states replaced. The society of states necessarily had to evolve a different normative base. Thus from the basis of an ethical community of mankind developed an ethical community of states in which individuals are not subjects.

---

[38] Ibid., p. 120.   [39] Bull and Watson (eds.), *The Expansion*, p. 6.
[40] Hedley Bull, 'European States and African Political Communities', in Bull and Watson (eds.), *The Expansion*, p. 108, and see Peter Raby, *Bright Paradise: Victorian Scientific Travellers* (London: Pimlico, 1996).

Contrary to this claim, Murray Forsyth has argued that 'the close identity of international law with the mutual definition of states' rights', up to at least 1914, 'did not mean that individual rights were ignored . . . On the contrary . . . increasing recognition [was given] during the Eighteenth and Nineteenth centuries to the rights of the individual within the state.' In support of this claim he refers to a 'growing tendency . . . to equate the "true" state not only with the attribute of sovereignty, but with the protection of the individual rights of life, liberty, and property'. And this, he further claims, was a tendency that had some influence on international relations by making states sensitive to rights 'in their external dealings with one another'. What Forsyth overlooks, in common with others, is that the individual rights he cites were those of the citizens of the European states that defined and controlled membership of the society of states. It is a view that does not address the indigenous and other non-European people who were not included in the society of states defined by the international law of Europe. Rather than Forsyth's picture of progress towards individual rights within the European state and in law governing relations between European states, the expansion of Europe resulted in a progressive erosion and denial of the rights of indigenous peoples.[41]

Why, if at all, does this matter for the argument of this study? To repeat an earlier point, the expansion of international society cannot be separated from dispossession, genocide and the destruction of cultural identity. In many cases this was part of a state building process. Once established, these same states then encased in them the survivors of indigenous peoples and first nations – the peoples that did not fit into the political societies created by settlers. International society is then inescapably a society that includes states built on domination by, in the first instance, Europeans. This throws into question the moral basis of individual states and in turn the moral basis of international society as a whole.

While the focus of this study is the expansion of European states and the subjugation of non-Europeans by Europeans, it is important to recognise that Europeans are not the only peoples who have colonised and subjugated others. By definition, international society includes non-European states. By the late nineteenth century international law

---

[41] All references to Forsyth are to Murray Forsyth, 'The Tradition of International Law', in T. Nardin and D. R. Mapel (eds.), *Traditions of International Ethics* (Cambridge University Press, 1992), p. 29.

defined international society as being composed of three tiers of states. The first included the American states, Turkey and Japan which were on an equal footing with European states. The second comprised the 'backward' but Christian states, such as Abyssinia and Liberia; the third was made up of the Congo, Morocco, Muscat, Persia, Siam and China – all of which had been 'admitted to parts of the law of international society without being admitted to the whole of it'.[42] Among these the Ottoman Turks and the Chinese, in Indochina, had certainly subjugated 'other' peoples. In the 1930s Japan subjugated first Chinese and then other peoples, and in the more recent past Indonesia, for example, has subjugated not only the East Timorese but the indigenous population of West Papua, while China continues to subjugate Tibet. An interesting question that will not be taken up in this study, therefore, is whether the practices of domination by non-Europeans over other non-Europeans differ significantly from European experience.

From the starting point of international society this book addresses three neglected aspects of international society. First, although thought about international society at first included individuals and non-state groups it has not since done so in any consistent or systematic manner, but the inclusion of individuals is an imminent element. The norms of international society developed in a way that has sought to deny international personality to individuals and sub-state groups. At this juncture many individuals and sub-state groups seek international legal personality as a defence against the states in which they are encased. This is especially true for many groups of the estimated 250–300 million indigenous peoples scattered around the globe. To the benefit of these peoples states are increasingly bound by human rights instruments which make it difficult for them to hide from international scrutiny by claiming that the treatment of their indigenous populations is a domestic matter.

Second, unlike most other approaches to international politics, the study of international society has included the story of its expansion from a society of European states to one that is supposedly global or all inclusive.[43] The story being told of encounters between European states and non-European entities is an incomplete one. It has excluded the story of peoples destroyed and dispossessed in the process of expansion. The story of these peoples needs to be recognised and recovered as a central part of the story of expansion.

[42] John Westlake, *The Collected Papers of John Westlake on Public International Law*, ed. L. Oppenheim (Cambridge University Press, 1914).
[43] Bull, 'The Emergence'.

Third, the moral basis of international society is not clear but it needs to be asked whether states that lack legitimacy, because of the way they treat the individual and collective rights of their citizens, undermine the legitimacy of international society. A major purpose of international society has been to maintain the autonomy of the state as a form of political organisation. If that means maintaining states that have contested and unresolved questions about their moral legitimacy, then the legitimacy of international society itself may be questioned.

The next section is concerned with defining and distinguishing between 'conquest', 'imperialism', 'empire', 'colonialism' and 'colonisation' as practices essential to the expansion of international society. In so doing it will not be my purpose to inquire into the veracity or explanatory power of the various theories associated with these concepts. Also, they are to some extent all cognate terms with overlapping meanings. Treating them separately, and in the order that follows, is not meant to imply any predetermined view of the relationship of one to the other. My essential point is that each was a vital element in the expansion of Europe and each involved practices that set up the opposition of superiority and inferiority. The dominant European culture was invariably represented as superior, with the result that the 'inferior' culture was devalued. Its members were typically dehumanised in ways that made domination easier.

Building international society

Conquest

Conquest refers to the subjugation of one people by another by means of force. The stipulation that the use of force be involved is recognition that subjugation can be achieved by other means and hence establishes the distinct meaning of 'conquest'. Force is important also because in the history of international law its use for the purpose of conquest has had to be justified. Conquest is, therefore, linked to the problem of whether war is just or unjust. Following the conquest of Mexico, for instance, the circumstances under which force could be used justly was a matter of considerable debate. Vitoria, as one of the protagonists in this debate, argued, as we shall see in Chapter 3, that the use of force in the Americas was justifiable only if the Amerindians hindered missionaries from propagating Christianity or refused to allow Spaniards the 'natural rights' of trade and travel. Provided the use of force it entailed was regarded as 'just' for one or more of these reasons, conquest was accepted as a legitimate means of acquiring the land of non-Christians. In the early phases of European expansion it could be used to occupy and then claim title over, lands occupied by non-European peoples.

By the early nineteenth century it was no longer accepted as a means to title. The opinion of Chief Justice Marshall of the American Supreme Court, and of many other jurists, was that conquest meant a change of sovereign but left property rights undisturbed.[44] Until early this century conquest was accepted in international law texts as a means of formally annexing territory. As a legal concept '[i]t was a . . . fiction employed to mask the conquest and transform it into a valid method of obtaining land under international law'.[45] Happily this phase of international law has been left behind. Contemporary international law defines conquest as 'the act of defeating an opponent and occupying all or part of its territory', but rejects conquest as 'a basis of title to land'. Conquered 'territory remains the legal possession of the ousted sovereign'.[46]

Imperialism

Benjamin Cohen defines imperialism as 'any relationship of effective domination or control, political or economic, direct or indirect, of one nation over another'.[47] It refers, he says, 'to that kind of international relationship characterised by a particular asymmetry – the asymmetry of dominance and dependence'.[48] It is a relationship between inherently unequal nations based on notions of inferiority and superiority. Towards the end of the nineteenth century 'imperialism' was, according to Cohen, 'equivalent to "colonialism" – the establishment and extension of the political sovereignty of one nation over alien peoples and territories'.[49] It did not include the extension of sovereignty over contiguous land areas, examples of which were the gradual extension of the Russian frontier across the Steppes to the east and the move westwards in North America. Rather than imperialism, these were instances

---

[44] Henry Reynolds, *The Law of the Land* (Harmondsworth: Penguin, 1992), p. 38, and M. F. Lindley, *The Acquisition and Government of Backward Territory in International Law: Being a Treatise on the Law and Practice Relating to Colonial Expansion* (New York: Negro Universities Press, 1969 [1926]), pp. 160–5.

[45] Malcolm N. Shaw, *International Law*, 2nd edn (Cambridge: Grotius Publications, 1986), p. 249.

[46] Ibid., p. 248.

[47] Benjamin Cohen, *The Question of Imperialism: The Political Economy of Dominance and Dependence* (London: Macmillan, 1974), p. 16. See also the discussion of imperialism and colonialism in Robert J. C. Young, *Postcolonialism: An Historical Introduction* (Oxford: Blackwell, 2001).

[48] Cohen, *The Question*, p. 15.   [49] Ibid., p. 10.

of 'nation building'. Regardless of what it is called the internal expansion of Russia and America involved the domination and decimation of indigenous peoples.

Cohen draws attention to the distinction made by others, between the 'old' and the 'new imperialism'. The old imperialism is typified by the Age of Discovery of the sixteenth and seventeenth centuries which peaked in the mid-eighteenth century. It was driven by mercantilist theories that emphasised the accumulation of wealth in the form of gold and silver as a pillar of national security. Colonies were thought to contribute to the accumulation of national wealth by shutting out commercial competition. This old imperialism waned and came to an end with the acceptance of Adam Smith's view that a better source of national wealth was an international division of labour that did not require colonies. The new imperialism was represented by the remarkable expansion of Europe in Africa and Asia between 1870 and 1900. The term 'imperialism' referred during this period to the 'colonialism of maritime powers' and 'the extension of political sovereignty overseas'.[50]

One of the most influential theorists of the new imperialism was J. A. Hobson. Of particular interest for the purpose of this book is the lengthy chapter entitled 'Imperialism and the Lower Races' in his 1902 classic study of the subject.[51] In common with the legal and social thought of the time Hobson distinguished between different kinds of non-European people in terms of the ' "lower races" of tropical and subtropical countries'; the 'manifestly unassimilable races' of places such as Australia; and the peoples of old civilisationss 'of a high type', like India and China.[52] The position assigned to a particular people in this spectrum determined the kind of treatment to which they would be subjected. The so-called 'lower races' were the most vulnerable. 'When the settlement approaches the condition of genuine colonisation, it has commonly implied the extermination of the lower races, either by war or by private slaughter, as in the case of Australian Bushmen and the Hottentots, Red Indians, and Maoris, or by forcing upon them the habits of a civilisation equally destructive of them.'[53]

Hobson first states a case for European governments establishing control over non-Europeans. It is one that resonates with the present-day claims by multinational corporations and states that regard indigenous

---

[50] Ibid.
[51] J. A. Hobson, *Imperialism: A Study* (Ann Arbor: University of Michigan Press, 1972 [1902]), ch. 4.
[52] Ibid., pp. 224–5.   [53] Ibid., p. 253.

peoples as standing in the way of economic growth. The argument was that because of the 'backward' nature of many native peoples there would not be any development of resources under a native government. Development of resources was 'for the good of the world' and European interference was thus justified in order to both develop natural resources and compel native inhabitants to do so. If governments did not step in then development would be left in the hands of 'private adventurers, slavers, piratical traders, treasure hunters, [and] concession mongers . . . [who would play] havoc with the political, economic, and moral institutions of the peoples'[54] in whose lands the resources were contained. More than the involvement of national governments Hobson favoured a supra-national body; having what he called 'some organised representative of civilised humanity' in charge of the development of hitherto undeveloped areas and, to use the language of the time, 'backward peoples'. His view was that 'every act of "Imperialism" consisting of forcible interference with another people can only be justified by showing that it contributes to the "civilization" of the world'.[55] He was profoundly sceptical that this would be the outcome and proceeded to argue against interference.

His reasoning began with the observation that the kind of civilisation Europeans sought to impose on others was simply imported from Europe without thought for the needs and nature of the societies on to which it was grafted. In the second place, imperialism did 'not even pretend to apply to them [the lower races] the principles of education and progress it appli[ed] at home'.[56] No attempt, he complained, was made to 'penetrate' the mind and culture of non-Europeans. In articulating this claim he is clearly out of step with his time by calling for a quite different mode of understanding and interaction with others. The core of his argument against imperialism, however, focuses on dispossessing non-Europeans of their land and then using them to exploit it. Hobson charges that whenever possible whites compelled non-Europeans to exploit the mineral and agricultural resources of their own lands: 'the most profitable use of the hired labour of inferior races is to employ them in developing the resources of their own lands under white control for white men's profit'.[57] Imperialism, he wrote, 'rests upon and exists for the sake of "forced labour", i.e., labour which natives would not undertake save under direct or indirect personal compulsion issuing from

[54] Ibid., p. 230.   [55] Ibid., p. 234.   [56] Ibid., p. 243.   [57] Ibid., p. 249.

white masters'.[58] This brings him back to the earlier hierarchy of 'lower' and 'unassimilable races'. 'If the "natives" are of too low an order or too untameable to be trained for effective labour they must be expelled or exterminated, as in the case of the "lower nomads" ',[59] among whom he includes Australian Aborigines and North American Indians. Finally, Hobson reiterates his theme that whites do not in fact confer the benefits of civilisation but instead inflict on non-Europeans 'a dominant male caste with little knowledge of or sympathy for the institutions of the people [whose presence was] ill-calculated to give to these lower races even such gains as Western civilisation might be capable of giving'.[60]

I have dwelt on Hobson because as well as telling us something about imperialism as an institution, and the representation of non-Europeans at the time, his analysis supports a previous point about the foundations of international society. Imperialism was one of the means by which international society was expanded from a European to a global society. To the extent that Hobson's account of subjugation can be accepted, it is one that begs serious questions concerning the moral practices involved in establishing at least some of the states that ultimately resulted.

Empire

Michael Doyle defines 'empire' as 'a relationship, formal or informal, in which one state controls the effective political sovereignty of another political society. It can be achieved by force, by political collaboration, by economic, social, or cultural dependence.'[61] The similarity between this and Benjamin Cohen's definition of imperialism will be immediately apparent. For Doyle, however, '[i]mperialism is simply the process or policy of establishing and maintaining an empire'.[62] 'The scope of imperial control involves both the process of control and its outcomes.'[63] Doyle is right to distinguish, in this way, between the characteristics of a relationship and the 'policy or process of establishing and maintaining' it. What should be noticed also is his care in specifying that a state controls the 'political sovereignty of another political society'. By using the term 'political society' he leaves open the question of whether the entity subordinated is a state. Cohen's terminology, which has nations dominating nations, pays insufficient, if any, attention to the distinction

---

[58] Ibid., p. 254.   [59] Ibid., p. 258.   [60] Ibid., p. 282.
[61] Michael Doyle, *Empires* (Ithaca: Cornell University Press, 1986), p. 45.
[62] Ibid., p. 45.   [63] Ibid., p. 40.

between state, nation and other entities and is too loose. Finally, at the same time as adopting Doyle's distinction between empire and imperialism, in terms of relationship and process, it is difficult to avoid using the term 'imperial relationship' when speaking of the relationship between the dominant or metropolitan power at the centre of an empire and the entities dominated by it.

In relation to the purposes of this book there are two important points to note about empires. First, it is not only European states that have established and maintained empires. An important example is the Ottoman Empire which, because of its proximity to Europe, became increasingly drawn into the international affairs of Europe. So much so that it was eventually given recognition, in international law, as a member of the society of states. A further example, already mentioned, is Japan and the empire it established in the inter-war years; though its history of overseas expansion goes back to its earlier 1906 occupation of Korea. China also, throughout its long history, has been an imperial power.

The second point is that at the very time that it became clearly discernible, international society was itself a society of empires. As it matured during the nineteenth century, the society of states, which, as we have already seen was in its inception a European society of states, distinguished between its 'civilised' members and the 'uncivilised' political entities that stood outside it. For states to be accepted as members of the society of states they had to attain an implicit standard of 'civilisation'. During the late nineteenth century this 'took an increasingly explicit juridical character. It provided a purportedly legal way to demarcate the "civilised" countries which qualified for membership within its ranks and the "semi-civilised" and "uncivilised" countries which qualified for only partial membership.'[64] By the end of the nineteenth century the society of states or international society had a quasi-legal definition. Each of the leading members of the society so defined had an empire. Foremost among them was, of course, Britain with the most extensive empire of all. France, Germany, Holland, Belgium and Portugal also all had overseas 'possessions' or, to put it another way, controlled a formal empire. Even in the late twentieth century when imperialism and empire had long since ceased to be politically and morally acceptable there are states that are essentially informal empires. Until 1989, eastern Europe was thought of as the empire of the former Soviet Union. Although it would not recognise it as such, the United States also had one in Central

[64] Gong, *Standard of 'Civilization'*, p. 5.

and South America. At the present time China can be seen as having an empire because of the nature of its presence in Tibet. Indonesia too resembles an empire, not just because of its recently ended annexation of East Timor, but also because of its continuing inclusion of West Papua, and of the peoples of Aceh who would prefer self-determination. France as well should not be overlooked. Its territories and colonies in the Pacific allowed it to continue testing the nuclear weapons it regards as essential to its national security.

Why should it matter if international society was and to some extent is a society of empires? There are at least two reasons. First, by definition, empire involves the limitation of sovereignty. The imperial government that controls an empire is generally always, to use Doyle's memorable phrase, 'a sovereignty that lacks a community'.[65] Though the imperial powers at the core of empires exercised sovereignty over the people they subjugated, the sense of community that is normally part of a legitimate sovereign state was absent. Empires have always resulted in subjugated peoples wanting to either regain, or establish for the first time, self-determination and sovereignty over their own affairs. Following World War Two the creation of new states as part of decolonisation and the end of empire did give millions of people self-determination and sovereignty. But for many it was an incomplete process that has left many indigenous peoples and minority groups still pressing for the right to self-determination and sovereignty over their own affairs. Decolonisation and these continuing claims to self-determination are discussed in Chapter 4.

Second, and related to the first reason, the fact that the society of states was and in important cases remains a society of empires harks back to the previously mentioned problem of the moral basis of international society.

Colonialism and colonisation

Colonialism has taken a variety of forms. Catherine Irons identifies three basic variations: *external colonisation; external colonisation by neighbouring states;* and *internal colonialism.* By external colonisation is meant so-called 'salt-water' colonisation in which 'aliens' colonised distant places. This characterises the expansion of Europe to the Americas, Asia, Africa and the Pacific. Colonisation imposed by neighbouring states differs from external colonisation in at least two respects: external colonisation

---

[65] Doyle, *Empires*, p. 36.

generally cannot be legitimated with the passage of time, and second, 'the present oppression faced by peoples that have been colonised in the past by neighbouring states does as much damage to the oppressed peoples as that presently faced by peoples once colonised by an overseas state'.[66] Finally, internal colonialism, 'or the political incorporation of culturally distinct groups by the core' is distinguished by Hechter 'from *internal colonisation*, or the settlement of previously unoccupied territories within state borders'.[67]

The primary concern in this book is with the first of these forms. In particular cases, the third, the concept of internal colonialism, is also relevant but it should be noted immediately that the idea of previously unoccupied territories that distinguishes internal colonisation is problematic. There have been some very important examples, of which the occupation of Australia is one, in which territory claimed to be uninhabited was in fact inhabited. At this point, however, the task is to define and say something about the nature of colonialism in general.

A helpful approach to colonialism is Georges Balandier's conception of it as a 'situation'.[68] The colonial situation is characterised by him as 'the relations of domination and subordination existing between the colonising and colonised societies'. It is 'a totality of conditions' that define the relationship between dominant and subordinate entities in which a foreign minority imposes domination on a 'racially' and culturally distinct majority, asserts racial (or ethnic) and cultural superiority over those subordinated, and is materially superior to them. The relationship is antagonistic because of the role of the subordinate society and the dominant entity may need to rely on force to maintain its position. It is a situation in which two heterogeneous civilisations are brought into relationship.[69]

Defined in this way the colonial situation is one in which there must be interaction between at least two cultures; a colonising or conquering metropolitan elite (or cosmopolitan culture) and the colonised or conquered 'indigenes' (or native culture). The former is 'promulgated by colonial authorities as being vastly superior for the realisation of universal ends: salvation in one age; industrialization in another'. The

---

[66] Catherine J. Irons, 'Indigenous Peoples and Self Determination: Challenging State Sovereignty', *Case Western Reserve Journal of International Law*, 24: 2 (1992), 298.
[67] Michael Hechter, *Internal Colonialism: The Celtic Fringe in British National Development, 1536–1966* (Berkeley: University of California Press, 1975), p. 52.
[68] Georges Balandier, *The Sociology of Black Africa: Social Dynamics in Central Africa* (London: Deutsch, 1970, orig. 1955).
[69] Ibid., p. 52.

assertion of superiority structures the relationship between the colonisers and the colonised. 'One of the consequences of [the] denigration of indigenous culture is to undermine the native's will to resist the colonial regime. – The native's internalization of the colonist's view of him makes the realisation of social control less problematic. Conversely, the renaissance of indigenous culture implies a serious threat to continued colonial domination.'[70] As Balandier puts it, European racialism could be countered by racialism on the part of the colonised – induced by the former.[71]

Essential to any colonial relationship were rationalisations meant to justify the position of the colonisers. These included the assertion of racial and cultural superiority; the argument that native peoples did not have the leadership skills needed to advance; that they were unable to exploit the natural resources of their countries; and that they lacked the finance. This meant, in effect, that colonial relationships were underpinned by ideologies that generated and were in turn generated by, stereotyped behaviour.[72] It was these ideologies and the rationalizations embedded in them that enabled a numerical minority of colonisers to establish social, political and economic power over the typically much greater numbers of people they subordinated.[73] But, as we shall see presently, the 'culture of colonialism', was, to repeat an earlier point, not simply a matter of subordination. Before coming to that the idea of internal colonialism needs to be considered; principally because it is something once again connected with the moral legitimacy of international society and has relevance for the contemporary situation of many indigenous peoples who claim that for them colonialism has not ended.

Internal colonialism

Michael Hechter's rigorous account of internal colonialism is one written to explain why particular ethnic groups are excluded from national development. Hechter defines national development as a process that 'occur[s] when the separate cultural identities of regions begin to lose social significance, and become blurred'. It is a process that creates a *national* culture in which 'core and peripheral cultures . . . ultimately merge into one all-encompassing cultural system to which all members of the society have primary identification and loyalty'.[74] His concern is with explaining why this does not always happen.

---

[70] Hechter, *Internal Colonialism*, p. 73.   [71] Balandier, *Sociology of Black Africa*, p. 47.
[72] Ibid., p. 47.   [73] Ibid., pp. 33–4.   [74] Hechter, *Internal Colonialism*, p. 5.

The expectation that the separate cultural identities of regions do actually lose significance is contained in the so-called diffusion model of development that posits three temporal stages of national development. The first of these is a pre-industrial phase in which 'core and peripheral regions exist in virtual isolation from one another'. With the onset of industrialisation this is succeeded by a period of more intensive contact in which the social structure of the core diffuses into the periphery with the result that the two eventually become culturally homogeneous. The 'economic, cultural and political foundations for separate ethnic identification disappear[s].'[75] In the final stage, a more even distribution of wealth between regions is achieved, 'cultural differences . . . cease to be socially meaningful; and political processes . . . occur within a framework of national parties'.[76]

The model of internal colonialism predicts instead that 'except under exceptional circumstances' national development does not necessarily follow industrialization. In contrast to the cultural conversion of the diffusion model, that of internal colonialism is one of cultural domination. The core seeks to maintain its social position. It reserves 'high prestige' social roles for its members and excludes from those roles individuals from 'the less advanced' periphery. There is no 'acculturation because it is not in the interest of institutions within the core'. Economically the pattern of development in the periphery remains dependent upon and 'complementary to that of the core'.[77] To the extent that the difference between the core and periphery is based on observable cultural differences 'there exists the probability that the disadvantaged group will, in time, reactively assert its own culture as equal or superior to that of the relatively advantaged core'. If it does, this may ultimately 'help it conceive of itself as a separate "nation" and seek independence'. Finally, the internal colonialism model is one in which political cleavages are largely a reflection of 'significant cultural difference between groups'.[78]

The reasons for this brief excursion into the concept of internal colonialism were its relevance to the moral foundation of particular states and to some groups of indigenous peoples. Taking these in turn: to the extent that a state incorporates structures of internal colonialism that disadvantages its citizens, it can be regarded as a politically and morally flawed state. As a protector of the sovereignty of such states, international society is something that condones and supports the social,

---

[75] Ibid., p. 7.   [76] Ibid., p. 8.   [77] Ibid., p. 9.   [78] Ibid., p. 10.

political and economic subordination within states. The moral basis of international society itself is, then, to reiterate an earlier suggestion, in need of critical appraisal. Concerning indigenous peoples internal colonialism presents a complicated picture. In the first place, it has a contemporary relevance no longer enjoyed by external colonialism. It is applicable to states that are not externally dominated, but which have indigenous populations making substantial claims against them.[79] Second, it is a way of conceptualising the marginalisation of indigenous peoples but in a way that sees the maintenance of cultural difference as something negative. Contrary to this, many indigenous peoples now see cultural difference as not only positive but fundamental to their identity and survival.

The culture of colonialism

So far this discussion of colonialism has emphasised relations of domination and subordination. Colonialism should not, however, be viewed as simply a story of denial and subjugation. At all times colonialism has involved complex interactions between cultures and there has not been simply colonialism but colonialisms. Nicholas Thomas argues that colonialism is not a uniform practice in all places at all times but instead a 'localised' 'plurality of colonising endeavours',[80] that differs from place to place. It is not 'a unitary project but a fractured one, riddled with contradictions and exhausted as much by its own internal debates as by the resistance of the colonised'.[81]

Thomas presents colonialism as a 'cultural practice' that varies greatly over time and involves a complex interaction between cultures, not only in the past but as a continuing practice. In order to develop this theme Thomas first refers to racism as a practice that has been regarded generally as 'a universal feature of inter-ethnic or inter-societal relations'.[82] The reality is instead more that the 'quality and intensity of racism vary in different colonial contexts and at different historical moments'.[83] Apart from that, race has also been falsely thought of as 'the only basis for representing others or representing them negatively'.[84] In the same way

---

[79] For a discussion of internal and external colonialism see James Tully, 'The Struggles of Indigenous Peoples for and of Freedom', in D. Ivison, P. Patton and W. Sanders (eds.), *Political Theory and the Rights of Indigenous Peoples* (Cambridge University Press, 2000), pp. 36–59.
[80] Nicholas Thomas, *Colonialism's Culture: Anthropology, Travel and Government* (Cambridge: Polity Press, 1944), p. 20.
[81] Ibid., p. 51.   [82] Ibid., p. 14.   [83] Ibid.   [84] Ibid., p. 54.

that racism has been incorrectly accepted as an unvarying and uniform feature of it, colonialism as a whole has generally been cast in negative terms that neglect its positive effects. It was a 'destructive process' that 'entailed inexcusable denials of the sovereignty and autonomy of the colonised' but 'this obscures the extent to which colonial projects were in many cases regarded as civilizing, progressive, necessary undertakings'.[85] Thus Thomas cites Johannes Fabian's suggestion that 'not only "the crooks and brutal exploiters, but the honest and intelligent agents of colonialism need to be accounted for"'.[86] To fully comprehend colonialism it is not sufficient to dwell on its denial and exploitation; there must also be some attempt to understand the minds of those who perceived themselves as having decent motives.

A second, related, point Thomas makes is that colonisation was not merely a matter of domination and assimilation. Colonisers were often troubled by their inability to fathom the minds of those they sought to control. Among colonisers there was no uniform 'imagining of, or will to, total dominance: colonial rule was frequently haunted by a sense of insecurity, terrified by the obscurity of "the native mentality" and overwhelmed by indigenous societies' apparent intractability in the face of government'.[87] Much later Thomas returns to this with the observation that colonialism could fail not only because it was resisted 'or because one colonial project undermined another, but also because colonisers were often simply unable to imagine themselves, their situations and their prospects in the enabling, expansionist, supremacist fashion that colonial ideologies projected'.[88]

The self-understanding of colonisers and colonial ideologies referred to here are vital elements of 'colonial discourse'. In the same way that contemporary foreign policies are often meant as much for domestic audiences in the states that pronounce them as for the states to which they are directed, much colonial discourse was 'addressed not at colonised populations, but at public opinion within colonising nations'. Given this, Thomas argues, 'it needs to be acknowledged that the discourse may not have impinged upon indigenous consciousness at all, or was at best indirectly related to discourses at the site of colonisation'.[89] It cannot, in other words, be assumed that the practice of colonialism matched the rhetoric of it. Further than this, it cannot be assumed, as it often has been, that there was any uniform imposition and adoption of practices such as Christianity, which 'has been indigenized in a great variety of

---

[85] Ibid., p. 14.   [86] Ibid., p. 15.   [87] Ibid.   [88] Ibid., p. 167.   [89] Ibid., pp. 57–8.

localised variants';[90] a point well made by Irene Silverblatt[91] with regard to Peruvian Indians of the sixteenth century.

Apart from enlarging on the claim that colonialism is not a single and unvarying practice, or 'unitary totality', this discussion of Nicholas Thomas is intended also to draw attention to the inter-subjective relationships inherent in the colonial situation. Colonialism is constituted by cultural difference. Colonisers construct or attempt to make sense of 'the other' in ways that reflect their own understanding of themselves. Their construction or account of what it is to be the other need not accord with the self-understanding of the other. Nevertheless, the other may in turn adopt aspects of the construction that has been made and use it to deal with the coloniser. The other may even use it to gain a degree of control in an otherwise inherently unequal relationship. This is in effect a form of the other constructing the coloniser. What is ultimately important about this process of inter-subjective understanding, is that in the distortions of mutual understanding and knowledge and the power relations inherent in it, the identity of the other is either submerged or lost. It is reconstituted for the purposes of the coloniser, or in the context of this book, Europeans. Consequently, aboriginality, the concept of what it is to be aboriginal, is defined by the European other.

This has important consequences and it will be helpful for later argument to summarise part of Thomas' discussion of post-colonial 'ways of subverting limiting constructions of Maoriness and Aboriginality'. For this purpose he refers to *Bran Nue Dae*, a 'musical written by Jimmy Chi of the Aboriginal community of Broome, in the far northwest of Western Australia.' *Bran Nue Dae* 'defines Aboriginality through the experience of assimilation and its rejection, as something that can be recovered through self-identification, rather than a quantity [*sic*] that "authentic" Aborigines possess more than others'.[92] Anthropology has constructed 'cultures that were often abstracted from the dynamics of interactions between colonisers and colonised, and which were constructed in terms of Western absences and viewers' interests . . .'.[93] Another way of saying this is that there is no essential quality that defines what it means to be an Aboriginal. In the contemporary context aboriginality is framed by the experience of first being assimilated and then by the process of

[90] Ibid., p. 63.
[91] See Irene Silverblatt, 'Becoming Indian in the Central Andes of Seventeenth-Century Peru', in G. Prakash (ed.), *After Colonialism: Imperial Histories and Postcolonial Displacements* (Princeton University Press, 1995).
[92] Thomas, *Colonialism's Culture*, p. 191.   [93] Ibid., p. 194.

rejecting the dominant European culture. Aboriginal identity can now be recovered only by self-identification as an Aboriginal and it will take a variety of forms. Essentially, Aboriginality is now the product of an interaction of cultures. Like Aboriginality 'culture' must also now be seen as something defined by the interaction of difference. For Thomas, *Bran Nue Dae* exemplifies post-colonial approaches to identity that seek to replace essentialist notions of Aboriginality with ones anchored in the 'experiences constitutive of contemporary indigenous life'. Its merit is precisely that it celebrates an Aboriginality as constituted by 'pluralized identities that emerge through historical dislocations rather than from a stable ethnicity'.[94] It can be known only by self-definition and in Chapter 4 it will be seen that this is crucial for the recovery of indigenous peoples' rights and the question of self-determination.

The language of international law

European exploration, conquest and colonisation raised fundamental questions about whether Europeans could lawfully claim sovereignty and/or title over the lands of non-Europeans; whether non-Europeans were the rightful owners of lands they occupied; and about the rights non-Europeans held against European sovereigns or states. Several terms essential to the discussion of these questions in the history of international law are at the same time ones that belong to the vocabulary of the expansion of international society. Those needing clarification in this context are *imperium, dominium, conquest, cession,* and finally, *terra nullius.*

Imperium is the Latin for sovereignty and is primarily an expression of authority over persons but includes also the relationship between a state and its territory. Sovereignty uncoupled from its Latin origin can refer to either persons or territory; only *imperium* denotes both forms of sovereignty.

Dominium is the Latin for property.[95] Whereas the 'acquisition of territory is chiefly the province of international law; the acquisition of property is chiefly the province of common law'.[96] The importance of this distinction is that when a European sovereign or state claimed sovereignty over non-Europeans this did not, in theory, necessarily extend to title over the property of those non-Europeans. In practice, however, it usually did result in the denial of native ownership.

---

[94] Ibid.   [95] Westlake, *Collected Papers*, p. 135.
[96] J. Brennan, in *Mabo* vs. *Queensland, The Australian Law Journal,* 66: 7 (1992), 423.

Conquest, cession and the *occupation* of territory that was regarded as
terra nullius were each ways of acquiring sovereignty. In the previous
section we saw that conquest was defined by the use of force. This
begged the question of the circumstances under which force was justified and is the reason why much early legal and moral argument about
European conquest centred on the conditions of Just War. Cession sig-
nified that title to territory had been ceded by its occupants, usually
in a treaty. This was the method by which Europeans gained title in a
number of cases in North America and in much of Africa. Whether the
Indian and African peoples who signed these treaties were aware of
their significance is open to question. James Crawford's opinion is that
the treaties were not 'always illusory or a mere sham'.[97] Treaties were,
nevertheless, a means of taking control of land and much else out of
the hands of indigenous peoples. That said, it should be recognised that
in the important cases of New Zealand (Aoteora) and Canada, historic
treaties are now the basis of negotiation between indigenous peoples
and the dominant white settler societies. In the case of New Zealand
the 1985 Treaty of Waitangi Amendment Act widened the powers of
the Waitangi Tribunal, set up under the 1975 Treaty of Waitangi Act,
enabling it to investigate claims dating back to 1840.[98] And in Canada,
the amendment of its Constitution in 1982 recognised and affirmed 'the
existing Aboriginal and treaty rights of Canada's Aboriginal peoples'.[99]

Territorium nullius is defined by Lindley as 'a tract of territory . . . not
subject to any sovereignty – either because it has never been so subject, or, having once been in that condition, has been abandoned – [in
which case] the sovereignty over it is open to acquisition by a process
analogous to that by which property can be acquired in an ownerless
thing'.[100] A land that was not *territorium nullius* was one 'inhabited by
a political society', which Lindley defined as 'a considerable number of
persons who are permanently united by habitual obedience to a certain

[97] James Crawford (ed.), *The Rights of Peoples* (Oxford: Clarendon Press, 1988), pp. 179–80.
Bull makes a different but nonetheless relevant point:'While it would be wrong to accept
the imperialist thesis of the time, that African political communities all over the continent voluntarily extinguished themselves, there is also danger in projecting backwards
into history the assumption of the present time, that no political community could know-
ingly prefer colonial status to independence.' Bull, 'European States', pp. 112–13.
[98] Claudia Orange, *The Story of a Treaty* (Wellington: Bridget Williams Books, 1990), p. 78.
[99] Hamar Foster, 'Canada: "Indian Administration" from the Royal Proclamation of
1763 to Constitutionally Entrenched Aboriginal Rights', in P. Haverman (ed.), *Indigenous
People's Rights In Australia, Canada, and New Zealand* (Auckland: Oxford University Press,
1999), p. 367.
[100] Lindley, *Acquisition and Government*, p. 10.

and common superior, or whose conduct in regard to their mutual relations habitually conforms to recognised standards'.[101] In theory this meant 'only "an unsettled" horde of wandering savages not yet formed into civil society', or more neutrally, only nomadic tribesmen lacking all regular political organisation could 'be regarded as not legal occupants of their territory'. Unoccupied territories defined in this way were, as Crawford observes, very few and confined mainly to Australia and New Zealand. In the case of Australia, *terra nullius* continued to have a life in legal discourse down to the 1992 *Mabo* vs. *Queensland* case before the High Court. In his judgment of that case Justice Brennan said: 'It was only by fastening on the notion that a settled colony was *terra nullius* that it was possible to predicate of the Crown the acquisition of ownership of land in a colony already occupied by indigenous inhabitants. It was only on the hypothesis that there was nobody in occupation that it could be said that the crown was the owner because there was no other.'[102]

Three points need to be made about *terra nullius*. First, it is hard to say when the actual term first entered legal and diplomatic language. It was used widely in the nineteenth century but in earlier times lands of the kind it was meant to describe were usually simply referred to as either 'uninhabited' or *vacuum domicillium*. Thus William Blackstone spoke of 'desert uninhabited countries'[103] rather than *terra nullius*. Second, by the time Lindley was writing the concept of *terra nullius* had been widened to include lands that were in fact inhabited. It had been enlarged by international law to justify the acquisition of the territory occupied by so-called 'backward' peoples who did not conform to European understandings of political society. Third, in the nineteenth century, especially during the 'Scramble for Africa', *terra nullius* was a reference not to whether territory was occupied by non-Europeans but, instead, another European state. At the time of the Scramble for Africa it was usual for European states to claim sovereignty over territory they did not actually occupy. For claims to be sustained against counter-claims from other European states the claimant had to 'effectively occupy' the territory in question within a reasonable time. *Terra nullius* in this sense served the role of international law in prescribing ways to avoid conflict between European states.

---

[101] Cited by Crawford (ed.), *The Rights of Peoples*, pp. 179–80.
[102] J. Brennan, in *Mabo* vs. *Queensland*, 424.
[103] William Blackstone, *Commentaries on the Laws of England, Vol. II, Of the Rights of Things (1766)*, Intro. H. W. Simpson (University of Chicago Press, 1979), p. 7.

The next and last section of this chapter addresses the question of why it should be 'peoples' rather than just 'people' or individuals that need to be brought into international society.

'Peoples' and international society

The term 'peoples' in the title of this chapter was deliberately chosen in preference to the singular 'people' for two reasons. First, because of both the nature of the claims made by indigenous peoples and the way they represent themselves. Indigenous peoples' rights are claimed as group rights. They are concerned with the rights due to a culture rather than to particular individuals located within it. In relation to this, Chapter 4 concerns, in part, the extent to which indigenous rights are adequately provided for by the major human rights instruments, which in theory do provide for indigenous peoples, but are essentially the rights of individuals. At the same time, it will be shown that 'peoples' is a politically problematic term in relation to the central issue of self-determination. A second reason for choosing 'peoples' is to draw attention to the plurality of indigenous peoples, already referred to in the Introduction. To speak only of an indigenous 'people' would be to ignore or at least obscure the differences between indigenous groups from one place to another. Indigenous peoples may be able to speak with a single voice on some issues affecting all of them but not on others.

Given that indigenous peoples are enclosed within the political, legal and moral boundaries of states, what does it mean to talk about bringing peoples into international society? Two senses are intended in this book. First, contemporary international society is by definition a society of states. This means that in crucial respects indigenous peoples, in common with non-indigenous individuals, generally have had a place in international society only as citizens of states. But one of the complaints of indigenous peoples is precisely that the states of which they are a part have deprived, and continue to deprive, them of political, cultural, and property rights. Consequently many indigenous peoples seek recognition of an international personality that will support their claims against states over issues not already covered in existing human rights instruments. To bring peoples into international society in this sense would be to give them a distinct international personality and ensure their group rights. A later task therefore will be to pay attention to the ways in which international society, having excluded indigenous peoples, either does, or might in future, support the group rights of indigenous peoples; especially the right of self-determination both within constitutional law and in international global law. The second sense of bringing indigenous peoples into international society is the more general one of making them a more prominent part of the story of the expansion of international society from, as Bull put it, a 'society of Christian or European states [to] one that is global or all inclusive'.[104]

With regard to the first of these senses the final chapter of the book considers the ways in which international society is already transforming itself or might in future be transformed into one that accommodates indigenous claims. We have already noted that Bull distinguished between international society and a future world society in which the interests of individuals are prior to those of states. In his 1984 Hagey Lectures he linked this to justice and the development of a 'cosmopolitan moral awareness' concerned with human welfare throughout the world that would extend 'our capacity to empathise with sections of humanity that are geographically or culturally distinct from us'. His argument was that

> the rights and benefits to which justice has to be done in the international community are not simply those of states and nations, but those of individual persons throughout the world as a whole. The world we live in is not organised as a cosmopolis or world state; it is a system of independent states. But within this system, the idea of the rights and duties of the individual person has come to have a place, albeit an insecure one, and it is our responsibility to seek to extend it.[105]

If the liberal tradition in the West is to be upheld, he continued, then '[w]hat is ultimately important has to be reckoned in terms of the rights and interests of the individual persons of whom humanity is made up, not the rights and interests of states into which these persons are now divided'.[106] And again on the following page: 'The world common good . . . is the common interest not of states, but of the human species in maintaining itself.'[107]

Bringing 'peoples', whether indigenous or not, into international society in the first of the senses identified above would require the extension of cosmopolitan moral awareness. What is not so clear is whether

---

[104] Bull, 'Importance of Grotius', p. 80.
[105] Hedley Bull, *Justice in International Relations*, The Hagey Lectures, Waterloo, Ont.: Waterloo University, 1984, p. 12. Reproduced in K. Alderson and A. Hurrell (eds.), *Hedley Bull on International Society* (London: Macmillan, 2000), pp. 206–45.
[106] Ibid., p. 13.   [107] Ibid., p. 14.

group rights, as part of the process, can be situated in the liberal tradition cited by Bull. Nor is it clear that the world common good can be advanced by the existing structures of the state and an international society constituted of states. The satisfaction of indigenous claims would mean acknowledging 'multiple identities' that may in turn require what Andrew Linklater calls, in another context, 'new political structures which go beyond efforts to maintain orders between settled bounded communities'.[108] This also will be taken up in the final chapter.

In conclusion, the purpose of this chapter has been to clarify the foundations laid by others for the chapters that follow. At the same time it has argued that the expansion of Europe was achieved through practices that involved not only the dispossession and subordination of non-European others but also complex interactions between cultures. In relation to this it has argued that the methods by which the expansion of international society was achieved and the ideologies that supported it call into question the legitimacy of states created as a result of expansion. To the extent that they were founded on genocide and dispossession they are morally flawed states and the moral foundations of the international society that is constituted by them is also called into question. Chapter 2 considers the conceptualisation of indigenous non-Europeans in the language of political theory.

---

[108] Andrew Linklater, 'Citizenship and Sovereignty in the Post-Westphalian State', *European Journal of International Relations* 2: 1 (1996), 99.

2   Wild 'men' and other tales

The expansion overseas of European peoples as explorers and settlers required them to respond, in some way, to 'other' peoples who were both culturally and racially very different from themselves. While there were differences between Europeans themselves, they belonged to an essentially common culture. The diverse peoples they encountered in the Americas, Africa, Asia and the Pacific represented a variety of cultures radically different from their own. Coming into contact with many of these peoples for the first time must have been an extraordinary experience for Europeans; as it would have been for those they encountered. On the part of both Europeans and non-Europeans alike, there were varying degrees of, if not total, incomprehension or lack of mutual understanding of each other. Cultural incommensurabilty, or the absence of a common measure between cultures, was a crucial element in the development of relations between Europeans and non-Europeans. Europeans generally either made no attempt, or else failed, to understand non-Europeans in their own terms. Instead, Europeans typically conceptualised non-Europeans in ways that regarded them as inferior; dehumanised them; and treated them as representing a lower stage of political, social and economic development that Europeans had themselves left behind.

This chapter considers some ways in which non-Europeans were conceptualised by Europeans. Its purpose is neither to write a history nor to present a novel argument but instead to understand some important concepts in the evolution of European thought concerning others. It first surveys three different but overlapping and suggestive accounts of European encounters with non-European others. Next it discusses the language used to classify others before rehearsing the stages of development theory and the purpose of categorising non-Europeans as either 'noble' or 'ignoble savages'. The final section discusses the state of nature, natural rights and property as concepts crucial to rationalising the dispossession of non-Europeans.

Conceptualising non-European others

Tzvetan Todorov's *The Conquest of America*, Anthony Pagden's *European Encounters with the New World*, and Bernard McGrane's *Beyond Anthropology: Society and the Other*[1] each, in their own distinctive way, provide insight into the dynamics of European encounters with non-Europeans.[2] The inquiries by Todorov and Pagden concern cultural incommensurability and are framed with reference to Amerindians, but their analysis is equally applicable to many other non-European peoples. McGrane has the broader purpose of working through changing European conceptions of otherness that necessarily extend to a larger range of peoples. These three books are of course not the only ones to deal with such themes, but they serve as well as any others to illustrate the dynamics of European encounters with non-Europeans.

Todorov: the failure to know others

The Conquest of America attempts to understand the reasoning and mental processes of people central to the discovery of the Americas, the conquest of the Mexican Empire and subsequent attempts to either understand or defend Amerindians. Todorov's method is to engage in a searching textual analysis of the actions and writings of these people. Ultimately his concern is not merely with Columbus and events in sixteenth-century Mexico but with the morality of European conduct towards those who are 'different' at all subsequent times and places. Mexico is, thus, as much a metaphor in a moral tale as it is a concern in its own right. It is, overall, a tale in which there has been a marked

---

[1] Tzvetan Todorov, *The Conquest of America: The Question of the Other* (New York: Harper Torch, 1992), Pagden, *European Encounters with the New World*, Bernard McGrane, *Beyond Anthropology: Society and the Other* (New York: Columbia University Press, 1989).
[2] Some other accounts include: Stuart B. Schwartz (ed.), *Implicit Understandings: Observing, Reporting, and Reflecting on the Encounters Between Europeans and Other Peoples in the Early Modern Era* (Cambridge University Press, 1994); J. H. Elliott, *The Old World and the New 1492–1650* (Cambridge University Press, 1992); H. Peckham and Charles Gibson (eds.), *British-Colonial Attitudes and Policies Toward the Indian in the American Colonies* (Salt Lake City: University of Utah Press, 1969); Boies Penrose, *Travel and Discovery in the Renaissance, 1420–1620* (Cambridge, MA: Harvard University Press, 1952); P. J. Marshall and Glyndwr Williams, *The Great Map of Mankind: British Perceptions of the World in the Age of Enlightenment* (London: Dent, 1982).

failure to 'know' others. For Todorov, we remain today in the position of Columbus, for whom the other remained to be 'discovered'.

Todorov's analysis is arranged in four parts, entitled *Discovery*, *Conquest*, *Love* and *Knowledge*. The first of these focuses on Columbus and his essentially medieval mode of thought. One characteristic of this was the acceptance of texts in preference to empirical evidence. Columbus had read texts such as Marco Polo's Journeys and despite ample evidence to the contrary believed he had succeeded in reaching the fabled Cathay. In a number of instances he chose to interpret what he saw as confirmation of what was already known or decided, thereby fundamentally misunderstanding what was before him. With regard to Indians, his way of thought prevented him from perceiving them as fully human like himself. Although he was himself able to speak several European languages, he neither recognised the variety of Indian languages nor the fact that they possessed speech in the way that he did himself. One consequence of this was that he took no interest in the Indian names for geographical and other natural phenomena, choosing instead to give them names that allowed him to relate them to his own mental universe. Columbus apparently was more interested in fauna and flora than in Indians and regarded them as specimens, much like the plants and animals that captured his interest. When it was to his advantage Columbus exploited his knowledge of natural phenomena, such as the immanence of an eclipse, to exercise power over 'natives'. That he was able to do this merely confirmed for him that Indians were not in the full sense 'human' beings.

In fact his attitude towards Indians was, according to Todorov, ambiguous. He fluctuated between two kinds of response to Indians:

> Either he conceives the Indians (though without using these words) as human beings altogether, having the same rights as himself; but then he sees them not only as equals but also identical, and his behaviour leads to assimilationism, the projection of his own values on the others. Or else he starts from the difference, but the latter is immediately translated into terms of superiority and inferiority (in his case, obviously, it is the Indians who are inferior). What is denied is the existence of a human substance truly other, something capable of being not merely an imperfect state of oneself.[3]

This ambivalence is, according to Todorov, found in the attitudes of colonisers down to the present day. And it is indeed something that

---

[3] Todorov, *Conquest of America*, p. 42.

crops up later in this book. For the moment we need note only that Todorov's fundamental point about Columbus is that while he might have discovered America he did not discover the Americans.[4]

The second part of *The Conquest of America* concerns the question of how a vastly outnumbered expedition of Spaniards was able to overthrow and subjugate the Aztec empire. For Todorov the answer lies neither in any superior technology nor military skills that the Spaniards may have possessed, nor in their ability to exploit divisions within the Mexican empire, but in the beliefs of the Aztecs. Of these the Spaniards gained some knowledge which they then used to exercise power. In this part of the story the key figures are Cortés as commander of the Spanish, and Montezuma, ruler and high priest of the Aztecs, and La Malinche, the linguistically gifted Indian woman who was for a time Cortés consort and the means by which the Spaniards were initially able to communicate with the Indians.

The society of the Mexican or Nahuatl peoples was highly ritualised. In the Aztec mind various practices had to be strictly observed if the natural and social order were to be prevented from collapse. Omens and the interpretation of them were regarded as essential guides to action. The year that Cortés began his expedition coincided with one in the Aztec calendar in which it was expected that the god Quetzalcoatl would return to Mexico. To have opposed his return would have meant the destruction of the natural and social order. As Cortés' expedition began various signs were interpreted by Montezuma and his seers as confirmation that Cortés was none other than Quetzalcoatl. Through La Malinche, Cortés was able to guess at what might be passing through Montezuma's mind and so exploit that knowledge to his own ends. 'The conquest of information', as Todorov puts it, 'leads to that of kingdom.'[5] The way that Montezuma interpreted signs was, Todorov points out, not at all unlike Columbus' insistence on seeing what he encountered as a confirmation of the texts he had read. Montezuma similarly chose to interpret omens that could be related to Spanish actions as a confirmation of expectations. Though in his case it was, according to Todorov, often as if the prophecy had been 'fabricated *a posteriori*'.[6] Despite these similarities, what was in the end crucial about the conquest was, as in any

[4] Ibid., p. 49.
[5] Ibid., p. 104. On the association of the Quetzalcoatl legend with Cortés, see Anna Lanyon, *Malinche's Conquest* (Sydney: Allen & Unwin, 1999), pp. 1120–1. Lanyon notes Pagden's observation in the introduction to his translation of Cortés's letters that the legend arose later in the sixteenth century as an evangelising device used by Franciscans.
[6] Todorov, *Conquest of America*, p. 86.

number of other examples, the contrary imaginations of the Spaniards and the Aztecs. The gap between the mental worlds of the two was too great to be bridged. For the Aztecs it meant that they did not resist the Spaniards as quickly, decisively and forcibly as they might have done. For the Spaniards it meant reacting with violence and greed against a culture of which they had little understanding, and to which they reacted with a mixture of admiration and disgust. Perhaps the Aztecs would in any case have succeeded only in staving off the destruction of their civilisation by others until a later date.

The third part of the book concerns the failure of those who achieved some understanding of and even admired the Indians, to accept them in ways that did not entail the assumption of European superiority. Instead of acceptance, understanding resulted in the rejection of what was different and it did so in one of two ways. On the one hand, people were regarded as different, inferior and not fully human. Difference in this case is 'corrupted into inequality'.[7] On the other hand, understanding resulted in accepting those who were different as equal; but this effaced difference. Indians were not accepted as both different and equal. To accept them as equal was to accept them in terms of a European identity and thus once again to impose a relationship of superiority and inferiority.

In the course of exploring the logic of these moves between equality and inequality/superiority and inferiority, Todorov coins the phrase: the 'paradox of the understanding-that-kills'. This, he says, is something that can be resolved once it is grasped that those who understand often form 'an entirely negative value judgement of the other'.[8] This judgement did not necessarily extend to the material culture of the Indians but denied them as the authors of it. According to Todorov, Cortés greatly admired the objects produced by the Aztecs. Indeed he 'goes into ecstasies about the Aztec productions but does not acknowledge their makers as human individualities to set on the same level as himself'.[9] Of the Conquistadors generally he argues that they did not regard Indians as full subjects 'comparable to the I who contemplates and conceives them'. Indians belonged instead 'to a series of "natural curiosities"'.[10] The admiration for their artifacts combined with the inability to accept the Indians as human individualities and as full subjects meant that Spaniards could 'speak well of Indians but rarely to them'.[11] Ultimately

---

[7] Ibid., p. 146. [8] Ibid., p. 127. [9] Ibid., p. 129.
[10] Ibid., p. 130. [11] Ibid., p. 132.

the Spaniards were apparently incapable of comparing themselves in a negative way with the Indians. They were, for instance, repulsed by the highly ritualised killing involved in sacrifice, but were totally uncritical of the random massacres perpetrated by themselves.

The last part of *The Conquest of America* analyses the people who came closest in the years immediately after the Conquest to getting inside the minds of the Indians and bridging the gap between Spanish and Indian cultures. These were the people who compiled dictionaries of the Nahuatl language and recorded Indian accounts of the Conquest, in particular Diego Duran and Bernardino De Sahagún. About Duran, Todorov concludes that while his empirical work was exemplary and he became 'Indianized', he remains ambiguous. He is in the final analysis unable to judge the Indians in their own terms, and does so from the perspective of Christianity. Sahagún saw that Indian beliefs could not 'be toppled without toppling the society itself' and that what the Spaniards sought to set in place of Aztec cosmology was, 'even from the Christian point of view', inferior.[12] Whereas Duran seemed to favour a hybridisation of cultures, Sahagún did not, preferring instead to juxtapose the two cultures and to write that either the 'idolatries' of the Indians or Holy Writ 'tells the truth, the other lies'. 'And yet', Todorov adds, 'we see here the first sketches of a future dialogue . . .'.[13]

Pagden: incommensurablity

In concluding *European Encounters with the New World*, Pagden observes that: 'If the discovery of America taught enlightened Europe anything it was, in the end, a form of despair: the recognition that the "savage", however defined, could ultimately have no place outside a world system whose character was already markedly European, yet could never survive as a "savage" within it.'[14] Earlier he makes the point that in the history of European encounters with non-European others 'the cultures of the West – do not merely respond to the presence of the "other": we actually construct him or her'.[15] All who encountered America were 'driven by their need to make some sense of the beliefs and the ethical lives of others. This may have resulted in an attempt to construct "others" better suited to the observer's own particular ethical life . . .'.[16] His conclusion is then a way of saying that the 'savage' – or non-European other – could not escape being drawn into a conceptual and actual world

---

[12] Ibid, p. 238.   [13] Ibid., p. 241.
[14] Pagden, *European Encounters*, p. 188.   [15] Ibid., p. 183.   [16] Ibid., p. 184.

created by Europeans; but equally, because Europeans 'construct' or define the identity of the 'other' according to their own understanding of the world, the non-European other is robbed of his or her own self-understanding of identity.

Pagden's departure point is that for Europe the 'discovery' of America posed 'the possibility, and for many the impossibility, of cultural commensurability'.[17] In pursuit of this theme he identifies and examines different modes of response adopted by Europeans from one time to another, in their attempts to understand the radically different culture of Amerindians. Each mode is a way of knowing that is in fact a failure to actually know Indians. The first is the *principle of attachment*. This is the idea that when Europeans attempted to understand the practices of others they commonly responded by translating 'varieties of experience from an alien world into the practices of [their] own'. It meant attaching an unfamiliar action of the other to a familiar European practice. It imposed on Amerindian actions a European significance and understanding that might have been utterly different from Amerindian understanding. For Europeans the strategy of interpreting actions in terms of apparently similar European actions imparted familiarity to the unfamiliar; it made 'the incommensurable seem commensurable'.[18]

As an example Pagden cites the way Columbus made the actions of the Taino Indians recognisable in his own terms and so 're-located them in a context which would have made them unintelligible to their original actors'. Even though Columbus' understanding distorted what the Indians might have intended, it 'offered at least an initial identification with humanity'.[19] The practices that he so interpreted were in fact too far from European practices to allow any 'direct assimilation of one to the other'.[20] Todorov similarly notices that Columbus neither grappled with Indian understanding nor was aware that Indians might not establish the same distinctions as Spaniards.

A second mode of understanding relied on what Pagden calls the *capacity for cognitive travel*. By this he means that Europeans imagined other worlds on the basis of representations by their compatriots and specimens transported from those other worlds. Indians were taken to Europe not because Europeans were interested in Indians as individuals but because they were representatives of a world unknown to and located in places difficult for Europeans to visit.[21] Europeans had no

---

[17] Ibid., p. 2. [18] Ibid., p. 36. [19] Ibid., p. 21. [20] Ibid., p. 24. [21] Ibid., p. 32.

interest in knowing them as persons but as objects of 'scientific' curiosity. Indeed, they were not accepted as being fully the same as Europeans. Pagden cites Jean de Lery, a Protestant missionary to Brazil between 1556 and 1558, as having held the view that Tupinamba Indians were men but only in the sense that 'the genus *homo sapiens* contain[ed] more than one species'.[22] Both the principle of attachment and the related phenomenon of cognitive travel are, in effect, ways of saying that what is assumed to be known is not actually 'known' at all.

Extending both of these, a third mode of understanding is what Pagden calls the *autopic imagination*. By this he means to encapsulate the idea of 'autopsy' and appeal to eyewitness accounts: the claim that the New World and its inhabitants could be known only by first-hand experience. When the Spaniards first began to go to the Americas they were burdened, as we have seen in the case of Columbus, with a collection of Canonical texts that conflicted with empirical evidence garnered by eyewitnesses concerning the nature of Amerindians. Officials in Spain were then confronted with the dilemma of whether to believe the texts or rather the eyewitnesses. This was not easily resolved precisely because different witnesses made different claims about the same thing. Gonzalo Fernandez de Oviedo and Bartolomè de Las Casas had both been to America, but whereas Oviedo saw Indians as beasts Las Casas saw them as people who would with 'instruction in the Christian faith and prolonged exposure to the more uplifting aspects of European culture [eventually] cease entirely to be "other"'.[23] In terms of contemporary understanding they would, in other words, eventually lose their cultural identity.

Las Casas, as we shall see in Chapter 3, was engaged in a defence of the humanity and consequently as well the 'full legal equality' of Indians with the Spaniards. His defence depended upon claiming the authority of his own first-hand experience in support of 'an interpretation of the canonical texts [that] . . . secure the human status of the Indians before a community for whom exegesis was the only access to knowledge'.[24] It meant that 'he had to present his experience of the facts as uniquely privileged'.[25]

A fourth kind of European response to Amerindians was to regard them as *representatives of an earlier stage of evolution* from which Europeans themselves had ascended. By arguing that Indians were 'no more "barbarous" than had been some of the remote cultural ancestors

---

[22] Ibid., p. 47.   [23] Ibid., p. 57.   [24] Ibid., p. 73.   [25] Ibid., p. 74.

of the modern Europeans', Indian cultures could be seen as resembling European ones. '[A]nalogies between the ancient Mediterranean and modern American worlds – made the seemingly incommensurable, commensurable'.[26] References of this kind to the Mediterranean were not confined to the Americas of the sixteenth century but continued until at least into the exploration of the Pacific in the eighteenth century.[27] Like the principle of attachment this translation of the unfamiliar into a common past represented a failure to engage with the difference of the other culture. It also was a way of avoiding really knowing.

These themes concerning the European response to Amerindians are contained in the first two chapters of Pagden's book. The remaining three include an analysis of how the discovery of America unsettled conceptions of knowledge; the role of language in distinguishing 'savages' from 'civilised' people; and finally the arguments of selected eighteenth- and nineteenth-century thinkers about the ultimate incommensurablity of all cultures and whether or not erosion of plurality was either desirable or moral. Of these, my immediate concern is with incommensurability and the threat to cultural pluralism posed by European expansion.[28] Colonisation, he points out, was conceived of as a process that 'could, with time, patience and sufficient force, make the incommensurable commensurable. But it could only ever do this by lessening and finally, perhaps, even eliminating the gap which lay between ourselves and the "other", by making the other entirely like us'.[29] In this way incommensurability of understanding between cultures was an important aspect of the expansion of Europe. The modes of understanding adopted by Europeans meant that in the long run some non-European peoples were progressively 'dehumanised' and conceptualised in ways that enabled their subordination by Europeans.

McGrane: changing constructions of the 'other'

Bernard McGrane examines the construction of otherness in the Renaissance, the Enlightenment and during the nineteenth century. Common to all three periods is the one-way process of understanding or failing to

---

[26] Ibid., p. 81.
[27] Bernard Smith, *European Vision and the South Pacific*, 2nd edn (Melbourne University Press, 1989), and Bernard Smith, *Imagining the Pacific: In the Wake of the Cook Voyages* (Melbourne University Press, 1992).
[28] Pagden, *European Encounters*, p. 178.   [29] Ibid., p. 168.

understand made amply clear by Todorov and Pagden. For McGrane, the history of anthropology has been one of 'an extremely subtle and spiritual kind of cognitive imperialism, a power-based monologue, a monologue about alien cultures rather than, and in active avoidance of, a dialogue with them in terms of sovereignty, that is, the untranslatability and irreducibility of one "culture" to the being and language of the other'.[30] What distinguished the other during the Renaissance was 'his' [*sic*] relation 'to the Christianity he lacks . . . The Other in the sixteenth century is, precisely, a non-Christian . . .'.[31] In the case of the Amerindian other this lack of Christianity justified the use of force by Europeans. It also supported the view that Amerindians were barbarians and hence to be treated as natural slaves, which, as we shall see in the next section, was opposed by Las Casas and Vitoria. But at the same time as they lacked Christianity the Amerindians were nevertheless potential Christians. This meant in turn that what made Indians different was recognised and evaluated from the standpoint of an implicit and unquestioned standard. That standard was European. It assumed European Christian culture to be superior to the culture of the Indian other.

In the age of the Enlightenment difference was located and accounted for not in terms of Christianity but instead in terms of 'man's relation to truth (light)'. It was a matter of knowledge. As McGrane puts it:

> Enlightenment knowledge consists in awareness of ignorance and ignorance consists of non-awareness of ignorance. Not knowing about ignorance is the very being of ignorance. The ignorance of the Other consists of the ignorance of ignorance. The alien Others are seen as ignorant because they don't know what they don't know. What they don't know is the nature of ignorance.[32]

By implication Europeans had access to truth and if they had not already done so could escape ignorance. They were consequently superior beings while the other was trapped in ignorance and inferior. This made it easier to discount non-European beliefs and customs.

In the nineteenth century the conjunction of Darwin's theory of evolution, genesis 'as a principle of classification' and the idea of progress

---

[30] McGrane, *Beyond Anthropology*, p. 127.
[31] Ibid., p. 10. On this period see also Dorinda Outram, *The Enlightenment* (Cambridge University Press, 1996), ch. 5.
[32] McGrane, *Beyond Anthropology*, pp. 71–2.

resulted in the other being seen as 'fundamentally primitive'. The alien other was no longer 'fundamentally pagan, savage, and demonic from a Christian frame of reference; nor fundamentally ignorant and superstitious from an Enlightenment reference point; rather the other is now *fundamentally primitive* from a progress and evolution frame of reference'.[33] After 1850 Social Darwinism fostered the growth of 'scientific racism'. The effect of this in Australia, for example, was that '[i]t made it so much easier to take Aboriginal land without negotiation or purchase, to crush resistance to the dispossession and then keep the survivors "in their place" '.[34] Europeans saw little need to take account of the rights of 'savages' and 'primitive societies'.

The problem with McGrane's typology is that the beliefs that characterise each of the periods cannot be confined to them. For many people today others are defined by their lack of Christianity, their ignorance or their 'savagery'. Of course the difference is that these are now minority views rather than the general outlook of a whole society. Nevertheless, periods are not self-contained; they do not have a clear beginning and end. All periods have antecedents linking them to earlier periods. Indeed Nicholas Thomas objects to McGrane on the grounds that 'an analysis that proceeds by identifying epistemological breaks and ruptures, that valorizes terms by establishing their distinctiveness, can suppress continuity across periods and ways of perceiving alterity that remain salient and available, if in varying forms, over time. . . .' Thus Thomas finds McGrane's 'sequence of constructions . . . unsatisfyingly crude', but he nevertheless concedes that 'on the other hand, there are important and fundamental contrasts between the ways of conceiving difference available to the conquerors of the New World and those expressed in the eighteenth and nineteenth centuries and subsequently'.[35] At the same time as being aware of the weaknesses inherent in McGrane's typology it remains, for this reason, useful and is referred to again later.

So far in this chapter I have been concerned with some of the ways in which Europeans conceptualised non-Europeans. The discussion will be extended in the next section by considering terms used by Europeans to classify others and frame discussion of them in political and social thought.

---

[33] Ibid., p. 98.
[34] Henry Reynolds, *Frontier: Aborigines, Settlers and Land* (Sydney: Allen & Unwin, 1987), p. 130.
[35] McGrane, *Beyond Anthropology*, p. 68.

Political language: classifying others
Wild men, barbarians and savages

These three terms are sometimes used interchangeably but each has a distinct meaning. 'Barbarian' and 'savage' are more closely related to each other than either is with the concept of 'wildness'. The essential distinction is that 'barbarians' and 'savages' are individuals or form societies that stand outside of the borders of the societies or states that refer to them by these terms. 'Wildness' refers instead to individuals found *within* ones' own society and ultimately within oneself. The term 'barbarian' has particular importance in connection with its place in the theory of 'natural slavery', articulated by Aristotle, which was used much later to justify the subjugation of non-Europeans. Hayden White argues that:

> [t]he notion of 'wildness' . . . belongs to a set of culturally self-authenticating devices which includes, among many others the ideas of 'madness' and 'heresy' as well. These terms are used not merely to designate a specific condition or state of being but also to confirm the value of their dialectical antithesis: 'civilisation', 'sanity' and 'ortho-doxy' respectively.[36]

Thus 'wildness' can be seen in terms of what White calls the 'technique of ostensive self-definition by negation'. In other words, '[i]f we do not know what we think "civilisation" is, we can always find an example of what it is not'. By appealing to the concept of wildness people were, in the past, able to identify subhumanity in relation to which they could define their humanity 'by everything they hoped they were not'.[37] The concept of wildness enabled those who labelled others as 'wild' to affirm their own 'basically contrived values and norms'.[38] But this was not all; it represented as well the 'repressed content of both civilised and primitive humanity'. The wild man was to be found 'lurking within every man – clamouring for release'.[39]

White traces attitudes to wild men through several phases of European intellectual history, beginning with Augustine for whom only

---

[36] Hayden White, 'The Forms of Wildness: Archaeology of an Idea', in Edward Dudley and Maximillian E. Novak (eds.), *The Wild Man Within: An Image in Western Thought from the Renaissance to Romanticism*, (University of Pittsburgh Press, 1972), p. 4. On the concept of 'wildness' see also Richard Bernheimer, *Wild Men in the Middle Ages: A Study in Art, Sentiment and Demonology* (Cambridge, MA: Harvard University Press, 1952), and T. Husband. *The Wild Man: Medieval Myth and Symbolism* (New York: Metropolitan Museum of Art, 1980).
[37] White, 'Forms of Wildness', p. 5.   [38] Ibid., p. 6.   [39] Ibid., p. 7.

God could know who belonged to the City of God: 'This meant that even the most repugnant of men – barbarian, heathen, pagan, and heretic – had to be regarded as objects of Christian proselytisation, to be seen as possible converts rather than as enemies or sources of corruption, to be exiled, isolated, and destroyed.'[40] Centuries after he had argued this, Augustine's basic propositions became an important element of debate about the treatment of Amerindians in the New World. During the Middle Ages the wild man was counterposed to the barbarian. The latter was seen as a 'threat to society in general' and as a threat to civilisation defined in terms of 'whatever the group's pride happened to be vested in'. Wild men were by contrast a threat to the individual. Unlike the intermittent threats posed by the external barbarian, the wildman was 'always present, inhabiting the immediate confines of community'.[41] The description White then gives of how wildmen were imagined in the Middle Ages is one that equally well describes the image of North American Indians and Australian Aboriginals held by many Europeans during the nineteenth century:

> He is just out of sight, over the horizon, in crevices, under great trees, or in the caves of wild animals, to which he carries off helpless children, or women, there to do unspeakable things to them. And he is sly; he steals the sheep from the fold, the chicken from the coop, tricks the shepherd, and befuddles the gamekeeper.[42]

During the fourteenth and fifteenth centuries this image gave way to one of the wildman as 'an object of open envy and admiration'.[43] White suggests that this may be the result of the influence of the classical culture of ancient Greece and Rome over the Renaissance mind. Finally, in the modern era, the wildman or 'primitive' man ceases to be either an ideal 'or a reminder of what we might become if we betrayed our achieved humanity'. Primitive cultures are instead 'seen as different manifestations of man's power to respond differently to environmental challenges'.[44] While it is not one of White's concerns, the association of primitive cultures with the environment has sometimes taken the form of assuming that indigenous peoples are related to the environments they inhabit in ways that give them a special custodial role.

In contrast to the psychological threat posed by the idea of wildmen, 'barbarians' represented an external threat to 'civilisation'. For the ancient Greeks, barbarians were people who did not speak Greek and were

---

[40] Ibid., p. 17.   [41] Ibid., pp. 20–1.   [42] Ibid.   [43] Ibid., pp. 22–3.   [44] Ibid., pp. 34.

consequently by definition 'uncivilised'. The Romans distinguished barbarians as those who did not live under Roman law; but by submitting
to Roman law 'barbarians' could gain citizenship and admission to civilisation. Later still, 'barbarian' became 'a word reserved for those who
neither subscribed to European religious views, nor lived their lives
according to European social norms'.[45] Barbarism was a 'cultural condition but frequently used simply to describe non-Christians'.[46]

Las Casas, whom we will encounter again in Chapter 3, distinguished
between four different groups of barbarians. The first consisted of individuals who had become detached from their cultural base. In this
he included 'all men everywhere who, momentarily and under special circumstances, have lost control of themselves, whose minds have
been overwhelmed by their passions'. Second was the group defined by
sharing a common language. Those who shared a language were 'civil
beings' able to ' "converse" adequately'. Barbarians, by contrast, were
'non-social men' and unable to converse adequately.[47] The third group
was 'the barbarian *simpliciter*', which included 'those men who, through
impious or perverse understanding (*impio et pessimo ingenio*), or on account of the miserable regions they inhabit, are savage, ferocious, slow
witted (*stoldi*) and alien to all reason'.[48] These were the natural slaves
of Book 1 of Aristotle's *Politics*.[49] Finally, the fourth group simply consisted of those who were not Christians.[50] Las Casas did not regard these
groups as mutually exclusive. While all Indians were the non-Christians
of the fourth group and many were probably the 'wild and merciless
men acting against reason' of the third group, they also formed cultural
groups that lived in the politic and social manner that distinguished the
second.

At the time Las Casas was writing the notion of barbarism was fundamental to the justifications given by some Spaniards for conquering and dispossessing the Indians of the New World. Non-Christians
were, as we have just seen, regarded by many as barbarians and as less
than fully human. The status of people as human beings was linked to
Christianity. Christian claims to sovereignty rested on the 'nature of the
people being conquered, instead of in the supposed juridical rights of

---

[45] Anthony Pagden, *The Fall of Natural Man: The American Indian and the Origins of
Comparative Ethnology* (Cambridge University Press, 1982), p. 24.
[46] Ibid., p. 124.   [47] Ibid., p. 127.   [48] Ibid., p. 132.
[49] In relation to this discussion see G. L. Huxley, 'Aristotle, Las Casas and the American
Indians', *Proceedings of the Royal Irish Academy* 80 (1980).
[50] Pagden, *Natural Man*, p. 132.

the conquerors'.[51] Book 1 of Aristotle's *The Politics* was appealed to as supporting the argument that Indians were natural slaves. Unlike civil slaves who became slaves either as a punishment for some 'illiberal act' or because they had been captured in a 'just' war; natural slavery was 'a matter of the psychology of the slave himself'.[52] A natural slave was one who was a barbarian in the sense of being 'a man whose intellect has, for some reason, failed to achieve proper mastery over his passions'.[53] Indians were depicted as 'obviously barbarians and thus the natural slaves described by Aristotle in the Politics'. As an example of this reasoning Pagden cites Gregio's assertion that '[t]yranny is the appropriate mode of government for the Indians because "slaves and barbarians . . . are those who are lacking in judgement and understanding as are these Indians who, it is said, are like talking animals"'.[54] Such was the view of many Spaniards in the early phases of the conquest.

Pagden demonstrates how this view began to change between 1520 and 1530 with the emergence of the School of Salamanca. Under the influence of its members, who included Francisco de Vitoria, Domingo De Sato and Francisco Suarez, attention was paid to the work of Thomas Aquinas.[55] His version of natural law was one that uncoupled Christianity from humanity. 'For the Thomists all men, whether Christian or not, were human.'[56] Even so the 'aberrant behaviour' of the Indians raised the question of whether they were 'fully human'.[57] Vitoria argued that they were and that the Indian 'problem' was essentially 'the problem of the nature of relations between the different groups of men within, as Vitoria termed it, "the republic of all the world"'.[58] Vitoria's particular contribution was to demolish the theory of natural slavery. In *De Indis*[59] he asserted that the only reasons for denying that the Indians were the rightful owners of their lands before the Spaniards arrived were that they were sinners, infidels, foolish, or irrational beings. Claims that they were either the second or third of these relied 'on Aristotle's hypothesis that "there are those who are by nature slaves, that is those for whom it is better to serve than to rule. They are those who do not possess sufficient reason to even rule themselves, but only to interpret

---

[51] Ibid., p. 39.   [52] Ibid., p. 41.   [53] Ibid., p. 42.   [54] Ibid., p. 48.
[55] See Bernice Hamilton, *Political Thought in Sixteenth-Century Spain: A Study of the Political Ideas of Vitoria, De Soto, Suárez and Molina* (Oxford: Clarendon Press, 1963), and Anthony Pagden, 'The "School of Salamanca" and the "Affairs of the Indies"', *History of Universities*, 1 (1981).
[56] Pagden, *Natural Man*, p. 63.   [57] Ibid., p. 64.   [58] Ibid., p. 65.
[59] Francisco de Vitoria, *Political Writings*, Anthony Pagden and J. Lawrence (eds.), (Cambridge University Press, 1991), pp. 231–92.

the orders of their masters and whose strength lies in their bodies rather than in their minds".[60] In relation to this Vitoria argued that the cities of the Mexica and the Inca could not have been built by people who were both barbarians and natural slaves.[61]

At the same time as denying in this way that the Indians were barbarians and consequently natural slaves, Vitoria delineated what he regarded as the limits of their rights against Christians. In Chapter 3 we will see that Vitoria and Las Casas parted company over the issue of forced trade and sociability. Vitoria argued that the biblical injunction to 'love thy neighbour' had the force of natural law. It obliged Christians to love Indians as they would their neighbours. If the Indians rejected Spanish attempts to fulfil this obligation they were violating natural law. The Spaniards were then under the further obligation to uphold the natural law by engaging in the forced evangelisation to which Las Casas so doggedly objected.

Vitoria accepted that the Indians had a civil way of life and were not natural slaves or barbarians in Aristotle's sense. Nevertheless, he saw them as exhibiting elements of 'barbarism'. Though not natural slaves, they were, in his mind, not so far removed from the 'foolish' and consequently it had to be asked whether they were 'able to constitute [or] administer a legitimate republic in civil or humane terms'.[62] In the end the condition of the Indians is, for Vitoria, one of 'barbarism' and it is what 'conferred on the Spaniards political *dominium* but only so long as it was exercised in the Indians', and not in the Spaniards', favour.'[63] Sepulveda's understanding of Aristotle was not so very different from Vitoria's but for him the Indians definitely were 'barbarous' in ways that did identify them as natural slaves. On the ground that they were natural slaves he argued that the use of force against the Indians was just war. For him it was their barbarism that justified their subjugation and dispossession. Las Casas, on the other hand, did not see them as barbarians and his struggle with Sepulveda ultimately resulted 'in a serious attempt to negotiate for the Indians a definite and unassailable position in the human community as a "civil" and "human" being'.[64]

To describe others as 'barbarians' was to claim one's own culture and values as superior. In the context of European expansion it also meant a Eurocentric approach to the non-European world and the belief that

[60] Ibid., p. 67.   [61] Ibid., p. 71.
[62] Ibid., pp. 79–80.   [63] Ibid., p. 105.   [64] Ibid., p. 119.

European values were or should be universal. Barbarism as defined by Europeans justified the imposition of European norms and control. A notable exception to this way of viewing barbarians was Montaigne, who recognised that 'everyman calls barbarous anything he is not accustomed to; it is indeed the case that we have no other criterion of the truth of right-reason than the example and form of the opinions and customs of our own country'.[65] Montaigne was critical of Eurocentric understandings of non-European peoples and a relativist in the sense of recognising that while their values were different they were perhaps no less valid. He conceived of barbarians as people still close to the state of nature: 'still governed by the laws of nature and . . . only slightly bastardised by ours. . . .'[66] He was, he said, not saddened by the barbarity in the practices of others, but by the failure of Europeans to recognise that 'while judging correctly of their wrong-doing we should be so blind to our own'.[67] Europeans, he observed, outstripped the barbarity of the people they called barbaric in comparison with themselves.[68] This was essentially the point made by Todorov about the Spaniards being horrified by the human sacrifices of the Aztecs but uncritical of their own massacres.[69]

The term 'savage' appears to have entered usage in writing about non-Europeans mainly in the eighteenth century. Like barbarity and barbarism, with which it is closely associated, it refers to more than one characteristic of non-Europeans. Savages share with barbarians an inability to 'understand the benevolence and humanity inculcated by the Christian religion'.[70] What sets the use of the term 'savage' apart is its place in Enlightenment writing concerning the state of nature. In essence, the Enlightenment view of the state of nature was the state of a rational being responding to the physical conditions of his or her existence. In the eighteenth century savages were those who lived outside of civil society and forms of government recognised by Europeans. Savages found their way into European political and social theory as either *noble* or *ignoble* savages. The noble savage formed part of a critique of society and was held up as an example of a desirable condition from which European society had fallen. Ignoble savages were instead a negative example and represented a stage of development Europeans had rightly left behind.

---

[65] Michel de Montaigne, *The Complete Essays*, trans. M. A. Screech (Harmondsworth: Penguin, 1991), p. 231.
[66] Pagden, *Natural Man*, p. 232.   [67] Ibid., p. 235.   [68] Ibid., p. 236.
[69] Todorov, *Conquest of America*, pp. 143–4.   [70] Reynolds, *Frontier*, p. 43.

During the eighteenth century it became common to distinguish between different types or races of men and to arrange them in a hierarchical structure. One consequence was that by the end of that century
'savages' became implicated in the idea of the Great Chain of Being.
The thrust of this was that all living matter is arranged in a hierarchical
pattern with mankind at the top.[71] Thus, in an address in 1795 to the
Manchester Literary and Philosophical Society, Charles White asserted
that '[n]ature exhibits . . . an immense chain of beings, endowed with
various degrees of intelligence and active powers, suited to their sta-
tions in the general system'.[72] At the top of the hierarchy in the Great
Chain of Being, above all other human races, stood Europeans. Savages
belonged to races that were at a lower level in this hierarchy. By the
middle of the nineteenth century this idea of hierarchy was reinforced
by the advent of Social Darwinism and then 'scientific racism', which
appealed to evolutionary theory and the spurious findings of craniol-
ogy and phrenology to claim that the so-called 'lower races' of 'savages'
were not fully human.

To summarise, wild men, barbarians and savages are each categories
that serve to set apart the 'civilised' from the 'uncivilised' and to establish the superiority of European culture and political organisation. The
wildman is in a category apart from either the barbarian or the savage
but is an element in the psychology of the European response to people
labelled as barbarians and savages. Barbarians perhaps may be usefully
distinguished from savages as Montesquieu did when he argued that
'[o]ne difference between savage peoples and barbarian peoples is that
the former are small scattered nations which, for certain particular reasons, cannot unite, whereas barbarians are ordinarily small nations that
can unite together'.[73] Alternatively barbarians might represent organised groups that have the capacity to effectively disrupt European states;
for example, the Mongols. Savages on the other hand are more likely

---

[71] Ibid., p. 109. See also Arthur O. Lovejoy, *The Great Chain of Being. The History of an Idea*
(Cambridge, Mass: Harvard University Press, 1948).
[72] Cited by Reynolds, *Frontier*, p. 110.
[73] Montesquieu, *The Spirit of the Laws*, trans. and ed. A. M. Cohler, B. C. Miller and H. S.
Stone (Cambridge University Press, 1989), p. 290. According to Pagden, Diderot thought
barbarians were 'those who have been cursed by "that sombre disposition which makes
man inaccessible to the delights of nature and art and the sweetness of society". "Savages"
exist only in a particular cultural milieu, but "barbarians", in common with Hobbe's
homo homini lupus, are with us always no matter how civilised we may appear to have
become.' See Pagden, *Lords of all the World*, p. 168. For a critique of Montesquieu's handling
of culture see Bhikhu Parekh, *Rethinking Multiculturalism: Cultural Diversity and Political
Theory* (London: Macmillan, 2000).

to have been peoples that could threaten individual Europeans but could not hope to triumph over the states to which those Europeans belonged. In addition to setting apart the 'civilised' from the 'uncivilised' and providing a justification for the actions of Europeans, these concepts also had an important role in the theoretical underpinning of state building in Europe. The next section considers the stages of development theory that also relegated non-European peoples to the condition of being 'uncivilised'.

Stages of development: noble and ignoble savages

In his *Social Science and the Ignoble Savage*, Ronald Meek argues that by 1780 it was accepted, by social and political theorists, that European and other 'advanced' societies had passed through four stages of development: each of which was distinguished by a different mode of subsistence. Corresponding to each of these modes were 'different sets of ideas and institutions relating to law, property, and government, and also different sets of customs, manners and morals . . .'[74] The first mode was hunting, followed successively by pasturage, agriculture and finally commerce based economies. According to Meek the theory that all societies pass through these four stages had, by 1780, 'become so important an element in the intellectual scheme of things; so much an integral part of the social thought of the Enlightenment, that there were very few historians and social thinkers who remained unaffected by it'.[75] It was, in particular, thought to help explain how mankind made the transition from savagery to civilisation.

One important source of the theory was Montesquieu's discussion in Book 18 of *The Spirit of the Laws*. There he posited a causal relation between the natural resources of particular lands and the degree of liberty, the form of government and the laws likely to be found in each.[76] He associates climate with different modes of subsistence but there is little to indicate that he thought of these as 'successive stages of development through which societies normally progressed over time'.[77] Meek finds other precursors in Hugo Grotius, Samuel Puffendorf and John Locke and argues that the theory became clearly discernible only in the 1750s

---

[74] Ronald L. Meek, *Social Science and the Ignoble Savage* (Cambridge University Press, 1976), p. 2.
[75] Ibid., p. 174.　　[76] Montesquieu, *The Spirit of the Laws*, book 18, pp. 285–301.
[77] Meek, *Social Science*, p. 35.

in the writings of Adam Smith, Sir John Dalrymple and Lord Kames, and was unmistakable in the 1760s in the work of Adam Ferguson.

North America and its native inhabitants were the primary reference for writers associated with the 'stages theory'. As already mentioned, Mexico and Peru were explicitly rejected as examples on the grounds that both were civilisations when the Spaniards arrived. North America, by contrast, was taken as representative of the first stage of development. It followed from this that the indigenous inhabitants of America had remained at a stage long since surpassed by civilised European societies. It took no great leap of imagination to conclude from this that as the Indians had not progressed from this primitive stage, as had the Europeans, they were lesser beings than were Europeans. For those who were satisfied with European society they were a negative example; they were 'ignoble savages' who represented a less desirable state of existence. Those, like Rousseau, who were instead dissatisfied with contemporary society regarded them rather as 'noble savages' and as a positive example. Contrary to others, Rousseau held that progress had stopped with the American Indians.[78] Implicit in the stages theory was, once again, the assumption of European superiority which provided support for the ideas about property attached to the theory.

By asserting that the laws and institutions of society were dependent on the mode of subsistence it was fundamentally materialist. Thus Adam Smith used the stages theory 'to explain the changes in "laws and regulations with regard to property" which occur as society develops'.[79] Chapter 4 shows how Locke's theory of property required that ownership be dependent on the labour invested in tillage, animal husbandry and general improvement. This attached property rights to a 'higher' stage of development than that attained by Amerindians. And since they were at a 'lower' stage, it was believed that European settlers were justified in ignoring both indigenous patterns of land use and the native rights attached to these patterns, and in dispossessing the original occupants. This association of property with a particular stage of development was given recognition in jurisprudence by Blackstone, who accepted and endorsed the stages theory in his influential *Commentaries*.[80] Essentially he accepted that those at a 'lower' stage of development were to be subjected to the property laws of the 'higher' stage, and this had

[78] Ibid., p. 64. See also J. J. Rousseau, 'Discourse on Inequality', in Alan Ritter and Julia Conaway Bodanella (eds.), *Political Writings* (New York: Norton, 1988).
[79] In Meek, *Social Science*, p. 119.
[80] Ibid., p. 179 See also Blackstone, *Commentaries on the Laws of England*, vol. II.

implications not only for Amerindians but also for the peoples in all lands colonised by the British.

The division between civilised society and the uncivilised world of barbarians and savages; the notion of stages of development with ignoble savages suspended in the lowest stage; and the rights to title over land issuing only from the highest stage all helped justify the dispossession of non-Europeans and the denial of rights. They also aided the development of theories of the state and of rights that supported European state-building through the sixteenth, seventeenth and eighteenth centuries. In these theories the concepts of the 'state of nature' and of 'natural rights' had an important place and implications for non-Europeans.

The state of nature and natural rights

The concept of the 'state of nature' is important for the purposes of this book in four respects: it is counterposed as an inferior condition to the superior one of civil society; it is essential to Locke's influential definition of property which, it can be argued, was devised to justify England's colonisation of the New World; it was crucial in the determination of whether particular non-Europeans had 'natural rights'; and, finally, it is fundamental to the imagery of classical international relations theory.

Taking these in turn, the state of nature is contrasted with the situation of people living within a civil society, in which there is a regime of civil laws and a structure of political organisation. European theorists regarded people they perceived as having no developed civil life or proper political organisation as living in a state of nature and typically described them as 'savages'. The state of nature was a vital element in the codification, by classical political theorists, of the state as a form of political organisation. A state of nature, according to Grotius was one 'in which all men must find themselves simply *qua* men, and on to which would be grafted the various appurtenances of developed civil life, including benevolence'.[81] Amerindians, in particular, represented a negative example used to illustrate the benefits of the state as a unit of political organisation in which there was a sovereign authority, a civil society, and a regulated relationship between the two. The state of nature was one from which European political communities had escaped. An exception to this was, as already mentioned, Rousseau, who

---

[81] Richard Tuck, *Hobbes* (Oxford University Press, 1989), pp. 21–2.

thought of civil society as a regression from the life of savages: 'The example of savages . . . seems to confirm that the human race was made to remain there always; that this stage is the true youth of the world; and that all the subsequent advances have apparently been so many steps towards the perfection of the individual, and in fact, towards the decrepitude of the species.'[82]

In this way Rousseau employed the example of savages to criticise European political society. The savages he had in mind were primarily the Indians of North America and for him they represented noble savages rather than the negative example of the ignoble savages. For Rousseau and others, the state of nature was, as much as anything else, an imagined world invoked to highlight the benefits of civil society and the European state as a form of political organisation.[83] Contrary to this, Barbara Arneil argues that for Locke, at least, far from being 'a mirror to reflect the origins of civil man and his society', the state of nature 'was a historical reality which existed in the Americas of his day'. She claims 'that the Two Treatises were written as a defence of England's colonial policy in the new world', and that the chapter 'On Property', in particular, 'was written to justify the seventeenth-century dispossession of aboriginal peoples of their land.'[84] As well as this Richard Tuck has more recently observed that 'the fundamental arguments of the Second Treatise develop point-by-point an answer to Pufendorf's critique of the ideology of the commercial nations'.[85]

Second, Arneil demonstrates that there is a vital link in Locke's work between the dichotomy of *savage* and *civil* and the concept of property. Before Locke, Grotius had articulated the view that '[t]here is no ownership in things which are of no use to their owners, and therefore other people have a perfect right to occupy them'.[86] Uncultivated land suggested, to many European minds, that it was of no use to its owners;

---

[82] Rousseau, 'Discourse on Inequality', p. 39. See also Robert Wokler, 'Perfectable Apes in Decadent Cultures: Rousseau's Anthropology Revisited', *Daedalus*, 107 (1978).
[83] See, for instance, C. B. Macpherson's assertion that 'Hobbes's state of nature, as is generally recognised, is a logical not an historical hypothesis', in *The Political Theory of Possessive Individualism: Hobbes to Locke* (New York: Oxford University Press, 1964), p. 20. See also his introduction to Hobbes's *Leviathan* in which he calls the state of nature a 'hypothetical condition [that] would exist if there no common power able to restrain individuals, no law and no law-enforcement'. Thomas Hobbes, *Leviathan*, ed. C. B. Macpherson (Harmondsworth: Penguin, 1968), p. 40.
[84] Barbara Arneil, *John Locke and America: The Defence of English Colonialism* (Oxford: Clarendon Press, 1996), p. 2.
[85] Tuck, *The Rights Of War And Peace*, p. 168.
[86] Ibid., p. 105.

and for Grotius, in particular, 'whatever remains uncultivated, is not to be esteemed a Property'.[87] Locke, as we shall see in more detail in Chapter 3, argued that property, understood as the possession of land, derived from the labour invested in it. Hunter-gatherers and nomadic peoples who did not enclose or cultivate land in the manner of European agriculture remained for that reason in the state of nature. Only by adopting European and particularly English agricultural practices could they have rights to property and progress to the establishment of a civil society. Arneil argues that Locke adopted the idea of civil society in order to make claims about the rights of men living in it. Those living in a state of nature did not have property rights. Civil society was consequently defined, at least in part, by the concept of agrarian labour. It was this that both set apart natural man in the state of nature from the civil man and gave the latter rights to property. In this way, Locke's representation of Amerindians was 'a distorted inversion of civil society'.[88]

Third, a critical question for political theorists in the seventeenth century was whether men living in a state of nature possessed natural rights. The answer to this was crucial to the further question of whether natural man had property rights, which took two forms: rights over land and the rights people possess as individual human beings against other human beings.[89] Property rights of the latter kind are 'rights as *dominia*'. They are, as Tuck puts it, 'active rights expressing their possessor's sovereignty over his world' and can 'be defended against other men . . . and transferred or alienated by [their] possessor'.[90] In dispute was whether there were such rights before there was social organisation; in other words, in a state of nature. Grotius held that natural man was the subject of rights prior to any contact,[91] and that the most fundamental of these rights was the right to preserve life, provided this did not involve 'wanton or unnecessary injury to another person', which was unjusitifable.[92] For Grotius 'an individual in nature (that is, before transferring any rights to a civil society) was morally identical to a state, and that there were no powers posssessed by a state which an individual

[87] Cited by Tuck, *Rights of War*, p. 105.
[88] Arneil, *Locke and America*, p. 70. See also Parekh, *Rethinking Multiculturalism*. Parekh (p. 39) cites Tully in support of the point that Locke 'unilaterally universalised the emerging European, especially English state, and condemned other societies for failing to be like it'.
[89] Grotius distinguished between these in terms of *property* and *jusrisdiction*. See Richard Tuck, *Rights of War*, p. 106.
[90] Tuck, *Natural Rights Theories*, p. 16.   [91] Ibid., p. 61.   [92] Tuck, *Hobbes*, p. 21.

could not possess in nature'.[93] This, Tuck explains, meant that the rights individuals possessed *'vis-à-vis* one another (outside the arbitrary and contingent circumstances of their civil arrangements)' could best be understood 'by looking at the rights which sovereign states seem to possess against one another'.[94]

In the state of nature, rights were enjoyed by 'atomic individuals' who, just as states did not, had no sovereign standing above them. For Thomas Hobbes a civil society required a sovereign charged with ordering relations between individuals. This was because there was no 'clear and objective truth about the external world', which meant men would 'make different decisions about what counts as a danger to them'; there would be no agreement about what was to be done and conflicts would be bound to ensue.[95] The problem was how a sovereign could be established without depriving his or her subjects of their right to self-preservation, regarded by Grotius and Hobbes as a fundamental natural right. Hobbes' solution was that men in a state of nature should surrender the right to self-preservation and indeed 'that the law of nature oblige[d them] to renounce their right of private judgement over what is to count as dangerous in dubious cases, and to accept for themselves the judgement of a common authority'.[96] In this way conflict between them would be avoided. Thus in *Leviathan* he proposed a *theory of authorisation* which proposed that natural men should appoint 'one man, or Assembly of men' to act on their behalf 'in those things which concerne the Common Peace and Safetie'. Tuck comments that as a result the sovereign would not be simply defending himself but acting 'as agent for the defence of each member of the community, and . . . thus capable of performing all the interventionary actions associated with sovereigns'.[97]

The assumption by Hobbes and Grotius that individuals in a state of nature did possess rights as *dominia*, meant that the establishment of civil society required a theoretical justification for transferring any of those rights – especially the primary one of self-defence – to a sovereign authority. And this was what Hobbes provided. Locke, on the other hand, was more concerned with property rights understood as rights over land. Chapter 3 discusses his notion of property, understood as the right to land derived from labour invested in it. This imposed European concepts of how land should be used on Amerindians in a way that

---

[93] Tuck, *Rights of War*, p. 82.   [94] Ibid., p. 85.   [95] Tuck, *Hobbes*, p. 64.
[96] Tuck, *Hobbes*, p. 64.   [97] Tuck, *Natural Rights Theories*, p. 130.

denied rights over land to people living in a state of nature. Property in this sense could be fully realised only in the civil society that inevitably replaced the state of nature. Hobbes's concern over natural rights was, in part, with the obstacles they posed for transferring the rights of European peoples to a sovereign. For Locke it was a matter of whether whatever natural rights inhered in the state of nature were an impediment to dispossessing Amerindians of their land. In either case it amounted to a loss of rights for non-Europeans; the absence of civil society justified both the assertion of sovereignty, albeit without their consent, over non-Europeans and the dispossession of their lands.

Pufendorf, who is also discussed in Chapter 3, disagreed with the account of natural rights given by Grotius and Hobbes. Rights were not possessed by individuals in isolation he claimed but instead were the result of individuals having claims on one another. He rejected the idea of possessing rights or property 'in themselves outside the network of social obligations, [as] fundamentally misleading';[98] thus repudiating the 'history of rights as dominia'.[99] Tuck points out that it was once common to stress the similarities between Grotius and Pufendorf and that he had indeed done so himself. His view now is that Pufendorf used 'some of Grotius's theoretical assumptions in order to undermine the practical implications of the Dutchman's ideas for the international realm – particularly where those ideas resembled those of Hobbes'.[100] Pufendorf rejected Hobbes' concept of the state of nature[101] and attacked Grotius' theory about 'the fundamental natural right to possess bits of the material world which are useful for our personal consumption'.[102]

Natural rights and the state of nature are not the only connections in which non-Europeans have figured in classical political theory. Denis Diderot and Johann Herder, as Pagden shows, were exercised by cultural difference, but once again the state of nature is a crucial reference point. Diderot argued that each culture was the result of a distinct environment and thus each was unique. In common with Herder he believed that cultures were incommensurable in the sense that individuals from one culture could not comprehend the mental world of those from another culture; one culture could not be understood in terms of another. Like other theorists who represented non-Europeans as living in

---

[98] Ibid., p. 161.   [99] Ibid., p. 160.   [100] Tuck, *Rights of War*, p. 142.

[101] In Tuck's words: 'nations could and often did live in peace with one another without the necessity of a common power over them, and the same could be said about individuals in a state of nature'. *Rights of War*, p. 142

[102] Ibid., p. 155.

a state of nature both Diderot and Herder regarded Europeans as having moved from that condition to civil society. Diderot thus thought that by travelling to faraway places Europeans were going backward in time. 'The faceless European traveller has, in a sense, reversed the journey that his ancestors once made from the state of nature to civil society.' Both Diderot and Herder objected to colonialism on the grounds that it threatened to disrupt the natural order of the social world by reducing the variety of cultures. But whereas Diderot thought there was 'a unity of the human race' that would eventually allow the emergence of hybrid cultures, Herder maintained that cultural forms were impenetrable and that common humanity would not result in common understandings. Cultural pluralism was a natural state that should not be tampered with in the manner of colonialism. For Herder, European empires were, in Pagden's words, Trojan horses that sought to subvert the naturally plural world.[103] A further difference between Diderot and Herder was that Diderot shared 'the Hobbesian and Grotian model of sociability', which held that 'all societies have their beginnings in the general recognition of the desirability of an escape from the state of nature'. Diderot thought of this process of social evolution as being the inevitable result of 'a rational calculation of interests', which was a proposition Herder rejected.[104]

Finally, the fourth way in which the 'state of nature' was identified as important to the purposes of this book is that it is fundamental to the realist tradition and consequently much that has been written about relations between states. Realists depict international life as resembling the 'state of nature'. Their argument is that in contrast to life within states, in which there is a central authority, a police force and courts to settle disputes and maintain order, there is no such authority standing above states. States are essentially self-interested and none of them can be relied upon to act always in ways that do not harm other states. Given the lack of overarching authority, each and every state must, ultimately, rely on itself to protect its perceived interests.

In the international society or rationalist perspective the absence of over-riding authority and civil society is mitigated by the rules and norms that regulate relations between states, but it too assumes the state

[103] Pagden, *European Encounters*, p. 145.
[104] Ibid., p. 143. See also Parekh, *Rethinking Multiculturalism*, F. M. Barnard, *Herder's Social and Political Thought: From Enlightenment to Nationalism* (Oxford: Clarendon Press, 1965), and Denis Diderot, *Political Writings*, Ed. Mason, J.H. and Wokler, R., (Cambridge University Press, 1992).

of nature as the basic condition of international life. Martin Wight makes this clear when discussing his assertion that a fundamental question for international theory is: 'What is international society?' This, he argued, 'resolved itself into the question "What is the state of nature?", and the answer to both questions will be the same.' According to Wight, international society equals the state of nature. His reasoning, following Locke, is that society within states rests on a social contract between individuals. This means first, that those who have not contracted – such as the American Indians – live in a pre-contractual condition which is a state of nature. And second, that states also are in a pre-contractual condition. For rationalists, unlike realists, the state of nature in this sense does not mean that states are not able to act in concert. As part of his defence for using the term 'rationalism' Wight refers to Locke's statement that a state of nature is one in which 'Men liv[e] together according to reason without a common superior on earth, with authority to judge between them . . .' Locke's premise', he comments, 'is that men are reasonable and that they live together according to reason even when they have no common government, as in the condition of international relations'. Thus states exist in a state of nature but are able to coexist through the application of reason.[105]

In accepting Locke's argument that the state of nature entailed a pre-contractual condition illustrated by Amerindians, Wight perpetuates the European denial of Amerindian social and political organisation. Locke's conception of the state of nature was one inhabited by individuals rather than groups or nations. In relation to the 'decision to enter into a state of war', Barbara Arneil convincingly argues to the contrary that:

> One of the greatest flaws of the state-of-nature device, when it is used as a mirror to European civilisation, is its complete obliteration of any special characteristics of the individuals themselves. Thus natural man belongs to no nation and has no political or ethical codes associated with the collectivity. Rather he is amongst an undifferentiated and ahistorical mass of non-European, civil savages.[106]

Amerindians acted as nations and groups rather than as individuals and by ignoring this theorists such as Locke denied the existence of political society; the absence of which was later taken as evidence for the lack of civilisation.

---

[105] Wight, *International Theory*, p. 14.   [106] Arneil, *Locke and America*, p. 38.

In conclusion, non-Europeans were conceptualised by Europeans in ways that dehumanised them and represented their cultures or civilisations as inferior. Classical political theory, with relatively minor exceptions, has had little concern with problems arising from the lack of mutual understanding between Europeans and the peoples they perceived as 'different' or 'uncivilised'. That cultures might be incommensurable was, as a problem to be overcome, largely ignored. With the exception of Diderot and Herder, theorists were untroubled about whether one culture could understand another. Given the underlying assumption of European superiority it was not necessary either to comprehend others in their own terms or to attempt to deal with them as equals. Political theory codified difference and invoked the state of nature as a negative example that served to demonstrate the superiority of civil society coupled with state sovereignty as a form of political organisation. Whether in the case of barbarism justifying 'natural' slavery; being located in a stage of development transcended by Europeans; lacking the entitlement to property rights; or being beyond the pale of civil society, non-European first nations were almost inexorably cast as inferior peoples. In many ways these claims merely project contemporary concerns back to an earlier and different context. The final chapter argues that while classical theory sheds light on how the dispossession of non-Europeans and dominance of them by Europeans was rationalised, it is, at the outset of the twenty-first century, an inadequate basis for the development of an international political theory that would both situate indigenous peoples in international politics and provide a normative framework for extending their rights. Chapter 3 concerns the status of non-Europeans at different junctures in the history of thought about international law.

3   Dispossession and the purposes of international law

Over a period of 400 years following the conquest of Mexico there was a progressive retreat from conceding sovereign rights to particular non-European peoples. During this time international law had the major role of defining the normative foundations of the global society of states created by the expansion of Europe. It defined and codified the terms for membership in the society of states. It marked the boundaries between those who belonged to the society and those that did not. Those that did formed a moral community bound by mutually agreed rules of conduct. And fundamental to this community was the idea that its members were not obliged to treat non-members according to the norms that applied to relations between themselves. It was consequently a form of cultural imperialism that served to aid and to justify Europeans in subjugating non-Europeans and dispossessing them of their lands and other rights. International law can for these reasons, be seen as a 'universalising discourse' that simultaneously sought to include and exclude some but not all non-Europeans. It was universalising because the rules and norms it codified were intended to have universal application, but by setting the terms for inclusion in international society according to European standards it necessarily excluded many non-Europeans. From the vantage-point of the early twenty-first century it is easy to criticise international law for having been insensitive, even oblivious to other cultures and mores. International law reflects the normative order of the European states that made it, and expecting non-Europeans to conform to it was clearly a form of cultural imperialism. But this is not to say that some values inherent in imperialism are not worth defending as universal values. There may be some core values that deserve to be universalised, regardless of whether they are culturally specific to Europe and the international society that created it or to some other civilisation.

Not all international law was either a universalising discourse or a form of cultural imperialism. Parts of it applied only to particular non-European entities and did not involve the imposition of European cultural values. International law regulated, for instance, relations between the Ottoman Empire and Europe, but was not used to justify European domination and to deprive the peoples of the Ottoman Empire of their rights. The development of international society brought with it different kinds of international law depending on the nature of the relationship it was meant to regulate. As Henry Wheaton put it, 'the international law of the civilized, Christian nations of Europe and America, is one thing; and that which governs the intercourse of the Mohammedan nations of the East with each other, and with Christians, is another and very different thing'.[1] What was applicable to relations between European states was not necessarily appropriate to relations between those states and other civilisations. Relations with peoples not recognised as possessing civilisation were another matter again. Consequently there developed law specific to relations between particular entities. My interest in this chapter is confined to peoples Europeans referred to at different times as 'barbarians', 'savages', 'backward' and 'uncivilised', and whom they generally regarded as lacking political society. Before proceeding to this the nature of a 'universalising discourse' needs to be clarified.

By a 'discourse' I mean a body of evolving thought or an ongoing conversation in which there is agreement between those who are party to it about underlying ontological, epistemological and moral assumptions. The effect is that those who share these assumptions have a shared world view and do not either perceive or have a need to renegotiate a fresh mutual understanding of them each time something is to be agreed upon or discussed. Understood in this way, a discourse may, for instance, be about a group of people who do not share the underlying assumptions of the discourse and are excluded from effective participation in it. A discourse that becomes the predominant mode of understanding a particular subject or object is a hegemonic discourse. It holds sway over alternate discourses or modes of understanding. A 'universalising discourse' is one that either has pretensions to, or is regarded as having,

---

[1] Henry Wheaton, *Elements of International Law* (New York: Da Capo Press, 1972, orig. 1836), p. 44. See also M. W. Janis, 'American Versions of the International Law of Christendom: Kent, Wheaton and the Grotian Tradition', *Netherlands International Law Review*, 39 (1992), and James Crawford, *The Creation of States in International Law* (Oxford: Clarendon Press, 1979), pp. 13, 146.

universal application. It is one that seeks increasingly to include more people, societies, organisations or states into its terms of reference as, for instance, does the discourse of human rights. A universalising discourse is accordingly one that either expands, or has the potential to expand, the boundaries of the community to which it refers. But this requires identifying those who do share the discourse and are therefore regarded as eligible to join the community from which it issues. Thus at the same time that international law established criteria for the expanding membership of the society of states it excluded other entities from membership. The more that it came to be defined as a body of rules to regulate relations between states, the more it excluded individuals, sub-state groups and political communities that did not meet European criteria for statehood. International law has been a universalising discourse in the sense of being one that, at the same time as laying claim to universal application, set limits to its universality.

The remainder of the chapter is in two parts. The first draws on M. F. Lindley's seminal 1926 study of the acquisition of territory in international law.[2] Lindley depicts the evolution of international law concerning acquisition as a gradual progression from regarding 'backward peoples' as the possessors of sovereign rights and title, to the denial of any such rights standing in the way of 'civilised' peoples assuming sovereignty over them and gaining title to their lands. Lindley distinguishes between three categories of writers: those who recognised sovereign rights in non-European peoples; those who recognised 'limited or conditional sovereignty'; and those who denied sovereign rights. Each of these corresponds with distinct phases of European expansion represented by the Conquest of Mexico in the sixteenth century, the occupation of North America in the seventeenth and eighteenth centuries, and the colonisation of Australia and Africa from the late eighteenth century down to the end of the nineteenth. These are phases that also correspond to the changing conceptions of otherness identified by Bernard McGrane, to which Nicholas Thomas objected because of the epistemological ruptures and breaks they involve.

Lindley's categories of writers and the idea of phases of expansion are open to similar objections. He overlooked important differences between the thinkers located in his first category, which included Grotius. Not only this, it will be shown that Grotius might have belonged more to Lindley's second category. I have nevertheless used Lindley's categories

---

[2] Lindley, *The Acquisition and Government of Backward Territory in International Law.*

as a heuristic device. The discussion of Grotius and Pufendorf in particular, relies heavily on Richard Tuck's *The Rights of War and Peace*,[3] which is indispensable to the purposes of this book and I shall return to him in a moment.

The second part of the chapter is concerned with what might explain the shift in status accorded to non-Europeans and suggests that a major factor was the gradual eclipse of natural law by positive international law. It suggests also that an additional factor was changing conceptions of otherness. The chapter concludes with some further observations about the relationship between international law and the moral legitimacy of international society.

International law and the rights of non-European peoples

From the outset of European expansion into the New World two important questions were whether Europeans had the right to occupy the lands inhabited by non-Europeans and whether the use of force against them was justifiable. The answers to these involved the determination, by Europeans, of the rights of non-Europeans and the principal thinkers engaged in this task were grounded in one of two traditions current in late sixteenth-century Europe: the 'humanist' and the 'scholastic'. Richard Tuck demonstrates the differences between the two by examining Alberico Gentili as representative of humanism and Juan Luis de Molina of scholasticism.

The humanist tradition defended war for self-protection; approved of war to enhance the glory of an empire; allowed pre-emptive strikes as a measure for self-preservation; endorsed the Aristotlean notion of natural slavery; held that war on less civilised people was permissible; and argued that war on people who leave land uncultivated was justifiable. Anticipating arguments later used by Locke and Vattel, Gentili argued that vacant spaces may always be colonised by those who need them and can use them.[4]

In contrast, scholasticism rejected wars in the pursuit of glory and forbade pre-emptive strikes. The tradition held that war could not be just on both sides and that warfare against barbarians was unjustifiable, unless its purpose was to protect innocent victims from the aggression of barbarians. Even then, the actions taken to protect the innocent should

---

[3] Tuck, *Rights of War*.   [4] Ibid., p. 36.

not lead to the occupation of their lands by a foreign power but to the liberation of their victims.[5] The kind of aggression that exercised European minds at the time included the human sacrifices practised by the Aztecs and cannibalism.

Richard Tuck gives a meticulously detailed account of how the divide between these two schools runs through the development of subsequent thought about sovereign rights and the right to occupy territory. He makes it quite clear that there were deep philosophical differences between thinkers in Lindley's first category, but also important continuities between them and Locke and Vattel in the second. Only with the third category, those who more decisively denied sovereign rights, is there a clear break. As much as anything else, that is a reflection of the historical changes that had taken place in the doctrinal basis of international law coupled with the growth of more overt racism. Tuck's location of particular thinkers in relation to humanist or scholastic antecedents enables him to revise previous conceptions of the intellectual relationship between them. Grotius has been thought of as building on the work of Vitoria, but his intellectual roots were in humanism, the tradition most distrusted by Vitoria. Pufendorf was thought to have ideas similar to those of Grotius, but used Grotius's own ideas to undermine the practical implications of them. Locke sought to defend Grotius's position against Pufendorf, and Vattel then inscribed a Lockean interpretation of Pufendorf, which is to say an endorsement of Grotius, into his *Law of Nations*. Bearing these differences and similarities in mind I will now turn to Lindley's classification.

Writers who recognised sovereignty in non-European peoples

The most prominent writers Lindley included in this group were Gentili, Vitoria, Las Casas, Grotius and Pufendorf. At the time of the Conquest of Mexico, in the sixteenth century, a distinct international law had not yet emerged. Prior to the seventeenth century the term 'law of nations' was a literal translation of the Roman *gens gentium* or *jus gentium*, which was a Roman national law 'concerned with relationships among individuals' and was law the Romans applied to themselves and to foreigners.[6] It was distinct from *jus civile*, which applied to Romans only, and 'had

---

[5] Ibid., p. 52.
[6] Francis S. Ruddy, *International Law in the Enlightenment: The Background of Emmerich de Vattel's 'Le Droit des Gens'* (Dobbs Ferry, NY: Oceana Publications, 1975), p. 3.

nothing to do with the modern law of nations'.[7] As well as *jus civile* and *jus gentium* the Romans distinguished *jus naturale* as representing the existence of an external criteria of right conduct.[8] During the middle ages *'jus gentium* came to mean "anything between developed natural law and a kind of universally recognised positive law" '.[9] It was then also that natural law was 'integrated . . . into Christian theology as a divine law above human law'. Natural law was discoverable by the application of right reason and its 'supreme principle . . . is to seek the good and to avoid evil'. The scholastic notion of it, according to Nussbaum, 'is not to be understood juridically' but as something that 'encompasses both moral (or ethical) and legal norms'.[10] Indeed 'the history of natural law is a history of painstaking efforts to delimit the two spheres and to get to the core of their difference'.[11]

It was in the framework of natural law that the debate over Amerindians and Spanish relations with them was conducted. The key protagonists were Bartolomè de Las Casas (1474–1566), Francisco de Vitoria (*c.* 1480–1546) and Juan Gines de Supulveda (1490–1573). None of them were concerned with legal argument as such but instead with rights and moral argument grounded in natural law. Vitoria was an exponent of basic natural rights rather than the *legal* rights of Amerindians. He was more a thinker 'related to the history of the law of nations'[12] than an international lawer. As Tuck puts it: 'Vitoria, Ayala, Belli, and Gentili were all trying to "clarify" some inchoate principles of international law.'[13] Both Las Casas and Vitoria have contemporary significance with regard to the 'questions of sovereignty and jurisdiction, and their recognition of indigenous societies as the "true owners" of their lands'.[14]

The Conquest of the New World involved a prolonged process of subjugation and dispossession. Indians lost their lands and were pressed into the service of Spanish settlers exploiting the so-called *Encomienda* system. Essentially, the Spanish Crown gave Indians to Spanish settlers who thereby became *encomenderos*. They then had the 'right' to extract

---

[7] Arthur Nussbaum, *A Concise History of the Law of Nations*, rev. edn (New York: Macmillan, 1954), p. 14.
[8] Ruddy, *International Law*, p. 2.   [9] Ibid., p. 15.
[10] Nussbaum, *A Concise History*, p. 38.
[11] A. P. D'Entreves, *Natural Law: An Introduction to Legal Philosophy* (London: Hutchinson University Library, 1972), p. 83.
[12] Ibid., p. 79.   [13] Tuck, *Rights of War*, p. 12.
[14] Greg C. Marks, 'Indigenous Peoples in International Law: The Significance of Francisco de Vitoria and Bartolomé de Las Casas', *The Australian Yearbook of International Law* 13 (1992), p. 51.

labour or tribute from the Indians in return for protecting the Indians and providing them with religious instruction.[15] This assumed that the Spanish Crown had sovereignty over the Indians, which was disputed, along with the justice of the *Encomienda* system, by Las Casas and Vitoria. The reality of Spanish colonisation was that it was brutal, and far from providing protection for the Indians begged important questions about the proper basis for relations between Spaniards and Indians; in particular, concerning the use of force to convert Indians to Christianity. Answers to these questions were divided between those primarily concerned with the aggrandisement of Spain and those concerned with the conversion and welfare of the Indians. It was in effect a split between those who represented Indians as little more than beasts and those who instead regarded them as rational beings sharing essential characteristics with all humankind.

The debate over the conquest and whether it should proceed was stimulated if not provoked by a sermon given by the Dominican Antonio Montesinos in Hispaniola shortly before Christmas 1511. Montesinos railed against the *Encomienda* system and the practices associated with it. He invited his audience, which included Las Casas, to consider whether they had a right and could with any justice 'keep these poor Indians in such cruel and horrible servitude. By what authority have you made such detestable wars against these people who lived peacefully and gently on their own lands? – Are these not men? Do they not have rational souls? Are you not obliged to love them as yourselves?'[16] Implicit in these questions was the view that Amerindians were human beings entitled to rights Spaniards claimed for themselves. In the debates about the status and rights of Indians in the ensuing years the answers to theoretical questions such as those asked by Montesinos had practical consequences:

> For example, if the Indians were rational beings, could they with justice be deprived of their lands and made to work or pay tribute? If [they] were cannibals, did not this unnatural vice make necessary their enslavement by Spaniards? Under what conditions could 'just war' be waged against the Indians? By what title or titles did the king of Spain exercise dominion in the New World?[17]

[15] Lewis Hanke, *The Spanish Struggle for Justice in the Conquest of America* (Boston: Little, Brown, 1965), p. 19. See also Charles Gibson, *Spain in America* (New York: Harper-Torch), 1966.
[16] Pagden, *European Encounters with the New World*, p. 71, and Hanke, *The Spanish Struggle*, p. 131.
[17] Hanke, *The Spanish Struggle*, p. 40.

Underlying these and other questions the central problem was, according to Hanke, 'always . . . to determine the capacity of the Indians. – In judging this capacity the Spaniards never doubted that their own standards were the logical ones to apply. The capacity to live like Spaniards was therefore the matter to be adjudged.'[18] It was, in short, a question of whether Indians were to be regarded as human beings.

For Las Casas, who had been an *encomendero*, Montesino's sermon was a personal turning point that progressively led him into defending the rights of Indians. At first he tried, unsuccessfully, to bring an end to the Encomienda system. What he is now most remembered for is his disputation with Sepulveda at Valladolid in 1550–51, in which he had to tackle the question of just war. Las Casas returned to Spain in 1547 from one of his periods in Mexico and Guatemala to find that Sepulveda had written a manuscript attempting to prove wars against the Indians were just. Las Casas vehemently objected to this and was instrumental in preventing the publication of Sepulveda's work. The upshot of this was that Charles V, who was concerned about the just treatment of Indians, arranged for a 'disputation' between the Las Casas and Sepulveda before a panel of judges.[19]

Sepulveda had presented four main justifications, very much set in the humanist tradition, for war against the Indians. First, he charged that Indians were barbarians, 'and therefore, following Aristotle, natural slaves, obliged by natural law to subject themselves to the (superior) Spanish'.[20] Or, as Hanke put it, 'the rudeness of their natures . . . obliged them to serve persons having a more refined nature . . .'[21] Second, the Indians had committed grave sins against both divine and natural law, especially by practising cannibalism and human sacrifice. Third, force or war was justified to rescue innocent victims from such practices: 'the weak among the natives themselves' needed to be rescued even if they were willing victims.[22] Finally, the use of armed force was justified if the end was the propagation of Christian faith.

Of these the first was the most important because it was the first step in a chain of reasoning that supported the subjugation of the Indians. The claim that Indians were barbarians challenged 'the concept of equality of mankind, on which human rights are based'.[23] If they were barbarians they were, to the European mind, inferior and irrational. From this

---

[18] Ibid., p. 41.   [19] Ibid., p. 117.   [20] Marks, 'Indigenous Peoples', p. 25.
[21] Hanke, *The Spanish Struggle*, p. 120.   [22] Ibid., p. 120.
[23] Marks, 'Indigenous Peoples', p. 26.

it followed that they were also incapable of self-government and consequently colonisation and the subjugation that went with it were justified. There was also a vital connection between the accusation of barbarism and the claim that lands were uninhabited. 'By defining away the essential humanity of the inhabitants, and by denigrating their capacity for self-government, it becomes possible to convert inhabited land . . . available for the first taker.'[24] Against this line of reasoning both Las Casas and Vitoria argued that the Americas were inhabited by human beings who were the equal of the Spaniards. For Las Casas all human beings were, in crucial respects alike: 'All the peoples of the world are men . . . all have understanding and volition, all have the five exterior senses and the four interior senses, and are moved by the objects of these, all take satisfaction in goodness and feel pleasure with happy and delicious things, all regret and abhor evil.'[25] This meant that their land could not be regarded as unoccupied and it followed that if they were indeed, by virtue of their essential humanity, the equal of the Spaniards they were also capable of self-government. For both Las Casas and Vitoria the Indians had native title to their lands, and it was neither lawful nor moral for the Spaniards to dispossess them.

Vitoria's two paramount concerns about the Indians of the New World were whether they had title to their lands, and the circumstances under which war against them would be just. The three central points in his argument were first, that the lands of the New World could not be regarded as unoccupied and empty; that these lands were not open to acquisition by occupation; and, in particular, that the Papal Grants on which Spanish title was based 'had no temporal power over Indians or other unbelievers'.[26] To his way of thinking '[t]here were . . . no grounds upon which the Pope could claim special rights over infidels'.[27] On this Grotius was in agreement with Vitoria. Second, *contra* Grotius, Vitoria held that 'the fact that an action was against the law of nature could not be pleaded as justification for intervention'.[28] Actions contrary to the law of nature included obstructing the evangelical mission of the Church and refusing the Spaniards their natural rights of trade and travel. Third, Vitoria argued that intervention to stop injury to the innocent was justified; even if the victims neither sought nor wished for help it was nevertheless lawful to defend them. But to this he added the important qualification that intervention for this purpose did not give

---

[24] Ibid., p. 28.　　[25] Hanke, *The Spanish Struggle*, p. 125.　　[26] Ibid., p. 151.
[27] Tuck, *Rights of War and Peace*, p. 73.　　[28] Ibid., p. 73.

'the belligerent . . . the power to eject the enemy from their dominions and despoil them at whim; he can act only as far as is necessary to ward off injustices and secure safety for the future'.[29] He did, however, allow that in cases where the Indians were incapable 'of forming a state, in their own interests, the King of Spain might acquire sovereignty over them in order to raise them in the scale of civilisation, treating them charitably and not for his personal profit'.[30]

It is important to be clear that in affirming prior Indian ownership Vitoria was not denying Spanish sovereignty over the New World. Pagden argues that the fundamental question for Vitoria was 'neither the limits of papal jurisdiction, nor of Roman law, but of the law of nature, the *ius naturae*, and the issue was consequently one not of juridic but of *natural* rights. What was at issue in the prolonged debates over the conquest of the Americas was not the Castilian crown's sovereignty in America – it was the nature of rights and, in particular, rights of property, which that sovereignty entailed.'[31] Neither Las Casas nor Vitoria sought to deny the sovereignty of the Spanish Crown. Their purpose was rather to establish that sovereignty did not subsume Indian ownership of the lands occupied by them. Because the Indians were men and rational, like the Spaniards themselves, they retained *dominium*, understood as 'the right . . . to govern themselves as they see fit as a consequence of the natural order . . .'[32]

Grotius (1583–1645) had a primary role in justifying Dutch commercial expansion and subsequently the annexation of territory. In both *De Jure Pradae Commentarius*, which Grotius himself called *De Indis*, and his later *De Jure Belli ac Pacis* he addressed questions related to the 'legal position of non-European peoples'.[33] As well as considering the property rights of native inhabitants, he discussed the issue of whether forcible evangelism was permissible and the question of natural slavery. In *De Indis*, Grotius 'endorsed the claim that we may punish men over whom we do not possess political rights'.[34] Richard Tuck explains that in discussing punishment Grotius accepted that some individuals

[29] Ibid., pp. 73–74.
[30] Lindley, *Acquisition and Government*, p. 12. See also de Vitoria, *Political Writings*, p. 290.
[31] Anthony Pagden (ed.), *The Language of Political Theory in Early-Modern Europe* (Cambridge University Press, 1987), p. 80.
[32] James Muldoon, *The Americas in the Spanish World Order: The Justification for the Conquest in the Seventeenth Century* (Philadelphia: University of Pennsylvania Press, 1994), p. 17.
[33] Hedley Bull, Benedict Kingsbury and Adam Roberts (eds.), *Hugo Grotius and International Relations* (Oxford: Clarendon Press, 1992), p. 43.
[34] Tuck, *Rights of War and Peace*, p. 87.

were by nature natural slaves over whom it was expedient to exercise sovereignty. 'In the critical struggle', Tuck continues, 'between humanist and scholastic over the right to inflict violence on barbaric peoples, Grotius (contrary to his popular reputation) supported its infliction', which he made 'even more explicit in *De Iure Belli ac Pacis*'.[35]

In *De Iure*, Grotius enlarged on the theme that 'the barbarians or natural slaves might rightfully be appropriated by civilized peoples'. He argued that sovereigns had the right to punish not only those who injured them, but also any persons who violated the Law of Nature or Nations. 'War', he wrote,

> may be justly undertaken against those who are inhuman to their Parents . . . [against those who kill Strangers that come to dwell amongst them] [a sentence found only in the 1625 edition] . . . against those who eat human Flesh . . . and against those who practice Piracy . . . And so we follow the Opinion of Innocentius, and others, who hold that War is lawful against those who offend against Nature; which is contrary to the Opinion of Vitoria, Vasquuez, Azorius, Molina, and others, who seem to require, towards making a War just, that he has some Jurisdiction over the Person against whom War is made. For they assert, that the Power of Punishing is properly an Effect of Civil Jurisdiction; whereas our Opinion is, that it proceeds from the Law of Nature . . .[36]

In commenting on this Tuck makes three points: first, that it 'is remarkable – and, [he thinks], completely unrecognized by modern scholars – that Grotius specifically aligned himself with Innocent IV and against Vitoria on this crucial issue'. Second, that '[t]he idea that foreign rulers can punish tyrants, cannibals, pirates, those who kill settlers, and those who are inhuman to their parents neatly legitimated a great deal of European action against native peoples around the world . . .' Third, in Tuck's opinion '[t]he central reason why Grotius developed his argument in this direction was . . . that the Dutch had begun to change the character of their activity in the non-European world since his earlier works, and in particular had begun to annex territory'.[37]

Following the establishment of Dutch settlements in the New World, Grotius turned his attention to 'the implications of his general theory for the occupation of and ownership of uncultivated land'. This resulted in him listing in II.2 of *De Iure Belli ac Pacis*,

---

[35] Ibid., p. 89.
[36] Grotius, *De Iure Belli ac Pacis* II. 20. 40, quoted by Tuck, *Rights Of War and Peace*, p. 103.
[37] Tuck, *Rights of War and Peace*, p. 103.

a number of qualifications on men's rights to enjoy ownership over terrestrial objects, which together represent a formidable set of constraints on property in land. The alleged owners of a territory must always permit free passage over it, both of persons and goods; must allow any strangers the right to build temporary accommodation on the seashore; must permit exiles to settle (all of these again rights which the Spaniards and other Europeans had pleaded against native peoples); and in particular, must allow anyone to possess things which are of no use to the owners. – There is no ownership in things which are no use to their owners, and therefore other people have a *perfect* right to occupy them.[38]

This notion of waste land that was assumed to be of no use to, or at least not being used by its owners, became, as we shall see shortly, a central element of Locke's theory of property and was then written into international law by Vattel. The argument Grotius developed about waste land distinguished between *property* and *jurisdiction*. Local political authorities had jurisdiction but did not, in Grotius's interpretation of the law of nature, have the right to prevent those with a use for waste land from settling on it. Settlers were obliged, in Tuck's rendition, to 'defer to the local authorities, assuming that they were willing to settle. If they were not, of course, then the situation is difficult, for the local authorities will have violated a principle of the law of nature and may be punished by war waged against them.'[39] Tuck elaborates on this by emphasising that 'jurisdiction is a right over people, not over things' and that 'the key point for Grotius was that jurisdictional rights could not be pleaded as a justification for stopping free passage or the occupation of waste . . .'[40]

In summing up his close reading of Grotius, Tuck makes the important claim that 'the view taken of Grotius in the conventional histories of international law badly misrepresents his real position'. What he then says bears quoting in full:

> Far from being an heir to the tradition of Vitoria and Suarez, as was assumed by writers at the beginning of this century [the twentieth], he was in fact an heir to the tradition Vitoria most mistrusted, that of huminist jurisprudence. – Grotius endorsed for a state the most far-reaching set of rights to make war which were available to the contemporary repertoire. In particular he accepted a strong version of an international right to punish, and appropriate territory which was not being used properly by indigenous peoples.[41]

---

[38] Ibid., pp. 104–05.   [39] Ibid., p. 106.   [40] Ibid., p. 107.   [41] Ibid., p. 108.

Pufendorf (1632–94) strongly disagreed with Grotius on the right to settle land that was of no use or at least 'not being properly used by its alleged owners'.[42] He did not accept Grotius' theory 'that there is a fundamental natural right to possess bits of the material world which are useful for our personal consumption – and that this natural right by extension develops into fully fledged property where property rights are necessary to produce commodities'.[43] Tuck rehearses the steps in Pufendorf's reasoning that led him to conclude that what was taken from the common store of material goods was not a matter of natural rights but of agreement between men. In Pufendorf's scheme all property 'even of the minimal sort Grotius had supposed to be natural, was artificial or contractual'.[44] It was up to human beings to determine 'what was to be owned by anyone. – They were therefore free to use the language of property in anyway they thought fit, consonant with the general end of advancing a "polished" common life.'[45]

In an argument that anticipated the territorial limits now part of the Law of the Sea, Pufendorf showed that it was difficult to say what should count as waste, but 'states might reasonably claim property rights in an area of the world's surface which they could not actually cultivate, if it was necessary for their defence or if they wished to hunt (that is, fish) over it. Applied to the land, this same agreement prohibited the kind of forcible dispossession of the Indians which Grotius's theory legitimated. . . .' In developing his argument, Pufendorf stated that where there was no apparent individual owner of land it was not to 'be looked upon as *void* and *waste*, so that any one Person may seize it as his *Peculiar*, but we must suppose it to belong to the whole People'.[46] Here and elsewhere Pufendorf made clear his belief that 'the inhabitants of the Americas are . . . members of nations who must be treated with respect'.[47] For property rights it meant that, in Tuck's words, 'the waste lands in a territory occupied by a people are owned by the people collectively, and may be disposed of in all sorts of ways'. Contrary to Grotius, Pufendorf did not believe that foreigners could 'claim a natural right to occupy . . . vacant territory, as long as they submit to the political authority of the local people'.[48]

---

[42] Ibid., p. 154.   [43] Ibid., p. 155.   [44] Ibid., p. 151.   [45] Ibid., p. 155.
[46] Samuel Pufendorf, *The Law of Nature and Nations* trans. Basil Kennet, 5th edn (London, 1749), pp. 386–88 (IV. 6. 3–4), quoted by Tuck, *Rights of War and Peace*, p. 158.
[47] Arneil, *John Locke and America*, p. 55.
[48] Tuck, *Rights of War and Peace*, p. 158.

Another related point of disagreement between Pufendorf and Grotius (and in this case Vitoria as well), was over the right of Europeans to unrestricted travel and trade. Pufendorf did not think that Europeans would be content to give others the right they demanded for themselves, 'to journey among us, with no thought of the numbers in which they come, their purpose in coming, as well as the question of whether . . . they propose to stay but a short while or settle among us permanently'. He argued similarly that rulers could and did limit trade if the interests of the state demanded it and would certainly do so if it meant having foreigners thrust 'upon us without our permission or will'.[49] The implication of his position on waste land is that Pufendorf did believe non-Europeans had sovereign rights.

Writers who recognised 'limited or conditional sovereignty' in non-European peoples

This category included Vattel, Philimore, G. F. De Martens and Bluntschli, all of whom, according to Lindley, admitted sovereign rights, 'but only with restrictions or under conditions'.[50] The discussion in this section focuses on Vattel and on Locke's labour theory of property as a major source of his ideas about property. Vattel published the *Law of Nations* some fifteen years after Locke's *Two Treatises on Government* appeared and was clearly influenced by it. The justifications for European possession presented by Locke and Vattel were, James Tully points out, referred to 'throughout the eighteenth and nineteenth centuries to legitimate settlement without consent, the removal of centuries-old aboriginal nations, and war if the native peoples defended their property'.[51] Vattel argued that it was permissible to take possession of lands that were 'uninhabited and ownerless, or [were] in excess of what would be required by a people leading a pastoral or roaming life if they cultivated the soil; but the occupying state [had to] be in need of more land'.[52] As

---

[49] Arneil, *John Locke and America*, p. 55.
[50] Lindley, *Acquisition and Government*, p. 11.
[51] Tully, *An Approach to Political Philosophy*, p. 169. See also James Tully, 'Aboriginal Property and Western Theory: Recovering a Middle Ground', *Social Philosophy and Policy* 11: 2 (1994), pp. 153–80.
[52] Lindley, *Acquisition and Government*, p. 17. Philimore, writing nearly a century after Vattel, agreed, while Martens argued that it was wrong to take lands 'already effectively occupied by savages against their will' but excluded nomadic peoples, and Bluntschli held that the territory of non-European peoples was 'open to occupation only so long as the [indigenous peoples did] not resist . . . by force'.

well as being a re-statement of Locke, the influence of Grotius' theories concerning the absolute right to occupy land not being used should be immediately apparent. As well as this, the links between Grotius, Pufendorf, Locke and Vattel spelt out by Richard Tuck should be remembered. His argument is that while Locke's Second Treatise is certainly about justifying English colonisation, insufficient recognition has been given to 'the way in which the fundamental arguments of the Second Treatise develop point-by-point an answer to Pufendorf's critique of the ideology of the commercial nations'.[53] Locke's purpose was in part to defend Grotius against Pufendorf's criticisms and, following him, Vattel endorsed Grotius by reinforcing Locke's interpretation of Pufendorf. Vattel's *Law of Nations* was thus 'a more or less faithful version of the Grotian arguments, as developed by Locke . . .'[54]

Tully persuasively argues that Locke's concepts of political society and of property served 'to justify the dispossession of Amerindians of their political organisations and territories, and to vindicate the superiority of European, and specifically English, forms of political society and property established in the new world'. Locke's definition of political society was such that Amerindian government did not qualify as a legitimate form of 'political society'. He defined property

> in such a way that Amerindian customary use is not a legitimate type of property. Rather it is construed as individual labour-based possession and assimilated to an earlier stage of European development in the state of nature, and thus not on equal footing with European property. Amerindian political formations and property are thereby subjected to the sovereignty of European concepts of politics and property.[55]

Locke identified America with the state of nature and the chapter entitled 'On Property' in Book II of the *Two Treatises on Government*, contains his famous comment that 'in the beginning all the world was America'. He defined political society by contrasting it with the actually existing state of nature in America that represented an earlier stage of development in which land was open to appropriation by settlers. Vacant land could be appropriated by means of labour that at the same time creates a property right. The effect of this was that

---

[53] Tuck, *Rights of War and Peace*, p. 168.   [54] Ibid., p. 195.
[55] Tully, *An Approach to Political Philosophy*, p. 139.

[a]s the English began to settle and plant, and not just trade, they began to argue that the Amerindians neither occupied and used in the appropriate manner the lands they claimed, nor did they live in civil societies. Hence, most of the land was vacant, no consent was required for its use, and the colonists claimed they signed formal treaties, not out of recognition of aboriginal rights, but only when it was necessary to appease the natives.[56]

The argument from agriculture, meant to legitimize dispossession, was qualified by the requirement that, ' "from the colonists" perspective, at the time of first European appropriation there was enough and as good land left for aboriginal peoples'.[57] To which was added the stipulation that the Europeans wishing to take over the land actually 'needed' it. Whose version of what was enough and what was needed were of course not questions resolved in ways that benefited Indians.

Situating America in a state of nature, as Locke did, meant disregarding both Amerindian political organisation and the Amerindian system of property. Tully comments that Locke's purpose, at least in part, must have been 'to legitimate and to celebrate the superiority of English colonial market agriculture over Amerindian hunting, gathering, and replacement agriculture that it forcefully displaced'.[58] More recently, Barbara Arneil has confirmed and extended Tully's line of argument. She argues that the *Two Treatises* were 'written as a defence of England's colonial policy in the New World' and that the chapter 'On Property', in particular, had the purpose of justifying 'the seventeenth century dispossession of the aboriginal peoples of their land'.[59] In order to mount this argument Locke made selective use of the many books on the Americas in his possession, omitting aspects of Indian life that were not congenial to his theory. For instance, in arguing for the superiority of European agriculture he 'disregard[ed] the fact that many English settlers in fact depended on the local Amerindian population and their technology for food'.[60] Arneil argues that 'Locke's objective in writing the Second Treatise was to articulate the ends of civil – that is, European – government. For Locke the most important

---

[56] Ibid., p. 148.   [57] Ibid., p. 151.
[58] Ibid., p. 162. He makes the further interesting suggestion (p. 165) 'that in arguing for the superiority of commercial agriculture over Amerindian hunting, trapping, and gathering, Locke may also be arguing for the superiority of English colonisation over the French fur-trading'.
[59] Arneil, *John Locke and America*, p. 2.   [60] Ibid., p. 40.

of these ends is the preservation of private property.' By making cultivation the criteria for property Locke was able to address 'the question
of how property may be claimed in land which lies in common – the
very question which settlers to the new world needed to answer'.[61]
Aboriginal nations could not claim title to their land unless they cultivated it in the manner of Europeans. 'Title to property – that is the
right to exclude others from it – [could] only be claimed, by definition,
by the individual.'[62] This necessarily meant ignoring Indian political
society, which, as previously mentioned, was based on the collectivity
of nations and patterns of land use that resembled European agricultural
methods.

In Book I, Chapter VII of the *Law of Nations*, Vattel first extols agriculture as a source of national wealth that is not served by rights of
common which prevent land owners from making the most productive
use of their land.[63] Having in this way endorsed enclosure and agricultural reforms that discourage subsistence farming, he next asserts that
cultivation of the soil is 'an obligation imposed by nature on mankind'
as a whole. 'Every nation is . . . obliged by the law of nature to cultivate the land that has fallen to its share; and it has no right to enlarge
its boundaries, or have recourse to the assistance of other nations, but
in proportion as the land in its possession is incapable of furnishing it
with necessities.'[64] Apart from sanctioning the occupation of the land
of others if that land is 'needed', it follows from this that nations that
did not cultivate their land according to European criteria were not con-
forming to the law of nature. Indeed Vattel states that whereas it might
once have been permissible for the occupants of fertile land to hunt and
keep flocks, instead of cultivating it by hunting and herding, that was no
longer acceptable. People who pursued such a life used more land than
they needed if they used it efficiently, and had, 'therefore, no reason to
complain if other nations, more industrious and closely confined, come
to take possession of part of those lands'.[65] He concludes his discussion
of this by saying that while the conquest of Mexico and Peru was 'a
notorious usurpation, the establishment of many colonies on the continent of North America might, on their confining themselves within just
bounds, be extremely lawful. The people of those extensive tracts *rather
ranged through than inhabited them.*'[66] It is clear from this that indigenous

---

[61] Ibid., p. 61.   [62] Ibid., p. 141.
[63] Emmerich de Vattel, *The Law of Nations* (Philadelphia: Johnson and Co., 1863, reprinted
New York: AMS Press, 1982), para 78, p. 34.
[64] Ibid., para 81, p. 35.   [65] Ibid., p. 36.   [66] Ibid., p. 36 (emphasis mine).

peoples leading the life of hunter gatherers did not, according to Vattel, have a right to all of the land over which they roamed and might have considered to be their own.

In a later chapter Vattel directly addresses the specific question of a nation establishing itself in another land. Like Locke before him, Vattel argues that the 'earth belongs to mankind in general',[67] but as population grew cultivation became necessary and from this came the 'rights of property and dominion'. The right that had been common to all mankind was then progressively 'restricted to what each lawfully possesses' as a result of cultivation. This in turn determines the meaning Vattel gives to whether or not a country was occupied. An unoccupied country is one that is not cultivated and in which the inhabitants are not united into a political society.

> All mankind have an equal right to things that have not yet fallen into the possession of any one; and those things belong to the person who first takes possession of them. When, therefore, a nation finds a country uninhabited, and without an owner, it may lawfully take possession of it: and after it has sufficiently made known its will in this respect, it cannot be deprived of it by another nation.

Once again 'the possession of anyone' and 'uninhabited' meant settled and cultivated in the European manner. It tells us nothing about whether or not there actually were indigenous inhabitants. Indeed, throughout the expansion of Europe there must have been very few places on earth that were genuinely uninhabited.

Nevertheless, Vattel continues by stating that when navigators took 'possession' of uninhabited lands in the name of their sovereign they established at the same time title which was respected 'provided it was soon after followed by real possession'.[68] Real possession meant effective occupation and his view was that the Law of Nations does 'not acknowledge the property and sovereignty of a nation over any uninhabited countries, except those of which it has really taken actual possession, in which it has formed settlements, or of which it makes actual use'.[69] Once again uninhabited really meant that the lands claimed by navigators had not been occupied by Europeans, which is implicitly made clear by him in the section that follows.

Vattel asks whether it is lawful for a nation to take possession 'of some part of a vast country, in which there are none but erratic nations whose

---

[67] Ibid., p. 97.   [68] Ibid., para 207, p. 98.   [69] Ibid., para 208, p. 99.

scanty population is incapable of occupying the whole'.[70] In answer to this he refers back to his earlier argument, in Paragraph 81, that nations were entitled only to land they need and were able to settle and culti-vate. 'Their unsettled habitation in those immense regions cannot be ac-counted true and legal possession; and the people of Europe, too closely pent up at home, finding land of which the savages stood in no particular need, and of which they made no actual and constant use, were lawfully entitled to take possession of it, and settle it with colonies.' The earth, he reiterates, belongs to mankind and if every nation had continued to live by hunting and gathering the earth would be unable to support 'a tenth part' of its population. From this he thought it followed that 'confining the Indians within narrower limits' was in keeping with the 'views of nature'.[71] This was of course to ignore completely indigenous patterns of land use, belief, custom and law.

Thus in the conclusion to *The Rights of War and Peace* Tuck comments that:

> The moral failure of the Europeans lay . . . in their indifference to the facts about North Americans – facts such as the actual prevalence of a form of agriculture among them (screened from view, often, by the circumstance that it was *women* who tilled the fields, and that their activity was promptly labelled gardening), the acute danger to the aboriginals posed by European diseases, and the inability of hunting societies to adapt to the loss of their hunting grounds. The attempt to save the lives of Europeans [by migrating to the New World to escape conditions in Europe] resulted in the mass slaughter of aboriginals on a scale far beyond even the great famines of the fourteenth century in Europe.[72]

Writers who denied sovereign rights to non-Europeans

In this category Lindley included John Westlake, William Edward Hall, Lasca Oppenheim[73] and T. J. Lawrence. All wrote in the nineteenth or early twentieth centuries, during or in recent memory of the extraordi-nary phase of expansion that began with the Scramble for Africa after 1885 and included the Scramble for Concessions in China. Gerrit Gong portrays this expansion as 'fundamentally a confrontation of civilisa-tions and their respective cultural systems. At the heart of this clash were standards of civilisation by which these different civilisations identified

---

[70] Ibid., para 209, p. 99. [71] Ibid., p. 100. [72] Tuck, *Rights of War and Peace*, p. 233.
[73] Lasca Oppenheim, *International Law: A Treatise*, 8th ed. H. Lauterpacht (London: Longmans, 1967), vol. I.

themselves and regulated their international relations.' A 'standard of civilisation' is, he explains, 'an expression of the assumptions, tacit and explicit, used to distinguish those that belong to a particular society from those that do not'.[74] In the late nineteenth century, in particular, the European society of states espoused a standard of civilisation that 'took an increasingly juridical character'.[75] The term 'standard of civilisation' was framed with reference to relations between European states and non-European peoples. It 'demanded that foreigners receive treatment consistent "with the rule of law as understood in Western countries" '.[76] The late nineteenth and early twentieth centuries were, according to him, a transition period between the expansion of the international system and the establishment of a 'civilised' international society.[77] International law incorporating the standard of 'civilisation' had a crucial role in that process. At the same time as it 'was by definition expanding to include all "civilised" nations, the countries qualified to come within its scope remained limited in practice'.[78] To enter the international society of 'civilised' states non-European entities had to meet the requirements of the standard set by European states. With the perspective of time we can recognise this as a form of cultural imperialism.

In the work of Westlake and Hall the notion of 'civilised' and 'semi-civilised' states was fundamental to determining the scope of sovereign rights in international law. The legal rights and duties of states were based on the 'legal capacity their degree of "civilisation" supposedly entitled them to possess'.[79] Westlake's opinion was that the only 'territorial titles recognised by International Law [were] those . . . held by states' sufficiently well organised to be able to 'protect the white settler in the pursuits of civilised life'. Hall regarded territory that had not been appropriated ' "by a civilised or semi-civilised state" [as] open to Occupation'. For Oppenheim, land occupied by indigenous peoples, but whose community could not be considered a state, was open to occupation; but 'the territory of any State', even one outside the 'family of nations', was not open and could be acquired only if it were freely ceded by its inhabitants or they were subjugated. Finally, Lawrence held that all territory that was 'not in the possession of States [accepted as] . . . members of the Family of Nations and subjects of International Law' was *territorium nullius*.[80]

[74] Gong, *Standard of 'Civilisation'*, p. 3.   [75] Ibid., p. 5.   [76] Ibid., p. 14.
[77] Ibid., p. 10.   [78] Ibid., p. 59.
[79] Ibid., p. 55.   [80] Lindley, *Acquisition and Government*, p. 18.

The problem with all of this was, as Lindley recognised in 1926, how the term 'state' should be understood and what it was that distinguished 'savage from civilised peoples'. His answer was that 'no accurate distinction' could be drawn between what was civilised and what was uncivilised and that the more sensible distinction to draw was that 'between one kind of civilisation and another', with the crucial deciding factor being whether there was evidence of political organisation.[81] The test of civilisation at the time was whether there was a sufficient degree of political organisation to allow European settlers to live in much the same degree of personal safety that they had enjoyed in their countries of origin. According to Westlake, this required a government able give Europeans the protection they needed to 'carry on the complex life to which they have been accustomed in their homes, which may prevent that life from being disturbed by contests between different European powers for supremacy on the same soil, and which may protect the natives in the enjoyment of a security and well-being at least not less than that they enjoyed before the arrival of strangers'.[82] If 'the natives' could not provide a government equal to this task then they were to be regarded for the purposes of international law as 'uncivilised'. Territory that did have political society was not open to occupation, but tracts of land 'inhabited only by isolated individuals who were not united for political action' could be considered *territorium nullius* and open to occupation.[83]

The *Collected Papers* of John Westlake illustrate very well the importance, at the time, of this distinction between the 'civilised' and the 'uncivilised' for the status of non-Europeans in international law. He is, for that reason alone, worth considering at length. Among the topics he identified as bearing on the status of non-Europeans in relation to the dichotomy between the civilised and uncivilised are territorial sovereignty; the position of uncivilised nations with regard to international law; government and the international test of civilisation; treaties with uncivilised tribes; and discovery and occupation as titles.

Taking these in turn, the question Westlake asks about territorial sovereignty concerns native title. It is whether, once a 'civilised' state turns a country into a colony, the title to the land continues according to the customs of the inhabitants before civilised government was established. What concerns him, in particular, is the situation where a

[81] Ibid., p. 22.   [82] Westlake, *Collected Papers*, p. 143.
[83] Lindley, *Acquisition and Government*, pp. 23, 47.

colony is 'formed among natives of some advancement'. In his view it was up to the coloniser to either accept or reject native custom and law. The title to land was regarded as issuing from a grant by the colonising state, the authority of which derived from territorial sovereignty. Consequently, it was open to colonisers to dispossess the 'less advanced' or 'uncivilised'. Acquiring sovereignty meant the colonising state acquired all land that 'it was not morally compelled to acknowledge as belonging to natives' or to European pioneers who occupied territory before the establishment of state sovereignty. Essentially property was viewed as issuing from sovereignty but that raised the question of the origin of sovereignty itself. What, Westlake asked, allowed the conclusion that 'an uncivilised region may be internationally recognised as appropriated in sovereignty to a particular state?'[84] Only, he answered, 'recognition of such sovereignty by the members of international society'. Whether the sovereignty claimed by the colonizing state was recognised by the inhabitants was irrelevant because international law took no account of 'uncivilised' natives. But this didn't mean that all rights they might have were denied. Whether they were recognised was a matter for the conscience of the state into which they had been incorporated: 'the rules of international society existing only for the purpose of regulating the mutual conduct of its members'.[85]

Two important implications of this were, first, that the establishment of a colony meant the inhabitants prior to colonisation were now contained within a state. They henceforth had, as a result of the logic of international law, no international personality and no sovereign rights other than as citizens of the states which now exercised sovereignty over them. Second, the idea that it was up to the colonising state to determine title brings us back to the question of the moral basis of the state and of international society. States might do dreadful things to 'uncivilised' people, such as take away their land, but as long as it did not transgress the norms of behaviour with fellow members of international society, it was of no concern to international law. Protecting the rights of a non-European society against a European state would, in all likelihood, have required the intercession of one or more other European states. Such action could have resulted in the kind of conflict between European states that the Berlin Conference of 1885 sought to avoid and it would have undercut the colonizing activities of all European states.

---

[84] Westlake, *Collected Papers*, p. 137.   [85] Ibid., p. 138.

Westlake begins his discussion of the position of 'uncivilised' nations in international law with an argument against natural law. It is that a theorist who entertains the idea of a 'state of nature independent of human institutions cannot introduce into his picture a difference between civilised and uncivilised man'. Westlake's theory is that certain institutions determine whether people are civilised or uncivilised, rather than abstract laws of nature such as those Vitoria had relied upon to draw the conclusion that there is a fundamental equality between all humankind. In what is obviously a reference to Vattel, Westlake asserts that when an 'uncivilised' people occupied more land than they needed, their presence was not a barrier to 'civilised' people occupying it as if it were *terra nullius*. In support of this he suggests that Vitoria was not questioning the title of Spain but instead wanted to influence its actions towards Indians.[86] If it was a matter of rights and making rights the starting point for law with rights regarded as common to both 'civilised' and 'uncivilised humanity', then this was not something for international law to 'develop and protect'. The Berlin Conference, convened to lay down the ground rules for European expansion into Africa, had not endorsed the idea that 'an uncivilised population has rights which make its consent necessary to the establishment of a government possessing international validity'.[87] In other words, 'uncivilised' populations had no rights against states accepted as members of international society. On balance, states were not well advised, if they wished to preserve harmony in their relations with one another, to question too closely how the one or the other actually had come to acquire the territory of 'uncivilised' people. This was not to deny the rights of those that were not party to agreements; but they were moral and not legal rights. 'The moral rights of all outside the international society against the several members of that society remain intact, though they have not and scarcely could have been converted into legal rights.'[88]

The test of civilisation articulated by Westlake was that of most if not all publicists of his time. Civilisation had nothing to do with the personal or cultural attributes of non-Europeans but instead with whether they could provide a level of government that would allow European settlers to live with the level of personal safety that they would enjoy in their home country.[89] This did not necessarily require the degree of government found in Europe. 'If even the natives could furnish such a government after the manner of the Asiatic empires, that would be

---

[86] Ibid., p. 139. [87] Ibid., p. 141. [88] Ibid., p. 142. [89] Ibid., p. 143.

sufficient.'[90] But if natives could not provide such government then it was legitimate for Europeans or 'civilised' peoples to impose it on them. In support of this Westlake rehearses the standard imperialist arguments of the time concerning progress and European duty. Regardless of that, he impishly argued, if the 'uncivilised' wanted to keep Europeans out of their lands they would have to have a government to do it.[91]

In the course of discussing the status of treaties with 'uncivilised tribes' Westlake defends European acquisition on the grounds that hunting and nomadic tribes 'may have so slight a connection with any land in particular as to share but little, if at all, the ideas which we connect with property and the soil'.[92] This harks back to the earlier discussion of Vattel and simply ignores the beliefs and laws that native inhabitants might have had concerning their relationship with the land. It is in effect to claim the superiority of European ideas of property and on that basis justify the dispossession of hunting and nomadic tribes. At the same time Westlake discounts the importance of treaties by saying that it is not so much treaties with first nations that count as whether or not they have the capacity for government. It is noteworthy that Westlake explicitly excludes Mexico and Peru from his discussion because, when Europeans arrived, they were countries that 'had attained a degree of advancement ranking them rather as states than as uncivilised tribes'.[93]

Finally, in a section on discovery and occupation as a source of title, Westlake makes it quite clear that international law is concerned with titles to territory that 'states belonging to the society of international law are able to invoke against one another'. The 'uncivilised' inhabitants of the territory concerned were simply denied title. From the perspective of the late twentieth century the idea that international law recognised only the claims of members of international society against each other is troubling. Fortunately it belongs to a phase of international law that has long been left behind.

The eclipse of natural law

The preceding versions of sovereign rights demonstrate that the earlier writers were more willing to concede rights to non-Europeans.[94] As the expansion of Europe proceeded international law became

---

[90] Ibid., p. 144.   [91] Ibid., p. 145.   [92] Ibid., p. 142.   [93] Ibid., p. 149.
[94] Crawford, *The Creation of States*, p. 175.

simultaneously more universal and exclusionary. It aspired to universal application but, as we have seen, excluded 'primitive societies' from its community. Gong argues that this tension was the source of the first of two crises that challenged the development of international law. The first derived precisely 'from the contradiction inherent within the law's universal aspirations and its requirements that only "civilised" countries could fully be its subjects'. The second came much later when the 'newly independent non-European countries sought to use their new membership in the United Nations and other international bodies to modify the international law which they had earlier perceived to be both foreign and disciplinary'.[95] The retraction of sovereign rights of non-Europeans regarded by Europeans as 'uncivilised', which was the source of the first of these two crises, was partly a result of the gradual eclipse of natural law as international law evolved into the positive law of relations between states.

Las Casas, Sepulveda and Vitoria with whom we began, worked from the precepts of natural law in which the rights and duty of all humankind were paramount; the law of nations had no important role in their argument. Grotius also worked from the precepts of natural law, but by the time he wrote states had begun to loom larger and with them the need for a law of nations. According to him both the law of nature and the less specific concept *jus gentium* or law of nations encompassed more than simply Europe and Christendom. By *jus gentium* he 'meant the particular positive law which, with the consent of nations, supplements the law of nature and which together with it regulates the totality of international relations'.[96] *Jus gentium* included natural law and because the latter concerned all humans, everywhere, it supposedly had universal application. Unlike the laws of each state that were to do with the interests of that state the Law of Nations represented certain laws that originated 'between all states, or a great many states; and . . . had in view the advantage, not of particular states, but of the great society of states'. It was an expression of common consent.[97] Thus Cutler asserts that '[t]he most profound component of the Grotian world view is the assumption that there is a universal standard of justice and morality against which the actions of states may be judged'.[98] It is a universal standard grounded

[95] Gong, *Standard of 'Civilisation'*, p. 243.
[96] Peter Remec, *The Position of the Individual in International Law According to Grotius and Vattel* (The Hague: Nijhoff, 1960), p. 28.
[97] Grotius, *De Iure Belli ac Pacis*, see the Prolegomena 17 and Para 40.
[98] Cutler, 'Grotian Tradition', p. 46.

in natural law and the work of Grotius supports the view 'that individuals, alongside states, hold rights, and owe duties under international law'. As previously mentioned, Grotius' writings reflect 'the absence at the time of a clearly perceived distinction between individual and state personality'.[99] Indeed, in his theoretical framework states derived their rights from individuals; the one had the rights of the other.

Remec contends that the conception of international law as a positive law of nations supplementing the law of nature obscures the fact that Grotius had a very different idea of the law of nature from that of the so-called Grotians with whom Vattel is usually identified. He defends this proposition by first drawing a trifold distinction between 'naturalists', 'positivists' and then 'Grotians' who combined the first two. Naturalists are writers on international law who, like Hobbes, regard nations as existing in a state of nature, which leads them to 'equate the law of nations with the law of nature' and 'more or less deny the existence of a separate law of nations'.[100] In this sense Vattel's conception of the law of nature followed that of Hobbes. That states existed in a state of nature implied that relations between them were governed by the law of nature. In Vattel's construction of international law states are collections of men who, in a state of nature, are free, independent and governed by the law of nature. Because states are nothing more than collections of men they also are free, independent and in a state of nature. The law of nations therefore equates with the law of nature.[101] Vattel's conception of the law of nature, according to Remec's reading of it, is then individualistic and to do with self-preservation rather than the classical ideal upheld by Grotius that 'the primary bond between men is their common rational and social nature'.

Earlier discussion, in this chapter and in chapter 2, of Tuck's work on Grotius, Hobbes and Vattel shows that this is not correct. Not only was self-preservation a cardinal natural right in Grotius' theory, on the question of sociability there was little to chose between Hobbes and Grotius. If Tuck's understanding is correct, and I believe it is, Vattel's *Law of Nations* was a defence of Grotius' conception of it. In Book II of the *Law of Nations*, Vattel did, however, move away from Grotius's inclusion of individuals via natural law towards establishing states as the exclusive subjects of international law. It is here that he articulates the idea that the paramount duty of a nation towards itself 'is its preservation and

---

[99] Ibid.   [100] Remec, *Position of the Individual*, p. 53.
[101] Julius Stone, *Approaches to the Notion of International Justice* (Jerusalem: Truman Center Publications No. 4, Hebrew University of Jerusalem, 1970), pp. 41–2.

perfection, together with that of its state'.[102] He then elaborates on the duties of states towards other states. States have a duty not only to help preserve other states,[103] but also to contribute to the perfection of other states. Perfection he defines in terms of whether a state 'is more or less adapted to attain the end of civil society'. Helping other nations obtain perfection does not, however, include doing so by force, which would be a violation of the 'natural liberty' of others. Nations are 'free and independent' and not to be interfered with by other nations and in relation to this he criticizes both the Conquest of America and Grotius. In an unmistakable reference to the Spaniards he says that the Europeans who attacked the American nations, 'and subjected them to their greedy dominion', in order to civilise them and instruct them in the 'true religion' were 'usurpers . . . unjust and ridiculous'. Grotius, he says, was mistaken in defending the use of force to prevent 'transgressions of the law of nature' such as cannibalism. The use of force was permissible only by those whose safety was at risk. Grotius' position was one that would give vent to 'the ravages of enthusiasm and fanaticism' in numerous ways.[104]

Vattel's system of international law is one in which individual human beings are excluded as direct subjects of international law. People can only assert rights against the state and are therefore cut off from appeal to international society. Remec argues that although 'the individual man serves as the basis for Vattel's constructions of the society of states – The humanitarian concept of a great republic of all men [actually] serves as a disguise for the establishment of the concept of a society of nations which excludes from its ranks everything and everybody but sovereign states.'[105] Ultimately he provides the conceptual basis of an 'exclusive society of states, with no place left for the individual'.[106] Remec concludes that 'Grotius recognises but Vattel denies the possibility of international protection of human rights against one's own state.'[107]

The nineteenth century, which formed the views of people like Hall, Westlake and Lindley, was when natural law finally gave way to positive international law. Charles Alexandrowicz argues that as a consequence '[i]nternational law shrank into an Eurocentric system which imposed on extra-European countries its own ideas including the admissibility of war and non-military pressure as a prerogative of sovereignty. It also discriminated against non-European civilisations and thus ran on

---

[102] Vattel, *Law of Nations*, Para 14, p. 135.   [103] Ibid., Para 4.   [104] Ibid., pp. 136–7.
[105] Remec, *Position of the Individual*, p. 19.   [106] Ibid., p. 220.   [107] Ibid., p. 243.

parallel lines with colonialism as a political trend.'[108] His view was that the 'standard of civilisation' was applied because of the 'ascendancy of positivist theories of international law'. Gong objects to this on the grounds that it is not true that the standard of civilisation 'emerged as international law shrank from a universal into an exclusive Eurocentric system. On the contrary, the standard emerged not so much to ostracize the non-European countries from the Family of Nations as to include them within the domain of international law.'[109] Nevertheless, by the end of the nineteenth century there had been a 'shift to the view that international law did not exist outside the territories of the European and American states, or at least that international law was generated only by these states'.[110]

The defence of the rights of non-Europeans by earlier writers was grounded in natural law which did not draw any clear distinction between individual and state personality. The positivist view of the late nineteenth century was that the acquisition of territory was a matter of the rights of European states against each other; the rights of non-Europeans were over-ridden if their societies did not meet European criteria for political society and statehood. It was, as Westlake said, a 'law of European peoples',[111] and was intended to govern relations between European states. If non-European states and entities were to be included it was by adopting European modes of social and political organisation.

Overlapping with these changes in legal thought about the sovereign rights of non-Europeans, from Vitoria down to Westlake, were the changing conceptions of otherness outlined in Chapter 2. The Renaissance, Enlightenment and nineteenth-century conceptions of otherness discussed by Bernard McGrane correspond with the categories identified by Lindley that have formed the basis of this chapter. Spanish reasoning concerning Amerindians was predicated on whether they were capable of being Christians and therefore entitled, as decreed by natural law, to be treated as equal human beings. Through its connection to the dichotomy between the state of nature and civil society the theory of property adopted by Vattel conceived of savages as lacking fully the faculty of reason that distinguished the Enlightenment attitude to

---

[108] Charles H. Alexandrowicz, *The European-African Confrontation: A Study in Treaty Making* (Leiden: Sijthoff, 1973), p. 6.
[109] Gong, *Standard of 'Civilisation'*, p. 44.
[110] Bull, Kingsbury and Roberts (eds.), *Hugo Grotius*, pp. 48–9.
[111] Westlake, *Collected Papers*, p. 103.

otherness. The parallels between the nineteenth-century notion of the other as fundamentally primitive and the criteria of the standard of civilisation for excluding particular peoples from consideration under international law are obvious. It would be surprising if the development of legal reasoning at any given juncture did not in some way reflect prevailing political and social ideas. The exact nature of the connections between these is however difficult to specify and is beyond the scope of this book.

In conclusion, European expansion into the New World coincided with the need for a Law of Nations to regulate relations between the independent states of Europe that had successfully established themselves by the end of the reign of Frederic III in 1493.[112] The Law of Nations that resulted was transformed, in the eighteenth century, into international law. It was a product of Christian civilisation and was for a long time confined to the states of Christendom.[113] Through the expansion of Europe it became a 'criterion' of the modern states system.[114] International law presupposed the existence of, and is framed with reference to, a community. Conversely, the boundaries of international communities are set by international law. To the extent that international law has coincided with and been a vehicle for promoting international morality it has been largely a morality of states that, at times, has served to justify the imposition of European ideas of political society and community on non-European others. By codifying rules that long excluded many non-European entities and individuals, international law was constituent of, and supported, an international society that was unjust in the way it discriminated between different peoples and treated them as unequal. In Chapter 4 it will be seen that international law now has a major role in reclaiming and entrenching the rights of, in particular, indigenous peoples.

[112] Oppenheim, *International Law*, p. 79.   [113] Ibid., p. 6.
[114] Wight, *Systems of States*, p. 47.

4 Recovering rights: land, self-determination and sovereignty

So far I have been concerned with the past and have deliberately used the broad term 'non-Europeans'. The focus of this chapter shifts to the quest of contemporary indigenous peoples for the core right of self-determination. The bulk of non-European peoples that had been subjugated by European peoples achieved formal self-determination as a result of decolonisation following World War Two. Decolonisation did not, however, give self-determination to numerous indigenous peoples enclosed in new states such as India or Indonesia. For many of them decolonisation merely meant exchanging one set of colonial masters for another. In former colonies such as Australia, New Zealand and Canada, which had achieved independent status much earlier, it did nothing to change the situation of indigenous peoples who had been dispossessed of their lands and both lost control over their affairs and were often denied the full rights of citizenship. The loss of these was connected, in Chapter 3, with international law as a discourse that aided and justified the dispossession of land and rights, but it can no longer be viewed in this way. James Anaya shows that international law now 'includes a certain universe of norms and procedures that benefit indigenous peoples'. It now challenges the legacy of dispossession 'and the forces that would see it continue'.[1] The displacement of natural by positive law, also noted in Chapter 3, established states as the subjects of international law and gave individuals a place mainly as citizens of states. In the twentieth century there was at least a partial reversal of this with

---

[1] S. James Anaya, *Indigenous Peoples in International Law* (New York: Oxford University Press, 1996), p. 184. See also p. 4 where he writes that 'although once an instrument of colonialism, [international law] has developed and continues to develop, however grudgingly or imperfectly, to support indigenous peoples' demands'.

increasing recognition, in international law, of individual and group rights that pose a challenge to the state-centric logic of international society. In particular, indigenous peoples' claims to self-determination, as a group right, unsettle the way states understand self-determination and sovereignty. International lawyers appear, in this case, to be actively revising an understanding derived from their predecessors and to be doing so ahead of state leaders.

This chapter first outlines the United Nations international human rights regime and its impact on indigenous peoples. As a prelude to more extensive discussion of self-determination, it then explains the centrality of land in indigenous claims. Next it considers the concept of self-determination and argues that indigenous peoples' claims are resisted, in part, because of the way self-determination has been understood as an attribute of statehood. It argues that this understanding can and needs to be recast to include multiple loyalties. Following that, four issues concerning self-determination that need to be resolved if indigenous claims are to advance are canvassed. Finally, there is a brief discussion of some indigenous concepts and perspectives on self-determination and sovereignty.

The United Nations human rights regime

This book was written during the United Nations International Decade of the World's Indigenous Peoples (1995–2004). Two central goals for the decade were the establishment of a Permanent United Nations Forum for Indigenous Peoples and the adoption, by the General Assembly, of a declaration on indigenous rights. The first of these goals was realised in 2000, but in 2003 the second has yet to be achieved. In the recovery of indigenous rights, the transformation of indigenous peoples from being objects to being subjects of international law and the establishment of indigenous rights as international norms, the United Nations has had a major role. Through the framework of the United Nations international human rights regime, indigenous peoples have been able to participate in setting international standards for indigenous rights. As well as this, existing United Nations human rights instruments enshrine fundamental indigenous rights; foremost among them is the right of 'peoples' to self-determination. This section briefly outlines the United Nations international human rights regime in relation to indigenous peoples and has a particular interest in the impact of the international human rights regime on indigenous peoples.[2]

One of the principal purposes of the United Nations expressed in Article 1 of the Charter is the promotion and encouragement of 'respect for human rights and fundamental freedoms for all without distinction as to race, sex, language or religion'.[3] This 'ideal of non-discrimination in the enjoyment of human rights was reiterated, and elaborated, in later human rights instruments including The Universal Declaration of Human Rights, The International Covenant on Civil and Political Rights, and The International Covenant on Economic, Social and Cultural Rights'.[4] Both covenants enjoin states to uphold the rights contained in them 'without distinction of any kind, such as race, colour, sex, language, political or other opinion, national or social origin, birth or other status'. The International Convention on the Elimination of all Forms of Discrimination (CERD) further 'reinforces the prohibition on discrimination and the obligation on states to eliminate racial discrimination'.[5] Taken together, The Universal Declaration, The International Covenant on Civil and Political Rights (ICCPR), and The International Covenant on Economic, Social and Cultural Rights (ICESCR) comprise the so-called International Bill of Rights. Of particular significance for indigenous rights is the right of all 'peoples' to self-determination, proclaimed in Article 1 of both the ICCPR and the ICESCR, and Article 27 of the ICCPR, which provides for the right of minorities 'to enjoy their own culture, to profess and practice their own religion, or to use their own language'.[6] Indigenous peoples 'see their status as other than minorities in their own land' and should not necessarily be identified with minorities. Nevertheless, Article 27 has had considerable importance for indigenous rights.

So far the only binding universal instruments dealing specifically with indigenous peoples have been the International Labor Organisation (ILO) Conventions 107 and 169. ILO 107, dating from 1957, is

---

[2] For accounts of the United Nations system in relation to indigenous rights see Venne, *Our Elders*, and the earlier and briefer account by Delia Opekoew, 'International Law, International Institutions, and Indigenous Issues' in R. Thompson (ed.), *The Rights of Indigenous Peoples in International Law: Selected Essays on Self-Determination* (University of Saskatchewan, Native Law Centre, 1987).

[3] *United Nations Charter*, Article 1(3), see also Article 55.

[4] Lisa Mary Strelein, 'Indigenous Self-Determination Claims and the Common Law in Australia', Ph.D. thesis, the Australian National University, April 1998, p. 62.

[5] Ibid.

[6] Henry J. Steiner and Philip Alston (eds.), *International Human Rights in Context: Law, Politics, Morals* (Oxford: Clarendon Press, 1996), p. 992.

now regarded as an essentially assimilationist document that ignores the goals of cultural integrity, autonomy and survival. The later ILO 169, which became effective in 1991, imposed 'obligations on states to protect the recognised rights of indigenous peoples and to protect their social, cultural, religious and spiritual values'. It did not, however, 'indicate the means or forms of participation by indigenous peoples in national decision-making' and gave 'no effective rights of autonomy'.[7]

The organs of the United Nations relevant to indigenous peoples form a hierarchical structure in which those lower in the hierarchy report to a parent body standing above them. At the top of the structure is the General Assembly. Descending from it are the Economic and Social Council (ECOSOC), the Commission on Human Rights (CHR), the Sub-Commission on the Promotion and Protection of Human Rights (Sub-Commission) and the Working Group on Indigenous Populations (WGIP). With the exception of the WGIP each of these has oversight of groups charged with particular tasks. The most important of these have been the Special Rapporteurs and Working Groups appointed by and reporting to the Sub-Commission, The Inter-Sessional Working Group on the Draft Declaration on the Rights of Indigenous Peoples, reporting to the CHR and since 2000, the Permanent Forum on Indigenous Issues, for which ECOSOC is the parent body.[8]

The initiative to work towards the establishment of the Permanent Forum was an outcome of the 1993 Vienna Conference on Human Rights, which was attended by hundreds of indigenous people. 'With the establishment of the Forum, indigenous peoples have become members of a UN body and, as such, will help set the Forum's agenda and determine its outcomes [which is regarded as] unprecedented within the UN system.'[9] The Forum comprises sixteen experts. Eight are nominated by governments and elected by the ECOSOC and the remaining eight are appointed by its president 'following formal consultations with Governments which, in turn, have discussed prospective nominees with indigenous organisations'.[10] As well as this, organisations of indigenous peoples can participate in the Forum as observers.

---

[7] Ibid., p. 1008. Concerning the ILO see Chris Tennant, 'Indigenous Peoples, International Institutions, and the International Legal Literature from 1945–1993', *Human Rights Quarterly*, 16 (1994), 1–57.
[8] For an account of how these bodies relate to each other see Venne, *Our Elders*.
[9] World Conference Against Racism, United Nations Guide for Indigenous Peoples, Leaflet No. 6, The Permanent Forum on Indigenous Issues, p. 3. http://www.unhchr.ch/html/racism/00-indigenousguide.html, accessed 4/12/02.
[10] Ibid. p. 2.

From the time of its establishment the United Nations has been involved in indigenous issues through its overall human rights work. The beginning of its direct involvement may be dated from 1970 when the Sub-Commission on Prevention of Discrimination and Protection of Minorities recommended a study of the problem of discrimination against indigenous populations. José R. Martínez Cobo of Ecuador was appointed as Special Rapporteur to carry out this task. His study, which was not completed until 1984, 'addressed a wide range of human rights issues affecting indigenous peoples – and called on governments to formulate guidelines for their activities concerning indigenous peoples on the basis of respect for the ethnic identity, rights and freedoms of indigenous peoples'.[11] The conclusions, proposals and recommendations contained in the report are regarded as 'an important milestone in the United Nations consideration of the human rights problems facing indigenous peoples'.[12]

Cobo's study led to the establishment, in 1982, of the WGIP by the Economic and Social Council. The WGIP is described as 'the focal point in the UN system for the promotion of indigenous people's rights'.[13] It consists of five independent experts who, at the same time as being members of the Sub-Commission on the Promotion and Protection of Human Rights, represent each geopolitical region of the world.[14] Prior to the establishment of the WGIP '[u]sually only those non-governmental organisations (NGOs) having consultative status with ECOSOC [were] permitted to participate actively in meetings of subsidiary bodies'.[15] The WGIP departed from this practice by receiving information from indigenous organisations and groups that did not have this status. 'Meetings of the WGIP are open to representatives of all indigenous peoples, their communities and organisations. As such, they have become some of the largest human rights meetings held by the UN.'[16]

---

[11] World Conference Against Racism, United Nations Guide for Indigenous Peoples, Leaflet No. 1, Indigenous Peoples and the United Nations System: An Overview, p. 5. http://www.unhchr.ch/html/racism/00-indigenousguide.html accessed 4/12/02.
[12] United Nations, Office of the High Commissioner for Human Rights, Fact Sheet No. 9 (Rev. 1), The Rights of Indigenous Peoples, p. 3. http://www.unhchr.ch/html/menu6/2/fs9.htm accessed 14/3/02.
[13] United Nations Leaflet No. 1, p. 5.   [14] Ibid.   [15] Venne, *Our Elders*, p. 52.
[16] 'Indigenous people have come from all over the world to participate in the WGIP: Aboriginals and Torres Strait Islanders from Australia, Māoris from New Zealand, Native Americans from North and South America, Inuit from the Polar regions, Saami from Northern Europe, Ainu from Japan, and other groups from the Asia and African regions and the Russian Federation', United Nations Leaflet No. 1.

According to the Office of the High Commissioner for Human Rights as many as 700 people comprising observers for governments and indigenous peoples' and non-governmental organisations, as well as scholars and academics regularly attend sessions of the WGIP.[17] Through the WGIP indigenous people were for the first time in the history of the United Nations allowed to speak directly to one of its organs. This meant that in the important task of preparing the Draft Declaration the 'peoples most affected by the Declaration were directly and fully involved in every step of the process. . . .'[18] According to Pritchard, this is largely because indigenous peoples' representatives have enjoyed 'unrestricted access to [WGIP] meetings . . . its processes enjoy an exceptional level of legitimacy among Indigenous representatives'. Pritchard explains that, by contrast, 'working groups at the level of the CHR . . . do not permit participation of non-governmental organisations . . . unless these have obtained consultative status with the Economic and Social Council'.[19]

It is important to notice that the mandate of the WGIP 'does not authorise it to examine specific complaints of alleged violations of human rights with the purpose of making recommendations or taking decisions on such cases'. Its two formal tasks are instead:

> To review national developments pertaining to the promotion and protection of the human rights and fundamental freedoms of indigenous peoples; and
> To develop international standards concerning the rights of indigenous peoples, taking account of the similarities and the differences in their situations and aspirations throughout the world.[20]

[17] United Nations Office of the High Commissioner for Human Rights, Fact Sheet No. 9, p. 4.

[18] Venne, *Our Elders*, p. 151.

[19] Sarah Pritchard, 'The United Nations and the Making of a Declaration on Indigenous Rights', *Indigenous Law Bulletin* http://www.Austlii.edu.au/au/special/rsjproject/rsjlibrary/ilb/vol3no89/1.html p. 4 accessed 21/2/02. The sixteen bodies that do have consultative status are the 'Aboriginal and Torres Strait Islander Commission, Asociación Kunas Unidos por Nabguana, Four Directions Council, Grand Council of Crees (Quebec), Indian Council of South America, Indian Law Resource Centre, Indigenous World Association, International Indian Treaty Council, International Organisation of Indigenous Resource Development, Inuit Circumpolar Conference, National Aboriginal and Islander Legal Services Secretariat, National Indian Youth Council, Saami Council, Sejekto Cultural Association of Costa Rica, Yachay Wasi, [and the] World Council of Indigenous Peoples. UN Leaflet No. 1, p. 6.

[20] United Nations Office of the High Commissioner for Human Rights, Leaflet no. 9 and Robert A. Williams, 'Encounters on the Frontiers of International Human Rights Law: Redefining the Terms of Indigenous Peoples' Survival in the World', *Duke Law Journal*, 4 (September 1990), 676.

With regard to the latter task a major achievement of the WGIP has been the Draft Declaration on Indigenous Rights which it began to prepare in 1985. A final text was agreed to at its Eleventh Session in July 1993,[21] when it was submitted to the Sub-Commission on Prevention of Discrimination and Protection of Minorities. Once the Sub-Commission adopted the Draft Declaration in August 1994 it was submitted in turn to the CHR for consideration. The Commission on Human Rights decided not to accept the Draft Declaration as submitted 'because of states' concerns that the provisions concerning self-determination went further than the states were prepared to accept in an international document'.[22] Thus in 1995 it passed a resolution to establish 'an open-ended inter-sessional working group to consider the text submitted by the Sub-Commission and elaborate on a draft declaration for consideration and adoption by the General Assembly within the International Decade of the World's Indigenous People'.[23] As already noted, adoption of a declaration is a major objective of the decade, but with less that two years to its end a Declaration has, to repeat, yet to be adopted.

Two issues central to the deliberations of the CHR Working Group have been the definition of indigenous peoples and their participation. A lot of the politics of the decade has been taken up with the question of definition. At the first session of the CHR Working Group there was much discussion of the definition of indigenous peoples which ended in a stalemate. A number of Asian delegations argued for the need to define the term 'indigenous' and, with China, tended to the view that indigenous peoples do not exist in Asia:

> A number of Latin American and European States, including Brazil, Mexico, Norway, Ukraine and the USA suggested that defining the term 'Indigenous' might be useful as a way of distinguishing Indigenous peoples from minorities. Other State delegations, including Australia, Bolivia, Canada, Chile, France and Aotearoa/New Zealand, rejected the need to agree on a definition, at least at such an early stage of deliberations.[24]

[21] See Appendix.
[22] Catherine J. Irons Magellanes , 'International Human Rights and their Impact on Domestic Law on Indigenous Peoples' Rights in Australia, Canada, and New Zealand' in P. Haverman (ed.), *Indigenous Peoples' Rights in Australia, Canada, and New Zealand* (Auckland: Oxford University Press, 1999), p. 24.
[23] Resolution 1995/32 cited in United Nations Office of the High Commissioner for Human Rights, Leaflet No. 9, p. 5. See also Venne, *Our Elders*, p. 137.
[24] Pritchard, 'United Nations', p. 3.

At the second session of the CHR Working Group there was much less debate on definition, and indigenous access and participation emerged as critical issues. Unresolved were the questions of whether state delegations would accept the consensual working methods that had made the WGIP a success, and whether indigenous peoples would insist that no changes be made to the 1993 Draft Declaration. From discussion in the CHR Working Group, 'it became evident that state governments want to re-open all the articles and preambular paragraphs for redrafting'.[25]

Once a Draft has been accepted by the CHR it will be passed on to the ECOSOC which consists of fifty-four members elected by the General Assembly every three years. Indigenous peoples are able to lobby members of ECOSOC which has the mandate to draft treaties for submission to the General Assembly. It could thus submit either the Draft Declaration or a convention (treaty) for adoption by the General Assembly. A declaration would not have the same legal status as a treaty, 'which can be ratified by states and then become legally binding on them'. Venne explains that

> a resolution adopted by the GA, even in the form of a Declaration, is a recommendation only and is not binding on states. A Declaration is not considered to be a primary source of international law. However, a declaration becomes influential on the future role and action of states. Over time and with usage, a declaration can become accepted as an international law norm in that it becomes representative customary international law.[26]

She later cites Patrick Thornbury to reiterate the potential that resolutions of the General Assembly have to influence the development of international law. According to him, '[a] declaration is "a basic or minimum standard for the international community as a whole"'. When a declaration is passed by a GA resolution, such a declaration 'is not an "imposition" but is an expression of commitment freely entered into by States in full sovereignty, and may not be disregarded'.[27] The outstanding example of a 'declaration' that enunciated 'principles of great and lasting importance' is the Declaration of Human Rights.[28]

---

[25] Venne, *Our Elders*, p. 160. [26] Ibid., pp. 135–6.
[27] Ibid., p. 162. See also Patrick Thornbury, 'Some Implications of the UN Declaration on Minorities for Indigenous Peoples', in Eyassu Gayim and Kristian Myntti (eds.), *Indigenous and Tribal Peoples' Rights – 993 and After* (Rovaniemi: University of Lapland, 1995).
[28] Venne, *Our Elders*, p. 135. Venne is quoting Hanna Bokor-Szego, *The Role of the United Nations in International Legislation* (New York: North Holland Publishing Company, 1978).

The Office of the Commissioner for Human Rights describes the draft declaration as representing 'one of the most important developments in the promotion and protection of the basic rights and fundamental freedoms of indigenous peoples'. Sharon Venne calls it 'a precedent-setting international instrument'. It is, she writes, 'the first UN instrument to develop standards on Indigenous Peoples' rights. It is also the first UN instrument to be drafted with the direct participation by Indigenous Peoples in the process.'[29] For the Office of the Commissioner for Human Rights it is a document that

> covers rights and freedoms including the preservation and development of ethnic and cultural characteristics and distinct identities; protection against genocide and ethnocide; rights related to religions, languages and educational institutions; ownership, possession or use of indigenous lands and natural resources; protection of cultural and intellectual property; maintenance of traditional economic structures and ways of life, including hunting, fishing, herding, gathering, timber-sawing and cultivation; environmental protection; participation in political, economic and social life of the States concerned, in particular matters which may affect indigenous people's lives and destinies: self-determination; self-government or autonomy in matters relating to indigenous peoples' internal and local affairs; traditional contacts and cooperation across State boundaries; and the honouring of treaties and agreements concluded with indigenous peoples.[30]

In summary so far, the United Nations international human rights regime has been fundamental to both giving indigenous peoples international personality and the goal of establishing indigenous rights as international norms. As Robert Williams puts it:

> The discourse of international human rights has enabled indigenous peoples to understand and express their oppression in terms that are meaningful to them and their oppressors. Thinking in terms of rights has organized indigenous peoples on a global scale to combat their shared experiences of being excluded and oppressed by the dominant world order. The use of rights rhetoric in international human rights standard-setting bodies such as the Working Group illustrates the ways in which indigenous peoples can transform the dominant perception of their rights in the international context.[31]

---

[29] Ibid., p. 137.
[30] Office of the High Commissioner for Human Rights, Fact Sheet No. 9 (Rev. 1), The Rights of Indigenous Peoples, http://www.unhchr.ch/html/menu6/2/fs9.htm accessed 14/3/02.
[31] Williams, 'Encounters', p. 701.

The right of peoples to self-determination enshrined in both the International Covenant on Civil and Political Rights and the International Covenant on Economic, Social and Cultural Rights and Article 27 of the latter are essential foundations for indigenous rights. As well as these normative supports the United Nations has provided an organisational framework for the WGIP, the establishment of the Permanent Forum, and preparation of the Draft Declaration. It has facilitated and given legitimacy to the need for indigenous rights. The inclusion of indigenous peoples as participants in organs reporting to the Commission on Human Rights and ECOSOC, and through them the General Assembly, coupled with development of the Draft Declaration within the framework of the international human rights regime, has enlarged the scope of the regime. For this reason, at the same time that the international human rights regime has had an impact on indigenous peoples by advancing indigenous rights, it might also be said that indigenous peoples have had an impact on the United Nations system. Indigenous peoples and Non-Governmental Organisations representing them, have been able to harness UN resources to build domestic movements.[32] If it is finally adopted, the Draft Declaration will 'settle the question of indigenous peoples' legal personality'.[33] For indigenous peoples the state will no longer be 'the final arbiter in regard to those living under its jurisdiction; as a member of the international system, every state will need some legitimacy, and that legitimacy will be tested, among other things, on the basis of its human rights performance'.[34]

Land and culture

Land is a crucial element in the recovery and continuation of indigenous ways of life. As Taiaiake Alfred puts it: 'Land, culture, and government are inseparable in traditional philosophies; each depends on the others, and this means that denial of one aspect precludes recovery of the whole.'[35] For many indigenous peoples the dispossession of their land, as a result of the arrival of European peoples, either destroyed or seriously eroded their culture. Since at least the 1960s land rights, and, more recently still, the recognition of 'native title', have come to

---

[32] Richard Falk, *Human Rights Horizons: The Pursuit of Justice in a Globalizing World* (London: Routledge, 2000), pp. 139–40.
[33] Russell Barsh, 'Indigenous Peoples in the 1990s: From Object to Subject of International Law?' *Harvard Human Rights Journal*, 7 (Spring 1994), 85.
[34] Opekokew, 'International Law', p. 15.   [35] Alfred, *Peace, Power, Righteousness*, p. 2.

be seen by indigenous peoples as crucial to their identity. The view of many indigenous peoples is that only by having title to traditional lands can they hope to retain, keep alive and revitalise what is left of their culture.

The importance of the link between land and culture was recognised by the United Nations Human Rights Committee in its response to a complaint brought to it by the Lubicon Lake Cree

> about commercial development of their territory (in Alberta). The Lubicon Lake Cree complained that private oil, gas, and timber development of Cree lands allowed by the federal and provincial governments destroyed the Cree economic base and their ability to pursue their traditional way of life, and thus would destroy their culture. The Human Rights Committee agreed that the 'developments threaten the way of life and culture of the Lubicon Lake Band, and would constitute a violation of Article 27 [of the ICCPR] so long as they continue.[36]

Benedict Kingsbury argues that the Committee's judgement in this case implied 'that the right of members of a group to enjoy their culture may be violated where they are not allocated the land and control of resource development necessary to pursue economic activities of central importance to their culture, such as hunting or trapping'.[37] The Aboriginal and Torres Strait Islander Social Justice Commission (ATSIC) of Australia makes an even stronger claim about the link between land and culture by asserting that:

> Hunting, fishing and harvesting activities are not merely economic activities or the exercise of property rights. – The denial, loss or impairment of hunting, fishing and harvesting rights amounts to a denial, loss or impairment of the opportunity to maintain and participate in the enjoyment and exercise of indigenous cultural life and to transmit culture from one generation to another.[38]

[36] Irons Magallanes, 'International Human Rights', p. 256. For a first-hand account of the political and struggles of the Lubicon Lake Cree see Bernard Ominayak with Ed Bianchi, 'The Lubicon Cree: Still No Settlement after All These Years', in J. Bird, L. Land and M. Macadam (eds.), *Nation to Nation: Aboriginal Sovereignty and the Future of Canada* (Toronto: Irwin Publishing, 2002), pp. 163–74.
[37] Benedict Kingsbury, 'Claims by Non-State Groups in International Law', *Cornell International Law Journal*, 25: 3 (1992), 490. The scope of the connections is spelt out by Steven Perkins, 'Researching Indigenous Peoples Rights Under International Law 1', http://www.rci.rutgers.edu/~sperkins/ipr2.html accessed 31/7/2002.
[38] Aboriginal and Torres Strait Islander Social Justice Commission (ATSIC), *First Report 1993*, Australian Parliamentary Paper 261 (Canberra: Australian Government Printing Service, 1993), p. 29.

In this and in other ways it is claimed that land has special significance for indigenous peoples. Concerning Australian Aborigines, the late W. H. E. Stanner observed:

> No English words are good enough to give a sense of the links between an Aboriginal group and its homeland. Our word 'home' warm and suggestive as it may be, does not match the Aboriginal word that may mean 'camp', 'hearth', 'country', 'everlasting home', 'totem', 'place', 'life source', 'spirit centre' and much else all in one. – When we took what we call 'land' we took what to them meant hearth, home, the source and focus of life, and everlastingness of spirit.[39]

Clearly land and rights over it are, for many indigenous peoples, an essential element in the recovery of both their identity and rights.

For Australian Aboriginal and Torres Strait Islanders an important step towards rights over land was taken with the Australian High Court's Mabo decision of 1992, which overturned the legal fiction that Australia was *terra nullius* at the time of British occupation. It declared that the Crown's acquisition of sovereignty could not be challenged in a court but established that native title could be claimed over unappropriated Crown lands.[40] As a result of the Mabo judgment – which was far more conservative than both the debate over its implications and subsequent developments have suggested – native title 'exists only where there is an Aboriginal group that has maintained its connection with traditional lands. The group has to be able to prove that it is looking after its country, discharging obligations under traditional law, and enjoying as far as practicable the traditional rights of use and occupation'.[41] In spite of being limited in this way, the recognition of native title in the Mabo judgement was, for Australian indigenous peoples, a milestone in the recovery of identity and rights.

Following Mabo the Federal Government enacted the Native Title Act 1993, which was intended to be the judicial framework for claims to native title. For Aborigines and Torres Strait Islanders it was a 'bitter disappointment'. 'It legitimated past dispossession without compensation' and placed tight restrictions on what could be claimed. In 1996 a new conservative Coalition government less sympathetic to native title came to power. A few months later, in the *Wik* case, the High Court

---

[39] W. H. E. Stanner cited by ATSIC, *First Report*, p. 28.
[40] For an overview of the issues arising from this case see Peter Butt and Robert Eagleson, *Mabo, Wik and Native Title*, 3rd edn (Sydney: Federation Press, 1998).
[41] Frank Brennan, SJ, *One Land, One Nation: Mabo – Towards 2001* (St Lucia: University of Queensland Press, 1995), p. 36.

ruled that pastoral leases did not necessarily extinguish native title. The Coalition government adopted the view that this created intolerable uncertainties for pastoralists and responded by introducing the Native Title Amendment Act which further weakened native title.[42]

In Canada the case comparative to Mabo was the 1973 *Calder* case concerning the claim of the Nisga'a First Nation to traditional lands in the Nass Valley in northwestern British Columbia. The Supreme Court 'recognised native title on lands unceded to the Crown', but it was not until April 2000 that an agreement between the Nisga'a and the governments of Canada and British Columbia finally came into force. The outcome of this agreement was that '[t]hough the Nisga'a agreed to give up native title to ninety percent of their traditional lands, [it recognised] . . . the supreme power of the Nisga'a legislature to make laws concerning the constitution, citizenship, culture, language and the management of the lands of the Nisga'a First Nations'.[43] Further important Canadian cases were *Sparrow* vs. *the Queen* (1990) and *Delgamuukw* vs. *British Columbia* (11 December 1997). The *Delgamuukw* case involved one of the longest civil trials in Canadian history. '[I]t fleshed out as no common law court had ever done before the meaning of 'native title', insisting on its full proprietorial force, including ownership of sub-surface minerals and the right of native owners to develop traditional lands in non-traditional ways'.[44]

Native title to land is for many indigenous peoples, as we have just seen in the example of the Nisga'a, the first step towards more far-reaching claims to the right to self-determination. 'It is the next demand once land rights have been recognised.'[45] For the states against which it is claimed, self-determination raises the spectre of at least a challenge to the integrity of their sovereignty and at worst possible secession. For states in this situation indigenous peoples represent what Richard Falk calls

[42] Peter Russell, 'My Peoples' Courts as Agents of Indigenous Decolonisation?', *Law in Context*, 18: 1 (2001), 58. See also Butt and Eagleson, *Mabo, Wik and Native Title*.
[43] Peter Russell, 'Corroboree 2000 – A Nation Defining Event', *Arena Journal*, 15 (2000), 35. See also Rod Robinson, 'Nisga'a Patience: Negotiating our Way Into Canada', in Bird, Land and Macadam (eds.), *Nation to Nation*, pp. 186–94, and Michael Asch, 'From *Calder* to *Van der Peet*: Aboriginal Rights and Canadian Law, 1973–96', in Haverman (ed.), *Indigenous Peoples' Rights*, pp. 428–46.
[44] Russell, 'Courts and Decolonisation', p. 59. See also Kent McNeil, 'The Meaning of Aboriginal Title' in Michael Asch (ed.), *Aboriginal and Treaty Rights in Canada: Essays on Law, Equity, and Respect for Difference* (Vancouver: University of British Colombia Press, 1987), pp. 135–53. Also *Delgamuukw* vs. *British Columbia*, *Dominion Law Reports* 104 D.L.R. (4th). In relation to Calder and Delgamuukw see also Tully, 'Stuggles of Indigenous Peoples', in Ivison, Patton and Sanders (eds.), *Political Theory*, pp. 44–50.
[45] Brennan, *One Land, One Nation*, p. 138.

a 'collective identity', that is the nucleus of 'a competing nationalism within the state'.[46]

Self-determination

For indigenous peoples self-determination is a means to the end of regaining their identity in states that have in crucial respects simultaneously included and excluded them. At the same time as they incorporated indigenous peoples as subjects, settler society states denied them full rights of citizenship. They have, at different junctures, sought either to eliminate indigenous peoples or to assimilate them in ways equally destructive of their cultural identity. Consequently, the right to self-determination is seen as 'an inherent right of distinct peoples' with distinct identities to make decisions vital to the integrity of those identities.[47] The difficulty is that the aspirations of indigenous peoples in this regard conflict with the meaning given to self-determination by states,[48] but its meaning and status in either context is not easily stated. It is not clear whether it is best regarded as a political or rather a legal principle.[49] In either case, it is a principle without a clearly defined meaning and, according to Deborah Cass, '[c]urrent international law theory regarding self-determination – is inconsistent within itself, and it does not accord with state practice'.[50] Gerry Simpson more trenchantly calls the language of self-determination 'a discourse gone dead in [the] hands of the international lawyers who manipulate it'.[51] Because of the contradiction it 'contains . . . between state rights to self-determination, and the rights of minorities within states to dismember or challenge the state in the name of another competing norm of self-determination', it is a principle that both supports and undermines the state system.[52] Self-determination is thus implicated in the resurgence of ethnonationalism. Ethnic groups challenge the states in which they are encased by claiming a right to self-determination and are in turn rebuffed in the name of the same principle.

---

[46] Richard Falk, 'The Rights of Peoples (in Particular Indigenous Peoples)', in J. Crawford (ed.), *The Rights of Peoples* (Oxford: Clarendon Press, 1988), p. 18.
[47] Fleras, 'Politicising Indigeneity', in Haverman, *Indigenous People's Rights*, p. 187.
[48] Falk, *Human Rights Horizons*, pp. 97, 102.   [49] Ibid., p. 121.
[50] Deborah Cass, 'Re-Thinking Self-Determination: A Critical Analysis of Current International Law Theories', *Syracuse Journal of International Law and Commerce*, 18 (Spring 1992), 21–2.
[51] Gerry J. Simpson, 'The Diffusion of Sovereignty: Self-Determination in the Post-Colonial Age', *Stanford Journal of International Law*, 32 (1996), 256.
[52] Ibid., pp. 259–60.

Self-determination has its basis in the existence of groups that define themselves as nations. According to Anthony Smith, 'A nation [is] a named human population sharing an historic territory, common myths and historical memories, a mass, public culture, a common economy and common legal rights and duties for all members.'[53] Self-determination has, in turn, been defined in terms of the aspiration of a nation, as a cultural entity, to achieve political statehood. In his 1941 essay, *The Future of Nations*, E. H. Carr thus asserted that: '[t]he principle of self-determination, strictly defined, requires that a group of people of reasonable size desirous of constituting a nation should be allowed to constitute a state'.[54] Alfred Cobban similarly defined it as the principle that 'each nation has a right to constitute an independent state and determine its own government'.[55] And for Cass it is a concept that 'encapsulates three basic ideas: there has to be a group; that group has to be concerned about its political status; and, that group must be able to exercise its own choice with regard to its political future'.[56]

The concept of self-determination found expression in the aims of the French and American revolutions of the late eighteenth century but it was not until the close of World War I that it became common in the language of diplomacy. It was at that time given prominence as a vital element of President Woodrow Wilson's conception of the requirements for post-war order. For him it was identified with democracy and the right of every people 'to choose the sovereignty under which they shall live'.[57] The emphasis placed on self-determination in the peace process encouraged the creation of small nation states detached from larger multinational states. Motivated by democratic principles, the American peace-makers encouraged the disintegration of existing states.[58] Similarly, when President Franklin D. Roosevelt and officials in his war-time administration began planning for post-World War II order, self-determination, understood as the right of peoples to choose the government under which they will live, was, from the beginning of their deliberations, a cardinal principle.[59]

---

[53] Anthony Smith, *National Identity* (Reno: University of Nevada Press, 1991), p. 14.
[54] E. H. Carr, *The Future of Nations: Independence or Interdependence?* (London: Kegan Paul, 1941), p. 9.
[55] Alfred Cobban, *The Nation-State and National Self-Determination* (London: Collins, 1969), p. 39.
[56] Cass, 'Re-Thinking Self-Determination', p. 24.
[57] Cited by Carr, *Future of Nations*, pp. 13–14. [58] Ibid., p. 26.
[59] See, for example, the Principles of the Atlantic Charter and the Subsequent Declaration on Liberated Europe.

Although self-determination historically has been linked, particularly by Wilson, to democracy, there is no necessary connection between the two. The principle of self-determination requires, above all else, an *identity of nation and state* in which the one is the expression of the other. Self-determination aims to establish states that are coterminous with cultural nations. This can mean that the state attempts to compel all members 'to identify themselves culturally with the ruling nation', which as Cobban is careful to point out, can be an element in the development of totalitarianism. 'As a result of the belief that the political state must perish unless it can achieve cultural unity, all the democratic and national rights of minorities are swept away.'[60]

In spite of Woodrow Wilson's support for the principle of self-determination, the Covenant of the League of Nations established the Mandate system that denied or at least postponed self-determination for peoples living in colonies and territories that had 'ceased to be under the sovereignty of the States which formerly governed them and which are inhabited by peoples not yet able to stand by themselves . . . '.[61] General Smuts was probably representative of the predominant European view at the time when he said that '[t]he German colonies in the Pacific and Africa are inhabited by barbarians, who not only cannot possibly govern themselves, but to whom it would be impracticable to apply any idea of political self-determination in the European sense'.[62] In language typical of the period the Mandatory powers were enjoined by the League, as part of 'a sacred trust of civilisation', to safeguard 'the well-being and development of such peoples'.[63]

It was not until the main thrust of decolonisation after World War II that most of these territories were able to achieve self-determination. In the post-World War II era self-determination was fastened to decolonisation. For colonised peoples self-determination was about having the freedom to decide for themselves whether they wanted either to be independent or to associate with some state other than the one that had colonised and exercised sovereignty over them. In relation to the process of decolonisation 'self-determination . . . came to be interpreted almost as the right of peoples of colour not to be ruled by whites'.[64] In the immediate post-war period it was also important with regard to the states of

---

[60] Cobban, *Nation-State*, pp. 44, 112.   [61] Article 22.
[62] Cited by Cobban, *Nation-State*, p. 61.   [63] Article 22.
[64] Thomas M. Franck, 'The Evolution of the Right of Self-determination', Paper presented to the 'Peoples and Minorities in International Law' stream of the Second Amsterdam International Law Conference (1992), p. 10.

eastern Europe. True to its declaratory policy concerning post-war order, the United States insisted on self-determination for the states of eastern Europe. The Soviet role in thwarting free elections, first in Poland and then elsewhere in eastern Europe, was seen as a denial of the principle of self-determination and was consequently a source of the Cold War.

Whether in the case of free and democratic elections for the states of eastern Europe, or the right of colonised peoples to sovereign independence as states, the common issue was the freedom of nations to determine their future unfettered by external powers. In both cases the object of self-determination was the right of peoples to constitute themselves as a self-governing 'nation state'. What was to be determined was the sovereign authority and independence of states with jurisdiction over defined territory as the political expression of the people contained in them. A problem common to both cases was that these so-called 'nation-states' more often than not contained ethnic minorities that might themselves seek self-determination at some future juncture; as indeed happened in the resurgence of ethnonationalism following the end of the Cold War. Self-determination is thus an inherently ambiguous principle. On the one hand, it has been and continues to be interpreted in the context of relations between states. It is inextricably linked with the principle of sovereign *independence from* other states. On the other hand, it is the normative basis of claims from within particular states for independence from the jurisdiction of those states. As Cobban put it in the 1960s, '[t]he history of self-determination is a history of the making of nations and the breaking of states'.[65]

In the context of relations between states, self-determination is coupled to the control of a territorial state. Consequently, states tend to regard indigenous peoples' claims to self-determination as claims to territorial sovereignty that would dismember them. Precisely because 'it could lead to a very different world map', self-determination has, in the 1990s, been perceived, politically and legally, as the 'most problematic topic in indigenous peoples' rights'; one that 'strikes at the legitimacy of settler regimes'.[66] The problem is, as Kingsbury puts it, that of solving 'how the principle of self-determination can be reconciled with the concern of states to maintain their territorial integrity and with the concern of the international community not to risk unlimited fragmentation of existing states'.[67] This is an understandable and justifiable

---

[65] Cobban, *Nation-State*, p. 43.   [66] Perkins, 'Researching Indigenous Peoples'.
[67] Kingsbury, 'Claims', p. 485.

concern, but indigenous claims to a right to self-determination are not intended to result in the establishment of independent states.[68] Were that the aim it would face formidable political obstacles and would not, in any case, be legally feasible in the framework of current international law. Claims to self-determination that conflict 'with the world system of state sovereignty' are simply not recognised in international law.[69] And because of its historical encumbrances self-determination is almost inevitably regarded as being in conflict with the principle of state sovereignty.

For many indigenous peoples, however, self-determination is fundamental to the recovery of their rights. This is poignantly illustrated in the *First Report* of the Australian Aboriginal and Torres Strait Islander Social Justice Commission. It argues that 'every issue concerning the historical and present status, entitlements, treatment and aspirations of Aboriginal and Torres Strait Islander peoples is implicated in the concept of self-determination'. 'The right to self-determination', it continues, 'is the right to make decisions.'[70] 'Our entire experience since the assertion of British sovereignty over our country has been the experience of the denial of the right to self-determination. – The human experience was one of devastation and destruction, death and disease, brutalisation and misery. Our lives were utterly subject to the control, the decisions, of others.'[71]

Cast in this light it is understandable that regaining control over the decisions that affect them, via self-determination, is indeed a first priority for indigenous peoples, whether in Australia or elsewhere.

An illustration of the positive benefits that could possibly result from self-determination for indigenous peoples is the recommendation of the Australian Royal Commission into Aboriginal Deaths in Custody that it is 'fundamental to reducing the number of Aboriginals in custody'. In support of this opinion Commissioner Elliott Johnston QC referred to a report of the House of Representatives Standing Committee on Aboriginal Affairs

> which included: the devolution of political and economic power to Aboriginal and Torres Strait Islander communities; control over the decision-making process as well as control over the ultimate decisions about a wide range of matters including political status, economic,

[68] Alfred, *Peace, Power, Righteousness*, p. 57.
[69] Irons, 'Indigenous Peoples and Self-Determination, p. 203.
[70] ATSIC, *First Report*, p. 41.   [71] Ibid., p. 43.

social and cultural development; and having the resources and capacity to control the future of communities within the legal structure common to all Australians.[72]

Self-determination is, in these reports, the right to make decisions and have control over decision-making within the state rather than a matter of setting up new and separate sovereign states. But, as we have seen, states almost inevitably regard self-determination for indigenous peoples as being in conflict with the principle of state sovereignty. This tension is inherent in General Assembly Resolution 1514, which is a key document in support of indigenous peoples' rights. With reference to colonies it declares that 'the subjection of peoples to alien subjugation and domination and exploitation constitutes a denial of fundamental human rights'. Article 1 then asserts that 'all peoples have the right to self-determination by virtue of [which] . . . they freely determine their political status and freely pursue their economic, social and cultural development'. But Article 6 then makes it clear that self-determination cannot be interpreted in ways that oppose self-determination to 'the existing geographical delimitation of territorial boundaries of sovereign states'. It stipulates that '[a]ny attempt at the partial or total disruption of the national unity and the territorial integrity of the country is incompatible with the purposes and principles of the Charter of the United Nations'. Article 7 then follows with the injunction that it is the duty of all states to 'uphold the obligation to enforce the Charter of the United Nations and the Universal Declaration of Human Rights and this Declaration, on the basis of equality, non-interference in the internal affairs of all States and respect for the sovereign rights of all peoples and their territorial integrity'. In essence, coupling self-determination to decolonisation meant subordination of 'the notion of self-determination itself . . . to an over-riding conception of the unity and integrity of the state'.[73]

Governments are increasingly either willing or forced to accept that indigenous peoples should have control over the decisions that affect them, but they remain nevertheless concerned about the implications of claims to self-determination. Canada has accepted inclusion of the right to self-determination in the Draft Declaration, but for the majority of governments Article 3 is worrying. The reluctance of states to move beyond the legal meaning given to self-determination in the era of decolonisation makes them unwilling to accept the autonomy within the state sought by indigenous peoples as proper instances of

[72] Brennan, *One Land One Nation*, pp. 153–4.   [73] Falk, 'Rights of Peoples', p. 26.

self-determination. States are concerned over whether adoption of Article 3 would eventually mean 'separate legal systems covering all manner of things from taxation and gambling to criminal law and marriage relationships'. In response to the Draft the New Zealand government of the time, for example, declared its support for the 'right of indigenous people to exist as distinct communities with their own cultural identity', but did not regard this as implying self-determination in the sense enshrined in international law. For other states as well, the problem has been, to paraphrase Brennan, whether self-determination means the international legal definition of it developed by the United Nations with decolonisation in mind or, instead, a different concept.[74]

So far I have wanted to draw attention to three essential points concerning the principle of self-determination in relation to indigenous peoples. First, since World War II it has been linked to decolonisation and been regarded as primarily applicable only to the peoples within colonial boundaries. Second, it has inescapably involved tension between its internal and external senses. States have chosen to emphasise the latter which supports the principle that they should be able to conduct their affairs without interference from other states. In this sense the population contained within the boundary of a state is treated as whole. Focusing on the internal aspects of self-determination would instead necessitate asking whether particular groups within states have or should have self-determination. This in turn could lead to breaking up particular states. Third, the meaning of self-determination emphasised by indigenous peoples is not of statehood but control over decisions within the existing institutional structure of states. This sense of self-determination is fundamental to Anaya's account of the concept in which he uncouples it from decolonisation.

Anaya argues that the apparent tension between the internal and external aspects of self-determination results from a 'misconception that self-determination in its fullest sense means a right to independent statehood'. This is a misconception that stems from the identification of self-determination with the process of decolonisation, which did indeed result in the establishment of new states. For Anaya, limiting the application of self-determination to peoples in colonial situations 'denies its relevance to all segments of humanity' and overlooks its connection, as a principle, with human rights. It cannot now be separated

---

[74] Brennan, *One Land One Nation*, p. 151.

from the expression it has been given in a variety of human rights instruments,[75] the significance of which is illustrated by the situation of indigenous peoples in, for example, Australia and Canada. Understood as decolonisation resulting in the establishment of a new state, self-determination has not been a possibility for these peoples. To respond to claims to self-determination by indigenous peoples in these states by saying that they are not in a colonial situation and hence not entitled to make such claims would be to deny the entitlement to self-determination contained in a number of human rights instruments. It would also mean in some way denying the claim made by many indigenous peoples that they continue to live in a colonial situation. Further, to depict self-determination as an escape from colonisation is to invert the true relationship between the two. Colonisation is a deviation from self-determination. Self-determination is not, as it often seems, a principle invented as a response or corrective to colonialism. Anaya's point is that decolonisation should be seen as rectification of a departure from the norm of self-determination and not as something that defines it. This leads Anaya to distinguish between what he calls the substantive and the remedial aspects of self-determination. Decolonisation is a remedial measure that results in the formation of new states, but not all remedial measures necessarily result in new states.

The substantive aspect of self-determination is, according to Anaya, defined by recognition of 'a standard of governmental legitimacy within the modern human rights framework'. The substance of self-determination is expressed in 'shared opinion and behaviour about the minimum conditions for the constitution and functioning of legitimate government' meant to benefit all 'peoples'. Anaya proposes that substantive self-determination so defined 'consists of two normative strains' or aspects: a constitutive and an ongoing one.[76] The essence of the constitutive aspect is that 'the governing institutional order be substantially the creation of processes guided by the will of the people'. It should 'reflect the collective will of the people, or peoples, concerned'.[77] The ongoing aspect is defined as requiring 'that the governing institutional order, independently of the processes leading to its creation or alteration, be one under which people may live and develop freely on a continuous basis'.[78] 'Ongoing self-determination requires a governing order under which individuals and groups are able to make meaningful choices in matters touching upon all spheres of life on a

[75] Anaya, *Indigenous Peoples*, p. 77.   [76] Ibid., p. 81.   [77] Ibid.   [78] Ibid.

continuous basis.'[79] Anaya objects to the conventional understanding of self-determination as divided into internal and external aspects, as one that obscures and neglects the reality of the 'multiple and overlapping spheres of human association'. States are not constituted simply of a homogeneous collection of people whose only loyalty is to the state. They contain groups with overlapping and competing loyalties that demand participation in making decisions that affect them. Both the constitutive and ongoing aspects correspond to human rights instruments that enjoin parties to them to allow participation. The collective will of the people that defines the constitutive aspect is expressed in the injunction in the International Covenant on Civil and Political Rights that peoples are to 'freely determine their political status'. And in the case of the ongoing aspects, the stipulation in the International Covenant on Economic, Social and Cultural Rights that peoples are to 'freely pursue their economic, social and cultural development'.

Anaya criticises the remedial aspect of self-determination for involving crucial omissions. By emphasising territorial states, defined by colonial boundaries that ignored tribal and ethnic groupings, decolonisation left indigenous peoples locked up in political groupings in which they did not gain self-determination in the sense of participation in decision-making. Further, state sovereignty, to which self-determination is linked, both supports the status quo and deflects international scrutiny away from the internal conduct of the state. Intervention that violates sovereignty is at the same time a denial of self-determination as it is understood in relations between states. But to strictly observe the principle of sovereign independence would be to leave citizens at the mercy of the states in which they are encased.[80]

Having re-cast self-determination in this manner Anaya proceeds to the norms embedded in a variety of human rights documents that elaborate the elements of self-determination he has highlighted. His contention is that self-determination together with related human rights 'precepts' are the basis for a number of important norms concerning indigenous peoples. These norms in fact 'elaborate on the requirements of self-determination'. Anaya identifies them as non-discrimination, cultural integrity, lands and resources, social welfare and development, and self-government. He details the instruments in which these appear and it is clear from his presentation that each one can be seen as an expression of substantive self-determination centred on the collective will

[79] Ibid., p. 82.   [80] Ibid., p. 85.

of peoples and participation in decisions that affect them. In elaborating on self-government, Anaya returns to the idea of overlapping associations that challenge the view of the state bound up with the conventional view of self-determination. Against 'the traditional Western conceptions that envisage mutually exclusive states as the primary factor for locating power and community', Anaya's preference is 'a political order that is less state-centred and more centred on people in a world of distinct yet increasingly integrated and overlapping spheres of community and authority'.[81]

Will Kymlicka finds much to admire in Anaya's account but argues that it contains some serious problems. These stem, in Kymlicka's view, from Anaya presenting 'as an interpretation of "actually exisiting" international law' what is actually a normative theory for reforming international law. When it is regarded as the former the first problem for Kymlicka is that he sees 'no evidence that the international community accepts the right to self-determination for non-indigenous national minorities'. The burden of his argument is that states are willing to concede rights to indigenous peoples because they pose less of a threat than large minorities. Even if states do accord self-determination to indigenous peoples they are not likely to extend this to large stateless nations. Kymlicka finds no evidence for the international community having so far 'accepted any general principle of self-determination for national groups, and, *a fortiori*, such a general principle cannot be what underlies recent developments in the law regarding indigenous peoples'.[82]

This leads to the second problem of whether distinctive remedial rights to correct 'historic violations of self-determination . . . require or justify having separate conventions for indigenous peoples or stateless nations. Here his underlying concern is with whether there is any justification for 'establishing a system of differential rights between indigenous peoples and stateless nations'. It would only make sense to establish a permanent distinction between indigenous and stateless nations if they had different inherent rights of self-determination. Yet this is what Anaya seeks to deny.'

To Kymlicka's mind remedial rights meant to correct past mistreatment neither 'captures nor explains the emerging norms of international law'.[83] He proposes that the more likely explanation for the impetus to

---

[81] Ibid., p. 112.
[82] Will Kymlicka, 'Theorizing Indigenous Rights', *University of Toronto Law Journal*, 49 (Spring 1999), 288.
[83] Ibid., p. 289.

'international protection of indigenous peoples is . . . the scale of cultural difference'. Kymlicka finds Anaya curiously silent about cultural difference and suggests that relying on claims about radical cultural difference cut against self-determination: 'it would imply that as soon as indigenous peoples start driving cars, going to university, working in modern corporations, and adopting other aspects of modern western lifestyles, then they lose their claim to self-determination. They could only maintain a traditional way of life.'[84]

For Kymlicka a further difficulty is that Anaya steps away from confronting a 'major controversy concerning indigenous rights – namely, whether standard human rights norms apply to indigenous self-government, or whether it is a form of cultural imperialism to expect indigenous communities to abide by "Eurocentric" principles of individual civil and political rights'.[85] This involves a complex set of issues, some of which are touched upon immediately below and are taken up again in the conclusion to the book.

At this point it should be abundantly clear that self-determination is a contested concept, the meaning of which is not easy to pin down. The next section considers four related issues regarded by international lawyers as obstacles to establishing self-determination as an international legal norm. These are the tensions between individual and group rights, coupled with the adequacy or otherwise of human rights to establish indigenous rights; the semantics and legal implications of the terms 'people', 'peoples' and 'populations'; the contemporary scope of self-determination; and, the assumed conflict between indigenous self-determination and state sovereignty.

Issues to be resolved

Human rights and indigenous rights

In the United Nations system indigenous rights are an expression and extension of universal human rights. Indigenous rights are codified and formalised through the United Nations human rights system. The Draft Declaration on Indigenous Rights proclaims that 'Indigenous Peoples have the right to the full and effective enjoyment of all human rights and fundamental freedoms recognised in the Charter of the United Nations, the Declaration of Human Rights and international human rights law' (Art. 1). This, however, is not informative about the conceptual

---

[84] Ibid., p. 290.   [85] Ibid., p. 291.

differences between human and indigenous rights. In particular, it does not answer the question of why, given that '[a]ll present international human rights documents and doctrines apply to indigenous peoples throughout the world',[86] there is any need for a distinct set of indigenous rights.

It is a commonplace that the difference between these two is that human rights are held by individuals while indigenous rights are the collective rights held or claimed by groups or peoples. The right to self-determination, in particular, is a collective right that cannot be claimed by individuals.[87] From this it follows that one reason for needing to supplement human rights with a set indigenous rights is precisely that human rights do not comprehend the collective nature of key indigenous rights. A frequent claim is that human rights are Eurocentric and do not make adequate provision for indigenous customs and cultural practices. Implicit in the idea of indigenous rights is an affirmation of the existence of collectivities that have a distinct identity linked to their particular culture and place of belonging. A compelling reason for rights specific to indigenous peoples is thus that individual human rights do not give legal expression to the existence of unique groups or cultures. If there are just human rights then groups of indigenous peoples have no legally defined rights that set them, their culture and place of attachment, apart from others. Without safeguards for collective or group rights cultural identity is at risk. For this reason Article 6 of the Draft Declaration stipulates the collective right to live as distinct peoples.[88] Indigenous peoples argue that group rights are the only way to ensure protection against ethnocide.

In the absence of specific indigenous rights codified in international law indigenous peoples have appealed to and relied upon human rights. There are at least two reasons for them having done so. In the first place it is claimed that all major instruments of human rights, such as the UN Declaration, include indigenous peoples. Second, human rights are perceived to have been successful in transforming behaviour. Robert Williams, for instance, argues that '[m]oral suasion, shame, and the simple capacity to appeal to an internationally recognised legal standard for human rights have all done much to undermine the legitimacy of state-sanctioned domestic practices that deny human rights'.[89] His

---

[86] Perkins, 'Researching Indigenous Peoples' Rights'.

[87] Hilary Charlesworth, 'Individual Complaints: An Overview and Admissibility Requirements', in Pritchard (ed.), *Indigenous Peoples*, p. 79.

[88] See Appendix for the text of Article 6.   [89] Williams, 'Encounters', p. 670.

purpose in referring to the human rights process in this way, however, is to argue for benefits that could be expected from adoption of a Universal Declaration on Rights of Indigenous Peoples. In the same way that human rights discourse has affected the domestic behaviour of states the standards and principles laid down in the Declaration would 'enter into the domestic policy discourse of ... [settler state governments] as an urgent matter affecting their own moral standing and authority in the international community as progressive advocates of international human rights standards and values'.[90]

As well as anything else indigenous rights are an expression of the distinctive conception indigenous peoples have of political and social relations. In an illuminating discussion of indigenous peoples in relation to individual human rights, Russell Barsh contrasts the role of the state in indigenous and non-indigenous thinking. 'In the legal systems of states, a "right" is an argument against state power. In indigenous thinking, there is no state, only a web of reciprocal relationships among individuals. This renders "rights" in the classical sense meaningless, because there is no state to argue against, only relatives.'[91] Barsh points out that in indigenous societies, at least in the North American ones with which he is most familiar, kinship is paramount. Consequently 'the most important difference between Indigenous peoples and conceptions of "rights" and the notion of "human rights" in international law speaks to the question of who bears the duty to satisfy claims: the state or other individuals'.[92] The socialisation of indigenous peoples into a network of responsibilities to kin, clan and nation means that these formations are the source of rights and obligations. This implies that indigenous and non-indigenous peoples conceive of rights in quite different ways. In the non-indigenous framework ' "Rights" are essential to maintaining a social order based on a hierarchy of power, from the family to state. Indigenous peoples have been struggling to remain outside that kind of social order, and as such they are quick to dismiss the relevance of "rights" in the usual, individualised sense.' Barsh observes that this is changing as indigenous societies 'becom[e] more like the states that oppress them'. With the breakdown of tribal society (in North America), 'Indian communities are increasingly using law, force and punishment to manage insiders and outsiders.'[93]

[90] Ibid., p. 671.
[91] Russell Barsh, 'Indigenous Peoples and the Idea of Individual Human Rights', *Native Studies Review*, 10: 2 (1995), p. 41.
[92] Ibid., p. 43.   [93] Ibid., p. 48.

At least two kinds of problems result from indigenous rights being available only to certain groups within states. The first is that indigenous rights can be, and indeed have been, objected to as ones that discriminate against non-indigeneous people. This claim was a plank in the platform of the now disbanded populist One Nation Party headed by Pauline Hanson in Australia. In her view and that of her followers, indigenous rights unfairly privileged Aboriginal Australians in access to a range of government funded benefits. A second problem is that individual human rights sometimes clash with the collective rights of indigenous peoples. Legal cases involving variations of this clash include *Lovelace* vs. *Canada* and *Kitok* vs. *Sweden*.[94] Another example is *Thomas* vs. *Norris*, 'in which plaintiff David Tomas, a member of the Coast Salish People' of Canada's west coast 'objected to being initiated into the Coast Salish Big House tradition known as the Spirit Dance'. Council for the defendants in the case argued that 'the plaintiff's civil rights against assault, battery and false imprisonment are subordinate and must give way to the collective right of the Aboriginal nation to which he belongs and is protected by s.35(1) [of the Canadian Constitution]'.[95]

These are cases that pose fundamental questions concerning the tension between the desire to protect cultural integrity and the human rights of the individual. Thus Kymlicka asks, 'Does the norm of "cultural integrity" provide indigenous peoples with a right to ignore or set aside human-rights principles that conflict with their traditions? Or does the norm of cultural integrity only apply to cultural practices that are consistent with human-rights norms?'[96] In the final analysis indigenous rights raise that problem of whether and under what circumstances it is permissible to over-ride the rights of the individual in favour of collective interests and *vice versa*.

In a vigorous defence of the claim that 'the unit of human rights discourse is the individual human being',[97] Anna Yeatman acknowledges that '[a] people can be the collective subject of rights, and one of the fundamental rights contained in the United Nations Charter was the right of peoples to self-determination'. But she argues, that 'recognition of a people's right to self-determination cannot be at the expense

[94] Steiner and Alston (eds.), *Human Rights in Context*, pp. 1017–19, Anaya, *Indigenous Peoples*, p. 101 and Srelein, 'Indigenous Self-Determination Claims,' p. 75.
[95] Avigail Eisenberg, 'The politics of Individual and Group Difference in Canadian Jurisprudence', *Canadian Journal of Political Science*, 27: 1 (March 1994), 3.
[96] Kymlicka, 'Theorizing Indigenous Rights', p. 292.
[97] Anna Yeatman, 'Who is the Subject of Human Rights?' in D. Meredyth and J. Minson (eds.), *Citizenship and Cultural Policy* (London: Sage, 2001), p. 113.

of individual rights without undermining the nature of human rights, namely, their existence as inalienable rights that are not the privilege of any collectivity to grant or withhold'.[98] For her, 'Human rights . . . is a conception of rights driven by the idea of the integrity of the human individual. Put differently, for human beings to be accorded human rights means that they are accorded the right to unit status or the right to individuality.'[99] It follows from this that in cases where the assertion of indigenous rights would violate the integrity of the individual human there is a fundamental tension between the two.

In relation to this, a further complication is the charge that human rights are not universal but merely an expression of Western liberalism.[100] They can be seen therefore as a form of cultural imperialism. To favour the rights of the individual against those of the tribe or nation is thus to impose the political and moral preferences of one group of peoples on another. A response to this may be found in the arguments of Eisenberg and Kymlicka,[101] both of whom locate the ability of human individuals to fully realise their individuality and autonomy in membership of nations or peoples. I do not propose to pursue this line of argument at this juncture but will return to it in Chapter 5.

In closing this section I turn once again to Tim Rowse, whom we encountered at the very beginning of the book. Rowse candidly declares that he subscribes 'to an understanding of human rights in which individual autonomy is the supreme value'. Consistent with this he declares that he supports the assertion of sovereign rights to self-determination by nation states and peoples 'to the extent that it enables their members to enjoy autonomy as individuals'. He continues by stating that he is 'hostile to claims that human rights can be realised only through individuals' inclusion within any particular nation-state or people'. He is instead in agreement with Anna Yeatman's view that '[t]he individual as the subject of human rights belongs nowhere as far as any particular jurisdiction goes, but represents the substantive claim in relation to which any jurisdiction may be judged'. For Rowse, the assertion of rights to sovereignty and self-government by nation-states and 'peoples' are 'contingent and imperfect attempts to realise or mediate human rights'. By this route he is led to the observation that '[a]ny careful consideration

[98] Ibid., p. 112.   [99] Ibid., pp. 116–17.
[100] Brown, 'Universal Human Rights', in Dunne and Wheeler (eds.), *Human Rights in Global Politics*, p. 105.
[101] Eisenberg, 'Politics of Individual and Group Difference', pp. 3–21, and Will Kymlicka, *Liberalism, Community and Culture* (Oxford: Clarendon Press, 1989).

of "self-determination" policy must try to come to an understanding of the relationship between Indigenous rights and human rights'.[102] This is, I think, saying that in cases where the assertion of indigenous rights would violate the integrity of the individual human there is a strong case for over-riding collective rights, including that of self-determination at the sub-state level.

Another approach to this would be to ask what justifies the right to self-determination. Kingsbury suggests that one way to respond to this would be to '[begin] with the group, and with the proposition that the interests of the group itself are sufficient to establish a right'. But he argues that this 'is not the basis on which human rights analysis proceeds'. It concerns the interests of individuals. 'If self-determination is to be understood . . . as a human right, the starting point must be the value to the interests of individuals of membership of a particular kind of group.' He then cites Joseph Raz in support of the assertion that 'the well-being of the group is related to but different from, the aggregation of the interests of individuals'.[103] In the end indigenous rights might be a species of human rights, but if they are they require human rights to be redefined in ways that include the collective human rights of groups.

Peoples and populations

The right of 'peoples' to self-determination is inscribed in Article 1 of both the ICCPR and the ICESCR. Neither Convention was written with indigenous peoples explicitly in mind. Any appeal to these instruments must be made on the grounds that indigenous groups belong to the general category of 'peoples'. Consequently, the Draft Declaration on the Rights of Indigenous Peoples seeks to establish the right of self-determination as a specific right of 'indigenous peoples'. Article 3 of the Declaration is thus a repetition of Article 1 of the Convention except for the insertion of the word 'indigenous'.[104]

The problem with this is that 'peoples' is taken to refer to groups constituted as nations that were colonised. States see indigenous peoples differently and to circumvent separatist claims that would challenge

---

[102] All references in this paragraph are to Tim Rowse, *Indigenous Futures: Choice and Development for Aboriginal and Islander Australia* (Sydney: University of New South Wales Press, 2002), p. 18.

[103] Kingsbury, 'Claims', p. 502.

[104] Article 3 states: 'Indigenous peoples have the right of self-determination. By virtue of that right they freely determine their political status and freely pursue their economic, social and cultural development.'

their authority they have wanted to cling to a distinction between 'peoples' and 'populations'. This is far from being a mere matter of legal semantics. Indigenous peoples claim both that 'self-determination is an inherent right of peoples (including indigenous peoples)' and that 'this right entails sovereignty'. Representatives of indigenous peoples argue that this does not necessarily imply separatism or secession. But, as Irons points out, it does 'imply that indigenous peoples themselves have the right to determine their form and extent of government, including the right to choose independence'.[105] For just this reason, government representatives to the Working Group on Indigenous Peoples have tended to argue that indigenous peoples should be regarded as minority groups within the state. The task is then 'minority protection within the state'. Government representatives have maintained 'that indigenous peoples are not entitled to self-determination under international law as the legal right of self-determination is only appropriate to the process of decolonisation and liberation from foreign occupation'. It is for this reason that governments have preferred the term 'indigenous populations' to 'indigenous peoples' as a way of avoiding 'any implication that indigenous peoples are entitled to the right of "all peoples" to self-determination'.[106]

A further problem is the distinction between the singular 'people' and the plural 'peoples'. The text of the final declaration of the 1993 United Nations Vienna Conference on Human Rights uses 'people' rather than 'peoples'. Dianne Otto points out that this is a form of Orientalism. It 'collapse[s] all indigenous groups into a single category incapable of specific geographic or ethnocultural meaning, [hence it] reflects the continuing power of the global colonialist discourse'.[107] Simply put, it does violence to the differences between groups of indigenous peoples who are far from being all alike.

The contemporary scope of self-determination

A persistent argument about the right to self-determination, stated in various instruments, such as the International Convention on Civil and Political Rights, has been whether it includes minorities generally or just those in a 'colonial' situation. We have already seen that the meanings given to 'self-determination' have included freedom from colonial domination, the right to choose independence from or association with another state, and, the collective right of a people (nation) to determine

---

[105] Irons, 'Indigenous Peoples', p. 211.   [106] Ibid., p. 212.
[107] Dianne Otto, 'A Question of Law or Politics? Indigenous Claims to Sovereignty in Australia', *Syracuse Journal of International Law and Commerce*, 21 (1995), 718.

its own form of government. For much of the post-World War Two period it has been the first of these that has mostly defined the scope of the term. With the passage of time the question has increasingly become whether the principle of self-determination should be confined to people in colonial boundaries or instead applied to all 'peoples'. Anaya is, as we have already seen, one who thinks it should not. Cass similarly argues that there is a 'lack of correspondence between international legal theory and state practice' and 'that the exclusion of non-colonially based claims is confusing and no longer appropriate'.[108]

State practice is important in this connection as a counter to claims that self-determination is merely a political or rather a legal principle. Cass argues that there is evidence in state practice for regarding it as the latter. First, there has been actual decolonisation; second, there is recognition by UN member states of the right to self-determination; and third, there is an accumulation of statements encouraging the legitimacy of self-determination claims. Allowing that these are sufficient reason for regarding it as a legal principle, the next problem is to determine the scope and content of the principle and, in particular, whether it does apply only to people in *existing colonial boundaries* or rather has broader application. Cass contrasts a *conventional* with a *controversial* view of this problem.

As representative of the conventional view she cites David J. Harris, who 'believes that General Assembly Resolution 1514, the first to deal comprehensively with self-determination, contemplates self-determination within existing boundaries'. His view is that 'ethnic minorities, not within definite colonial boundaries, are not entitled to exercise a right of self-determination'.[109] In Australia the conventional view is represented by the Australian Law Reform Commission in its 1986 report on Aboriginal Customary Laws. The Commission stated that the principle of self-determination had '[s]o far ... been confined in international practice to situations involving separate ("colonial") territories politically and legally subordinate to an administering power'.[110] Representing the controversial view are Professor Ved Nanda and Professor John Collins. For Nanda, 'the right of self-determination extends beyond the colonial context' and for Collins, 'the principle

---

[108] Cass, 'Re-Thinking', p. 24.
[109] Ibid., pp. 29–30, and see David J. Harris, *Cases and Materials on International Law*, 3rd edn (London: Sweet and Maxwell, 1983).
[110] Cass, 'Re-Thinking', p. 30. See Australian Law Reform Commission, *Recognition of Aboriginal Customary Laws*, Report No. 31 (Canberra: Australian Government Publishing Service, 1986).

of self-determination should not be considered strictly as a colonial right'.[111]

Of these two, Cass supports the controversial view as the one that 'more accurately reflects state practice' and can be considered as 'a workable prescription for the future'. Her conclusion is that it is the interpretation that 'should . . . be formally recognised as the appropriate international law standard'. After reviewing *opinio juris* across a number of examples, she accordingly concludes that '[i]f self-determination is to have any contemporary relevance . . . it must be taken to include the situation where ethnic minorities may exercise this right'.[112]

On this argument it is not, as Anaya argues, something that can be confined by narrow interpretations that restrict its applicability to the largely outmoded category of peoples seeking sovereign independence in the form of a state. Given this, are there any grounds for the fear that states have that the right to self-determination for indigenous peoples is a challenge to state sovereignty?

A conflict between self-determination and sovereignty?

It is, as previously discussed, widely assumed by states that the right to self-determination implies the right to form a separate state. In that case, it is a challenge to the territorial sovereignty of states against which it is claimed[113] and cannot be recognised in international law as it is presently written. International law does not currently recognise the right to freedom of indigenous peoples because of secession implications. Rights for 'peoples' achieved through self-determination are countenanced 'only within the existing system of state sovereignty. No right of self-determination is recognised where it clashes with the rules of the system.'[114]

As previously mentioned, it is a mistake to see self-determination as having only the aim of establishing a separate territorial state. It may also be represented by a set of goals that can be pursued through life within the state. In this case it poses a challenge to the idea 'of a unified "nationality" juridically administered by governmental organs',[115] but is not about carving out a separate state. Brennan argues that it is

---

[111] See Ved P. Nanda, 'Self-Determination under International Law: Validity of Claims to Secede', *Case Western Reserve Journal of International Law*, 13 (1981), and John A. Collins, 'Self-Determination in International Law: The Palestinians', *Case Western Reserve Journal of International Law*, 12 (1980).
[112] Cass, 'Re-Thinking', pp. 31–8.   [113] See Falk, 'Rights of Peoples', p. 18.
[114] Irons, 'Indigenous Peoples', p. 285.   [115] Falk, 'Rights of Peoples', p. 18.

indeed not easy for a people within a state 'to constitute themselves as a separate nation state'. To do so, 'a "people" needs an identifiable land base, a social and economic system, and an identifiable group of consenting persons. Indigenous populations and minority groups within existing nation states cannot easily separate themselves from such nation states.'[116] For precisely this reason 'self-determination' should now be understood as referring 'to self-determination for indigenous groups within the life of the nation'. According to Brennan, it now means the 'entitlement of the indigenous groups to make decisions about their economic, social and cultural development without unwarranted interference by the state'.[117] Evidence for this, he suggests, is Article 31 of the Draft Declaration.

The Inuit and the Nisga'a First Nation of Canada and the Māori of New Zealand already have varying degrees of self-determination and constitutional recognition, which is sought also by other indigenous peoples including those of Australia. Thus Darryl Pearce, executive director of the Northern Lands Council, told a 1994 conference on regional agreements: 'It's about cutting out the Northern Territory Government. We could be talking about self-government, about an Aboriginal parliament on Aboriginal land . . . about self-governing territory. We will control the resources, we will control the access, we will set up the police forces, we will set up the legal system and move away from a system which . . . we don't fit into.'[118] While this would involve far-reaching changes to the relationship between Aborigines and the state it nevertheless does not mean a separate state.

Canada and the United States are cited as states that now accommodate 'the concept of multiple sovereignty'. In Australia 'it already exists . . . in the form of the constitutional delineation of the powers of the Commonwealth and the States'.[119] As much as anything else self-determination is 'a theory about the relationship that should prevail between the nation and the state'.[120] As a contemporary theory it is stating that indigenous claims are about rights within the state rather than carving out new states. This, however, is not a new way of interpreting self-determination. In his 1941 essay, *The Future of Nations*, Carr articulated the idea of 'divided but not incompatible loyalties'. His view

---

[116] Brennan, *One Land*, pp. 148.   [117] Ibid., pp. 148–9.
[118] *Sydney Morning Herald*, 30 November 1995, p. 4.
[119] See remarks attributed to Greg Crough, *Sydney Morning Herald*, 30 November 1995, p. 4.
[120] Cobban, *Nation-State*, p. 39.

was that 'people should be allowed and encouraged to exercise self-determination for some purposes but not for others, or alternatively that they should "determine" themselves into different groups for different purposes – [a]system of divided but not incompatible loyalties is the only tolerable solution of the problem of self-determination'.[121] Applied to the contemporary self-determination claims of indigenous peoples this clearly is an argument for self-determination expressed in ways that fall short of statehood. In other words, self-determination for indigenous peoples can be comprehended in ways that need not challenge state sovereignty.

Contrary to this line of argument, Dianne Otto believes that internal self-determination cannot comprehend and provide for the ideas of 'indigenous sovereignty' that are fundamental to indigenous identity. Otto argues that the definition of sovereignty has been restricted by international law and needs to be reconceptualised in a way that would enable the recognition of indigenous sovereignty. Law has had this effect because it is part of a liberal discourse that has denied 'diverse social realities by legitimating discourses that protect and promote the status quo, or allow only incremental changes to it'.[122] Without a concept of indigenous sovereignty that has so far not been part of legal theory there can, in her view, be no satisfactory 'recognition of a post-colonial indigenous identity'.

By 'indigenous sovereignty' Otto 'means the power for indigenous communities to imagine themselves . . . [and] To be creators of themselves as subjects rather than objects of law and history.'[123] Indigenous sovereignty would enable 'the reconceptualisation of Aboriginal identities as bearers of rights, obligations and unique nationhood, and as agents of their own destinies'.[124] The need to define and defend indigenous sovereignty as distinct from self-determination is because 'indigenous ideas of sovereignty [encompass elements] . . . which are not comprehended by the notion of internal self-determination'. Indigenous sovereignty would go beyond self-determination in three respects.

[121] Carr, *Future of Nations*, p. 50. See also Ralph Pettman's discussion of world society as something divided into many specific networks. Ralph Pettman, *International Politics* (Melbourne: Longman Cheshire, 1991), p. 16.

[122] Otto, 'Question of Law', p. 704. See also Dianne Otto, 'Subalternity and International Law: The Problems of Global Community and the Incommensurability of Difference', *Social and Legal Studies*, 5: 3 (1996), 337–64.

[123] Ibid., pp. 703–4.

[124] Ibid., p. 710. See also Henry Reynolds, *Aboriginal Sovereignty: Three Nations, One Australia?* (Sydney: Allen & Unwin, 1996).

First, it would give back to Aboriginal peoples the capacity to determine their Aboriginality instead of having to deal with white constructions of Aboriginality.[125] Second, it would give Aboriginal 'peoples international standing beyond the derivative personality of individual standing accorded by some human rights instruments'.[126] Access to international legal processes has been limited 'to those human rights fora which recognise the standing of individuals. [But to] deal with indigenous peoples as a collective of individuals is destructive of indigenous identities and culture'.[127] It represents a failure to take account of the differences between peoples. At worst it may be seen as a deliberate ploy to deny those differences for political purposes. Indigenous sovereignty would confer international legal personality on indigenous peoples as discrete groups, each of which may have needs that will not be met if all indigenous peoples are treated alike. Third, 'the recognition of indigenous sovereignty would provide a foundation for the acknowledgement of land-associated responsibilities and rights that are not adequately protected within a human rights paradigm'.[128] Indigenous relationships with land are not readily comprehended by non-indigenous legal systems. Fundamental to these relationships are spiritual connections that are not recognised by the non-indigenous concept of sovereignty embodied in international law. At the same time as recognising the spiritual aspects of land, indigenous sovereignty would contrast with the more restricted goal of self-determination within a framework in which sovereignty is not invested in indigenous peoples.[129]

While the reform of law proposed by Otto might be difficult to achieve, support for her concern with the concept of indigenous sovereignty may be found in the concepts and perspectives of indigenous peoples.

Some indigenous perspectives

Indigenous peoples reject European notions of sovereignty in which the state exercises authority over civil society. Taiaiake Alfred, for example, argues that European notions of sovereignty, in which there is 'a permanent transference of power and authority from the individual to an abstraction of the collective called "government"', are incompatible with the indigenous concept of governance founded on respect for individual autonomy.[130] In his view 'sovereignty is an exclusionary

---

[125] Ibid., p. 710.   [126] Ibid.   [127] Ibid., p. 712.
[128] Ibid., p. 710.   [129] Ibid., p. 713.   [130] Alfred, *Peace, Power, Righteousness*, p. 25.

147

concept rooted in an adversarial and coercive notion of power'[131] and is an inappropriate model for indigenous governance. Rather than giving indigenous people control over their lives sovereignty might simply result in placing structures of domination into the hands of indigenous administrators. In support of this he cites two Canadian scholars who write that

> by adopting the European-Western ideology of sovereignty, the current generation of Indian leaders is buttressing the imposed alien authority structures within its communities, and is legitimising the associated hierarchy comprised of indigenous political and bureaucratic elites. This endorsement of hierarchical authority and a ruling entity constitutes a complete rupture with traditional indigenous principles.[132]

Consequently, Alfred calls for a modified concept of sovereignty that will be consistent with indigenous understandings of power and authority.[133]

Māori leaders also articulate understandings of sovereignty that differ from orthodox European politico-legal conceptions. For Kara Puketapu, sovereignty is related to Māori 'searching their souls about what they are deciding for future generations'.[134] Areta Koopu similarly describes it as 'being in control of oneself' and as 'being who I am and remembering that I am Māori'. At the national level it is, to her mind, 'the ability of Māori to have their own programmes and to do things for themselves'.[135] And for Sandra Lee, Māori sovereignty predates the arrival of Europeans. 'Māori are a sovereign people. We are a nation of people.'[136] The Māori term for sovereignty is *tino rangatiratanga*, which has had a variety of meanings. Roger Maaka and Augie Fleras explain that 'at various times, *tino rangitiratanga* has encompassed the following: Māori sovereignty, Māori nationhood, self-management, iwi nationhood, (an iwi is a confederation of tribes) independent power, full chiefly authority, chiefly mana, strong leadership, independence, supreme rule, self-reliance, Māori autonomy, tribal autonomy, absolute chieftainship, trusteeship, self-determination'.[137] In short the term is contested but it is regarded as representing 'the most crucial and important means by

---

[131] Ibid., p. 59.   [132] Ibid., p. 56.   [133] Ibid., p. 57.
[134] Hineani Melbourne, *Māori Sovereignty: The Māori Perspective* (Auckland: Hodder Moa Beckett, 1995), p. 49.
[135] Ibid., p. 92.   [136] Ibid., p. 121.
[137] Roger Maaka and Augie Fleras, 'Engaging with Indigeneity: Tino Rangatiratanga in Aotearoa', in Ivison, Patton and Sanders (eds.), *Political Theory and the Rights of Indigenous Peoples*, p. 99.

which Māori can participate fully both in their affairs and in those of the country.'[138]

In New Zealand debate about sovereignty has centred on the difference between how Māori and Pakeha (the dominant white society) understand the meaning of the term in the 1840 Treaty of Waitangi (*Te Tiriti o Waitangi*). The provisions of this Treaty are regarded as the foundation for relations between the Māori confederation of tribes (iwi) and the state.[139] As J. G. A. Pocock puts it: 'The Treaty . . . is now considered fundamental, in the sense that it establishes the national sovereignty; it therefore furnishes a basis on which Māori may make claims against that sovereignty . . .'[140] Preceding the Treaty there had been a Declaration of Independence signed in 1835. It had been prompted by British concern over the possibility of the Frenchman Baron de Thierry attempting to establish an independent state on part of the North Island. To pre-empt this the British gave, in the Declaration, recognition to the sovereignty and independence of the Māori.[141] Having done that, Britain then needed a 'mechanism to justify imposing its own will on Māori and assuming governance'.[142]

The Treaty of Waitangi was to serve this purpose and its objectives were 'protection of Māori interests, promotion of settler interests, and the securement of strategic advantage for the crown'. In retrospect, the first two of these were bound to be in conflict. Protection of Māori interests meant in practice 'usurping sovereignty from the Māori'. Durie comments that 'within a decade the Treaty was used, not to protect Māori, but to separate them from their land and culture . . .'[143] Cases appealing to the Treaty brought before the courts mostly involved judgements concerning its legal status. For instance, in the 1877 Supreme Court case of *Wi Parata* vs. *Bishop of Wellington*, Chief Justice Prendergast ruled that 'the Treaty of Waitangi lacked binding force in law, precisely because the Māori signatories lacked the authority of sovereign statehood that alone could have made the terms of a treaty with them binding on the

---

[138] Ibid. Maaka and Fleras are quoting Maitu Rata.

[139] Maaka and Fleras, 'Engaging with Indigeneity', p. 204.

[140] John Pocock, 'Waitangi as Mystery of State: Consequences of the Ascription of Federative Capacity to the Māori', in Ivison, Patton and Sanders (eds.), *Political Theory and the Rights of Indigenous Peoples*, p. 26.

[141] Claudia Orange, *The Story of a Treaty* (Auckland: Bridget Williams, 2001), p. 11, and Ranginui Walker, 'Māori Sovereignty, Colonial and Post-Colonial Discourses', in Haverman (ed.), *Indigenous People's Rights*, p. 111.

[142] Mason Durie, *Te Mana, Te Kāwanatanga: The Politics of Māori Self-Determination* (Auckland: Oxford University Press, 1998), p. 176.

[143] Ibid., p. 176.

Crown and its subsequent judges, officers and subjects'.[144] In later cases the approach of the court differed and the question of the status of the Treaty was finally settled with the 1975 Treaty of Waitangi Act.

Of particular importance for the definition and location of sovereignty has been the fact that there is an English and a Māori version of the Treaty; both of which were accepted in the Treaty of Waitangi Act. The first article of the English version cedes to the Crown, 'absolutely and without reservation, all the rights and powers of sovereignty'.[145] The second clause granted the chiefs 'the absolute chieftainship of their lands, homes, and all their treasured possessions'.[146] In the Māori version the rights and powers of sovereignty granted to the Crown in the first clause are translated as *kāwanatanga*, and the absolute chieftainship stipulated in the second clause is rendered as *tino rangatiratanga*. The significance of this is that the *kāwanatanga* granted to the Crown did not, for the Māori, amount to sovereignty. *Kāwanatanga* is a transliteration for government or 'governance'. *Tino rangatiratanga* is not easily defined but 'refers to those indigenous rights to self-determination that Māori possess by virtue of their status as original occupants ("tangata whenua")'. For Maaka and Fleras it 'serves as a precursor of Māori sovereignty; it also provides the basis for, derives from, is contingent on, and is strengthened by claims to self-determination'.[147]

The essential point here is that the Māori understood the provisions of the Treaty to mean that power was to be shared with the British Crown. For the British it meant power was transferred with the 'Crown as sovereign and tangata whenua as subject'.[148] The intention of the British was to acquire sovereignty, but in negotiating the Treaty they failed to make clear to the Māori 'either the impact that settlement would have on their *rangatiratanga*, or the extent to which the Crown would further that process in the act of exercising sovereignty over it'.[149] Whether rightly or wrongly, the different meanings of sovereignty embedded in the Treaty meant that Māori inevitably thought they had

---

[144] John Pocock, 'Waitangi as Mystery of State', p. 28.
[145] Walker, 'Māori Sovereignty', p. 112 and Jeanette Jameson, 'Indigenous People: An American Perspective on the Case for Entrenchment of Māori Rights in New Zealand Law', *Pacific Rim Law and Policy Journal*, 2 (Summer 1993), 347.
[146] Walker, 'Māori Sovereignty', p. 112. See also Mary Kay Duffié, 'Goals for Fourth World Peoples and Sovereignty Initiatives in the United States and New Zealand', *American Indian Culture and Research Journal*, 22: 1 (1998), 183–212. For a comparison of the English and Māori versions see Orange, *Story of a Treaty*, p. 30.
[147] Maaka and Fleras, 'Engaging with Indigeneity', p. 101.
[148] Fleras, 'Politicising Indigeneity', p. 205.
[149] Pocock, 'Waitangi as Mystery of State', p. 29.

been deceived. Sovereignty is a potent and emotive concept and it is not surprising that divergent understandings have kept debate about it alive in New Zealand. Pocock encapsulates the importance of the term for Māori when he writes that 'sovereignty, legislative and political, is among other things a mode by which a human community seeks to command its own history: to take actions which shape its politics in the present and even – since a great deal of history has in fact been written in this way – to declare the shape of the historic past and process out of which it deems itself to be issuing'.[150] It is in this connection that Dianne Otto sees the urgency and importance in indigenous sovereignty.

Finally, in contrast to those, whether in Canada, New Zealand or elsewhere, who seek indigenous concepts of sovereignty, the Australian Aboriginal activist and barrister Michael Mansell makes political use of the conventional meaning. He has in the past claimed sovereignty for Aboriginal people as the basis of 'an independent nation as understood in international law'. His purpose in doing so has been in part rhetorical, but it is, as Noel Pearson points out, also 'based on the questionableness in international law of the validity of the British acquisition of sovereignty over Australia, and the implied extinguishment of any pre-existing Aboriginal sovereignty'.[151] Pearson, who is also an Aboriginal leader and lawyer, comments that Mansell clearly believes that to accept anything less than 'full-blown sovereignty, would be to sell [indigenous Australians] short and would be conceding legitimacy to the colonial invasion that left indigenous people dispossessed, destitute and pariahs in their own country'.[152] Pearson himself doubted both that this was effective strategy and that recognition of separate statehood was realistic. In his opinion 'advocacy of the sovereignty agenda reduces the gains that people could otherwise make via appropriate pragmatism'.[153]

This chapter has been concerned with self-determination and sovereignty as crucial elements in the recovery of indigenous peoples' rights. Because many of the issues and concepts involved are contested it is in many ways a necessarily inconclusive discussion. There are, nevertheless, some conclusions to be drawn concerning the obstacles inherent in establishing indigenous peoples' rights and the future direction of this struggle.

[150] J. G. A. Pocock, 'Law, Sovereignty and History in a Divided Culture: The Case of New Zealand and the Treaty of Waitangi', *McGill Law Journal*, 43 (October 1998), 496.
[151] Noel Pearson, 'Reconciliation: To Be or not To Be – Separate Aboriginal Nationhood or Aboriginal Self-determination and Self-government within the Australian Nation?' *Aboriginal Law Bulletin*, 3: 16 (April 1993), 14–17.
[152] Ibid., p. 14.   [153] Ibid., p. 16.

In the first place, satisfying indigenous rights claims that involve questions of self-determination and sovereignty does require a revision of the current understanding of these concepts. Self-determination carries the baggage of state building and decolonisation. States resist or are at least wary of self-determination because it suggests state breaking. For that reason some states continue to insist that they have indigenous populations rather than indigenous peoples within their borders; they cling to the position that human rights instruments are an adequate protection of indigenous rights; and are concerned about the implications of group rights as opposed to individual rights. All of these are, for states, pregnant with the possibility of a challenge to their integrity and over-riding authority.

More progressive states recognise that secession is not the goal of most indigenous peoples. Their aim is instead control over what they define as their own affairs in ways consistent with their location within the borders of a sovereign state. What this requires is the acceptance that self-determination can take more than one form. One of these needs to be specific to indigenous peoples and to allow for indigenous self-government at a sub-state level. It is at this point that self-determination shades into sovereignty.

Otto's account of sovereignty tied to particular indigenous cultural identities is clearly a radical departure from the orthodox understanding of it to which she objects. Her case for reconceptualising sovereignty is that the power to define, shape and maintain identity is fundamental to all indigenous rights. Sovereignty is constitutive of identity, and consequently if indigenous rights are to be fully realized sovereignty must be invested in indigenous peoples.

What is interesting about this is that she is not arguing for a new single definition of sovereignty. Instead, the argument is for different layers of sovereignty defining different areas of competence, not in competition with each other but as interacting parts of a whole. Her conception is one in which sovereignty is not the sole preserve of the state. It has sovereignty over some things but not others. In this scheme indigenous peoples would have control over legal and political systems that affect them, but would exercise such control within the boundary of the state. For indigenous peoples she is 'laying claim to an area of jurisdiction that previously belonged to the state' – not to all areas of jurisdiction.[154] In some matters it would free indigenous peoples from the jurisdiction of

[154] Ibid., p. 736.

the state, but not in others. There are clear parallels between her proposals and Anaya's reformulation of self-determination, which illustrates
the close relationship between the two concepts.

In practice, there are already varying degrees of 'multiple sovereignty'. Formal acceptance of the idea would, however, involve a leap
of imagination and a deliberate break from the cages of political and
legal thinking that do not cope well with multiple meanings. Politically
it would mean states being willing to relinquish control over particular
areas that have hitherto been in their jurisdiction, which could result in
disputes over the demarcation of authority. At a more general level the
idea of multiple levels of sovereignty is unlikely to appeal to and will be
resisted by people educated in traditions of thought that either prefer
or insist on analytic neatness and parsimony. Untidy though it may be,
'indigenous sovereignty' means thinking in terms of the sovereignty of
individuals and groups contained within the overarching sovereignty
of the state. The state retains control over external affairs and those matters that affect all groups within it. In relations between these groups its
role is that of mediator and arbiter. This involves not a radical departure
from the traditional role of the democratic state but a transfer of some
of its power to the hitherto dispossessed, which is perhaps the most
threatening thing of all to state leaders.

In many ways the difficulty over the meaning and scope of the concepts of self-determination and sovereignty are ones derived from the
fact that international law ties them to states. It is legal definition, as
much as anything else, that stands in the way of them being recon-
ceived in ways that would more readily accommodate indigenous peoples' rights. It seems, as Otto argues, that extending and formalising
the rights of indigenous peoples necessarily involves challenging the
centrality of the state in the 'discourse' of international law.

Richard Falk is prominent among those who have thought seriously
about the obstacles state-centric international law creates for indigenous peoples' rights. He proposes that an effective challenge to state-
centric international law would be the development and involvement
of an international civil society that would enlist domestic courts as
'agents of interpretation and implementation of critical norms in the
war/peace and human rights area of the international legal order'.[155]
Falk noted that at the time of writing, in 1988, the 'international legal

---

[155] Falk, 'Rights of Peoples', p. 30. See also Falk's later *Human Rights Horizons*, chs. 6 and
7, and Strelein, *Indigenous Self-determination Claims*.

framework [did] not give access to the main political arenas to the representatives of indigenous peoples themselves, nor [did] it seem to deal with their specific historic identity, their claims, nor with their special value to human society as a whole'.[156] Since then there has, as noted in the earlier discussion of the United Nations, been progress. Through the establishment of the Permanent Forum access to a major political forum has been gained. If the Draft Declaration on Indigenous Peoples' Rights is eventually adopted it will give some degree of legal definition to group rights, territorial rights, indigenous self-determination and the international legal status of indigenous peoples.[157] It is at the same time vital to the development of an international civil society that includes the achievement of indigenous peoples' rights in its purposes. It could, however, also have some negative aspects. Otto suggests that, in particular, some indigenous peoples could regard the Draft Declaration as part of a 'totalising discourse' that treats all indigenous peoples as alike, instead of recognising the substantial differences between them.

Equally, in response to attacks on statist international law it needs to be asked whether a defence of statist logic should be mounted. The answer to this, most consistent with the overall argument of the book, is that statist logic needs defending in some respects but not in others. It may well be acceptable to defend statist international law when it has a role in bolstering order and justice in relations between states. But this should not then be a reason for excluding from the competence of international law the conduct of certain of the internal affairs of states. There is not necessarily a clash between the order functions of international law and the role it can have in the protection of rights within states.

The reconceptualisation of self-determination and sovereignty in the ways discussed in this chapter necessarily involves an approach to law that will not be readily accepted by the legal traditions that prevail in many countries. It would mean a shift away from law as an established body of rules to an approach more closely associated with the view of law as a social process, in which the boundaries between law and politics are less clearly drawn. Law would, in this case, have a greater role in codifying rules and norms likely to promote social justice. It would require demystifying law of the kind that wanted to continue the fiction that Australia was *terra nullius*, based on the precedent of

---

[156] Ibid., p. 31.   [157] See Williams, 'Encounters'.

previous cases. One of the arguments in Australia concerning the Mabo decision was that it sullied the High Court because it blurred the boundaries between law and politics with the court assuming an essentially political role. This is to misunderstand that law is inherently political. To have continued the fiction of *terra nullius* would have been no less political.

5 The political and moral legacy of conquest

The preceding chapters have successively discussed European representations of non-Europeans, the way first nations were dispossessed of their property, and the struggle to have rights to land and self-determination restored to them. This chapter concerns some political and moral issues arising from European conquest. In relation to the preceding chapters three clusters of problems stand out as the most important: the ethics of constructing 'others'; the idea that 'the West' bears a collective responsibility for historic injustices that need to be redressed; the moral legitimacy of states with significant unresolved issues affecting their indigenous populations, leading in turn to the question of whether international society is legitimate. The underlying premise of the chapter is that if international society is to be regarded as worth preserving, either as an idea or in practice, then it must be a society that defends the whole community of humankind and not just the particular interests of dominant groups in particular states. This harks back to the suggestion in Chapter 1 that international society has a universal moral basis so long as it fosters the well-being of individuals everywhere, which is an argument that will be revisited in Chapter 6.

This chapter is arranged in three parts corresponding with the issues mentioned above. The first discusses the harms that can result from constructing others and which extend beyond colonial pasts and indigenous peoples to contemporary cross-civilisational relations in general. Next, the discussion turns to responsibility for past wrongs and what might be done to redress them. Historic injustices and how they are addressed have the capacity to politically divide the citizens of states with indigenous populations and so have an important bearing on the legitimacy of governments and of states. The third section considers not only the legitimacy of states with indigenous populations but also

of international society in relation to the moral purpose of advancing
world order values.

The ethics of constructing others

Anthony Pagden cogently argues that the 'need to make some sense
of the beliefs and the ethical lives of others' sometimes 'resulted in an
attempt to *construct* "others" better suited to the observers, own particular ethical life'.[1] Others are, as we have seen before, counter images
constructed in ways that define us by what we are not.[2] The construction of this image involves imagination and may not accord with reality.
Nevertheless, the 'other' that is constructed is assumed to exist and
to be representative of a culture. Once the 'other' – 'this or that real
"savage" or "barbarian" ' – has been set up as a counter image and
given a cultural identity 'his or her moral existence becomes a matter
of real concern'. This leads Pagden to assert that '[t]he discoveries by
modern Europe of a huge range of "other" worlds, of which America
was merely the first, if also the most striking, has made this the most
deeply troubling, the most unsettling of modern cultural and ethical
dilemmas'.[3] The construction of people, which often fails to understand
them in their own terms, complicates cross-cultural understanding. In
European encounters with non-Europeans it meant that 'conquest and
annihilation was the only way in which cultures could deal with the
differences between them'.[4] There has thus always been a lot riding on
the way others are constructed.

My concern here is with the nature of the ethical dilemma that is part
of and results from constructing others. The essence of the dilemma is
that we cannot avoid constructing others but in so doing we may do
them a variety of harms. What is more, these harms are not confined
to the past but are ones that continue to result from the practices of
contemporary international politics. This has been brilliantly demonstrated by Greg Fry in a searching critique of Australian images of the
South Pacific. Fry is concerned with the implications and consequences
of Australian media, officials and academics asserting the right to speak

---

[1] Pagden, *European Encounters*, p. 184.
[2] Ivar B. Neuman and Janet M. Walsh, 'The Other in European Self-definition: an addendum to the literature on international society', *Review of International Studies*, 17 (1991),
327–48, and Ivar B. Neuman, 'Self and Other in International Relations', *European Journal of
International Relations*, 2: 2 (1996), 139–74.
[3] Pagden, *European Encounters*, p. 185.   [4] Ibid., p. 187.

for the peoples of the South Pacific and to lead and manage them.[5] His interest is that one region, but his analysis is one that applies equally to all situations involving the construction of others. It should be abundantly clear from earlier chapters that the construction of non-European others by Europeans has frequently meant that the latter ascribed to the former characteristics that degraded and represented them as less than fully human. The images constructed by Europeans have been ones that disempower non-Europeans and are used to justify practices of domination.

Fry opens his critique by pointing out that Australian images of South Pacific peoples are two-edged. Not only do they provide an insight into the minds of those who hold them, they also 'affect the lives of the people they depict':

> It has mattered for Pacific islanders when, at various times over the past two hundred years, influential Australians have viewed them collectively as savages, noble savages, children, or full human beings, and whether the region was depicted as a defence shield, a frontier, empty or unstable. Each of these lenses allowed or encouraged different Australian behaviour towards Pacific islanders: from colonial control and exploitation, to protection, development, and the encouragement of self-determination.[6]

In explaining and developing this argument Fry draws on Edward Said's critique of orientalism.[7]

Said argues that the depiction of others is integral to the structure of power that binds those others into an inferior role and status. The way others are depicted or represented is part of the 'knowledge' that rationalises the exercise of power. His 'method for assessing whether knowledge practices might be regarded as inherently subordinating is to examine the unacknowledged epistemological premises' embedded in them. Consequently, Fry focuses on the concern Said has with 'first, the tendency to create a mythical collective identity – the Orient – and a mythical essentialised person – the Oriental – which it then becomes possible to characterize, and second, the tendency to consistently promote belittling, negative images of those identities'. Said argues that this knowledge affects those depicted 'not just because it informs and justifies colonial or neo-colonial practices through providing the lenses

---

[5] Greg Fry, 'Framing the Islands: Knowledge and Power in Changing Australian Images of "the South Pacific" ', *The Contemporary Pacific*, 9: 2 (1997).
[6] Ibid., p. 306.   [7] Edward Said, *Orientalism* (Harmondsworth: Penguin, 1985).

through which Europeans see the orient, but because it begins to be taken on as a self-image by those so depicted'.[8]

Fry is careful not to uncritically accept Said's analysis and draws attention to three different traps that the unwary can be led into by Said. The first is that of mirroring Orientalism with the concept of 'Occidentalism' and speaking of 'the West' as if it were a single entity. With the support of James Clifford[9] and Nicholas Thomas,[10] Fry argues that this 'simply does not reflect the complexity of Western approaches to the non-Western world'. It is not the case that all 'Westerners', or in the case of the Pacific, all Australians, should be seen as supporting structures of knowledge and power concerned with domination. Second, Said's critics have expressed concern about 'his ambivalence on the question of whether a critique of Orientalist practices implies that there is a true Orient which is missed by the distorting lenses of European preconceptions'.[11] What is interesting about this for Fry is the implication that those who believe European lenses are distorting, themselves 'think there can be one true reality'. The third trap or set of issues identified by Fry is Aijaz Ahmad's argument that 'the critique of Western representations of the non-European world becomes a new form of dependency theory, an attempt to place the blame for wrongs firmly on the outside world rather than sheet responsibility home to local elites'.

Taking care to avoid these traps Fry proceeds to uncover and rebut four epistemological premises suppressed in a series of influential media, policy and academic representations of the South Pacific. Each of the premises he examines points to the way harm can result from the construction of others. Fry himself is particularly interested in the ethical judgements that can be made about the exercise of power inherent in the practices associated with each. The first is the way mythical persons who are supposedly representative of all who resemble them are constructed and assumed to exist. Instead of, for instance, Pacific Islanders being seen as diverse peoples, they are essentialised and seen as one; diversity is suppressed. Pacific Island states are treated as if they were all alike and all facing the same problems. What is presented as knowledge actually 'bears little resemblance to the experience of any society, [and] this has implications for the claim to truth'.[12] Second, with

---

[8] Fry, 'Framing the Islands', pp. 310–11.
[9] James Clifford, *The Predicament of Culture: Twentieth-Century Ethnography, Literature, and Art* (Cambridge, MA: Harvard University Press, 1988).
[10] Thomas, *Colonialism's Culture*.   [11] Fry, 'Framing the Islands', p. 312.
[12] Ibid., p. 313.

regard to whether others are consistently dehumanised or belittled Fry finds a mixed record but concludes that, with regard to the South Pacific at least, there has been a return to 'subordinating images'.[13] Third, he deals with 'the relationship that the framers of the knowledge define between themselves and the frame'. His argument concerning this is that 'the construction of a division between a superior "us" and an inferior "them" is accentuated by the degree to which there is a denial of shared humanity on the part of the framer, in the sense of a preparedness of placing its own experience and problems up for depiction alongside the others about which it is constructing knowledge'. Finally, Fry considers 'preconceptions concerning certainty of knowledge . . .'. He is troubled in particular about 'the extent to which Australian representations claim to provide the one true reality of Pacific Island experience rather than a perspective built on particular epistemological and ideological preconceptions'.[14]

To recap, Fry's major argument is that the practices associated with each of these premises adversely affect the lives of the people they concern. They influence, even determine, both how those who frame the images behave towards those framed and the self-image of those framed. Each of the premises identified by Fry can be linked to either potential or actual harm; and because of this the construction of others is necessarily an act that has ethical implications. Stereotyping and the denial of diversity leads to the unjust treatment of some, if not a great many, individuals and whole social and cultural groups. It can involve the denial of rights and results in the perpetuation of false images used to justify oppression and domination. People are harmed by the false images and the denial of rights based on them. Similarly the dehumanisation of others has historically harmed those seen as 'uncivilised', 'savage' or less than fully human. Such terms undermine the self-esteem of individuals so categorised and can be used to justify the denial of rights. In extreme cases, the dehumanisation of others leads to cultural if not physical genocide. The presumption of superiority, including the ways of knowing of those who believe themselves to be superior, discounts or denies the belief systems of those named as inferior peoples. It is a further justification for a variety of harms. Last, claims to know reality compound the harm to others by disempowering them from determining the nature of the conditions that affect their lives.

[13] Ibid., pp. 313–14.   [14] Ibid., p. 314.

At stake in all of these is an underlying question of human dignity. Given that we cannot escape constructing others, the onus is on us to make sure we understand each other as well as possible. If the past and present harms associated with constructing others are to be dealt with and addressed there must be an effort to understand others in their own terms. However, in the final analysis this may be an impossible goal to attain. Apart from anything else, encounters between cultures can involve a clash of values that may be an insurmountable barrier to full comprehension of the other. Finally, in concluding this section it should be recognised that the construction of others need not be negative but can have positive outcomes. Just as others have been constructed in ways that denigrate, dehumanise or demonise them, it is possible to construct others in ways that praise, value and empower them.

Collective responsibility and historic injustices

Whether present generations have any responsibility for past wrongs to first nations is a complex and sometimes bitterly contested question. It can be approached from a number of standpoints, with some of them shaped by the historic circumstances of the country in which the question is being debated. In this section I propose to canvass four different approaches without in any way wanting to suggest that these are the only ones. The first is Tzvetan Todorov's discussion of responsibility as the obligation to understand others. The second is one provoked by recent developments in Australia in which Rob Sparrow grounds a defence of collective responsibility on a view of history that can be applied to other contexts and issues. The third is Chandran Kukathas' denial of collective responsibility as part of his concern to articulate a liberal theory of responsibility. Finally, Jeremy Waldron's argument that historic injustices can be superseded is canvassed.

Towards the end of *The Conquest of America*, Todorov refers to what he calls the 'half prophecy and half curse' Las Casas uttered when he asserted that the Spaniards had a collective responsibility for the death and destruction they had inflicted on the Indians of the Americas. It was, he said, a responsibility for all time and not just the past or the present. Todorov takes Las Casas' pronouncement as a cue for himself, suggesting that Spain can be substituted by 'Western Europe'. It is not only Spaniards who have a collective responsibility but also the peoples of all other European powers that formerly controlled overseas colonies – Portugal, France, England, Holland, Belgium, Italy and Germany. All of these states, he suggests, have collective responsibility for their former colonised peoples.[15] What he means by 'collective responsibility' is not entirely clear and needs clarification.

The idea that the Spaniards have a collective responsibility to Amerindians for all time is meant to convey, first, that it is not just the Conquistadors and colonists who had direct contact with the Indians who had this responsibility. It was the whole of the Spanish people – or the whole of the people of any other European former colonial power. The claim is that each and every Spaniard was responsible for actions taken in the name of Spain. Second, it was not just the responsibility of all Spaniards at a particular time in the past but remains a responsibility for Spaniards today and for those yet to be born. Third, it is not just the Spaniards who have this responsibility but 'Western Europe', which really amounts to the membership of international society at the outset of the twentieth century. Curiously he appears not to be concerned about the responsibilities of non-European colonisers, but that need not detain us here.

Todorov's claims concerning responsibility would clearly be extraordinary if they referred to dispossession, to intentional killing or to the deaths caused by the introduction of diseases such as smallpox, but they concern the more diffuse and continuing problem of knowing others. His concern is with the ability of Europeans to use knowledge of others to manipulate them, coupled with a paradoxical failure to attempt to understand those very same others in their own terms. As he puts it, the other remains to be discovered:

> Since the period of the conquest, for almost three hundred and fifty years, Western Europe has tried to assimilate the other, to do away with an exterior alterity, and has in great part succeeded. Its way of life and its values have spread around the world; – This extraordinary success is chiefly due to one specific feature of Western civilisation which for a long time was regarded as a feature of man himself, its development and prosperity among Europeans thereby becoming proof of their natural superiority: it is paradoxically, Europeans' capacity to understand the other.[16]

This passage comes after an extensive analysis intended to demonstrate that Cortés used language to gain knowledge of Indian beliefs which he then used to manipulate Indians, Montezuma in particular, into thinking

---

[15] Todorov, *Conquest of America*, pp. 245–6.   [16] Ibid., pp. 247–8.

that events were unfolding in conformity with the signs essential to their view of the world. Todorov's concern is then that 'Western Europe' has a responsibility not to use knowledge as power for the purpose of oppression and domination; a responsibility not to simply assimilate the other and so obliterate difference but to truly discover and to understand the other in his or her own terms. The introduction to his later book, *On Human Diversity*,[17] suggests that his concern is closely connected with his personal experiences of otherness and the systematic abuse of knowledge and power in his homeland.

One reason for understanding others in their own terms is that it may be necessary for sustaining international society. David Blaney and Nameen Inayatullah[18] compare Todorov's work with that of Ashis Nandy in relation to the challenge cultural pluralism poses for international society. They point out that in a world of many cultures there may not be agreement about the 'common assumptions, values, ways of life, and modes of communication' presupposed by the idea of international society. There is then the problem of how agreement can be reached, and their suggestions are drawn from 'Todorov's idea of "nonviolent communication" and . . . Nandy's notion of a "dialogue of visions".' Both of these are concerned with the process of 'othering' by means of which 'a self understands the relationship between itself and some other' and it is 'an understanding with practical implications'.[19] Their argument is that while both Todorov and Nandy offer richly rewarding insights into cross-cultural understanding and 'othering' their narratives are 'not situated within a complex of global cultures'. They then show how these narratives can be constructively situated in the framework of international society. For them the possibility contained in Todorov and Nandy is one that does not surrender to 'incommensurablity, disabling of conversation and international society', but is instead a conversation 'in the face of difference and in confrontation with power and domination'.[20] Together Todorov and Nandy provide ways of understanding self–other relations that 'make possible a conversational process in which participation by the postcolonial and non-European periphery does not require its inevitable subordination to the European core'.[21] Through a dialogue

---

[17] Tzvetan Todorov, *On Human Diversity: Nationalism, Racism, and Exoticism in French Thought* (Harvard University Press, 1993).
[18] David I. Blaney and Nameen Inayatullah, 'Prelude to a Conversation of Cultures in International Society? Todorov and Nandy on the Possibility of Dialogue', *Alternatives* 19 (1994), p. 24.
[19] Ibid., p. 41.   [20] Ibid., p. 42.   [21] Ibid., p. 42.

that does not assume 'Western' superiority it is possible to achieve a conversation between cultures and, if Blaney and Inayatullah are right, the degree of mutual understanding needed to sustain international society.

In essence, the responsibility that concerns Todorov is that of engaging in dialogue with 'the other' in order to understand those who are different in their own terms and that means avoiding repeating the same form of past injustices. The second sense of responsibility to be discussed uses an Australian example and requires some background.

At the beginning of the twenty-first century in Australia the question of responsibility for past injustices arises not only in relation to land rights but also the so-called 'stolen generations'. This refers to the practice of routinely removing half-caste babies and children from their families over a period that extended from the early 1900s down to the late 1960s. The intention underpinning this practice is debated but there is compelling evidence that during the 1930s in the Northern Territory and Western Australia it amounted to genocide. At that time it was believed that 'full blood' Aborigines were a doomed race and that if they were prevented from intermarrying with whites they would die out. By removing half-caste children from their families aboriginality could be bred out of them, resulting in an end to the 'problem' of Aborigines.[22] Regardless of whether or not genocide was intended, thousands of children were removed from their families.[23] Many were never reunited with their families and are today able to testify to the pain and suffering they have endured. As one result of an inquiry into the Stolen Generations released in 1997,[24] both Aboriginal leaders and concerned white Australians continue to call for an apology from the prime minister of Australia for the wrongs done to Aboriginal people throughout white occupation. So far, Prime Minister Howard and his government have refused to go further than to express regret for past harms.

[22] Robert Manne, 'The Stolen Generation', *Quadrant*, 42 (January–Frebrurary 1998), pp. 53–63.

[23] Australia was not the only country to have removed children from their families. In aid of assimilation indigenous Canadian children were also subjected to forcible removal and taken to residential schools set up and run by the churches. Like their Australian counterparts they were prohibited from using their own language and were deprived of their cultural heritage. As in Australia the effects on the individuals and their families was profound. See Maggie Hodgson, 'Rebuilding Community after Residential Schools', Bird, Land and Macadam (eds.), *Nation to Nation*, pp. 92–108.

[24] Human Rights and Equal Opportunity Commission, *Bringing Them Home: Report of the National Inquiry into the Separation of Aboriginal and Torres Strait Islander Children from Their Families* (Canberra: Australian Government Publishing Service, 1997).

An important question in the debate about this is whether non-Aboriginal Australians can be held 'collectively responsible' for the past wrongs done to Aboriginal people. Robert Sparrow argues from the nature of history to persuasively argue that they can.[25] Essential to his argument is the idea that we are not able fully to comprehend the present. It is only at some time in the future that historians are able to look back, separate the important from the unimportant and better understand complex events. Historical knowledge is in this sense a social construction. Not only that, in looking back to our present, future historians will not distinguish our present from our past as we do. They are instead more likely to see our present and past as just the one contiguous past. In his words, 'the distinction between our past and our present is not necessarily a historically significant one. – From the perspective of the future, our past and present are both merely the past. The backwards gaze of the future may well treat much of what we regard as the past as part of our present.'[26]

A second crucial element of the argument is that not only is Australia's past racist and replete with injustices towards Aboriginal Australians, there has been no fundamental change in the contemporary treatment of them by non-indigenous Australians. Their life expectancy is considerably lower, as are their levels of income, health and education. At the same time, they have a higher rate of unemployment, they represent a greater proportion of those in prison,[27] suffer more alcoholism and are more likely to commit suicide. It remains 'essentially continuous with a racist history'[28] with respect to dispossession, extermination and forced assimilation. So long as present day injustices are tolerated and there is no decisive break from past practices, 'our actions will be associated with those who have gone before'. Those 'who look back . . . will not see us independently of our history'.[29] By implication we have the capacity to bring about a fundamental change and it is by not doing so that we will be seen by future historians as sharing responsibility for historical injustices with those who have gone before us.

Sparrow anticipates that for some this merely prompts the question of why we should care about how we will be seen by future generations.

---

[25] Robert Sparrow, 'History and Collective Responsibility', *Australasian Journal of Philosophy*, 78: 3 (2000).
[26] Ibid., p. 348.
[27] For a comparison of indigenous rates of incarceration in Australia, Canada and New Zealand see chs. 9, 10 and 11 of Haverman (ed.), *Indigenous People's Rights*.
[28] Sparrow, 'History and Collective Responsibility', p. 350.   [29] Ibid., p. 350.

His answer to this appeals to the effects of our actions on the future coupled with the ethical character of those actions. 'The future', he argues,
'represents the continuation of our ethical projects.' If the earlier argument that the future determines 'the nature of past and current events' is
accepted, then it 'transform[s] our understanding of our current ethical
predicament'.[30] The knowledge that we are likely to be judged in the
same light as those of our forebears who were responsible for injustices
should bring us to the realisation that unless we effect a decisive break
we will share collective responsibility for historic injustices.

Kukathas focuses on who has or otherwise should be assigned, responsibility for historic injustices within states. In order to answer this
he contrasts individualist and collectivist views of responsibility and rejects collective responsibility as not only problematic but ultimately un-
desirable. Early on he states the individualist position that past wrongs
are not the fault of people living today and since it is not their fault they
bear no responsibility for such wrongs. The individualist position denies
any responsibility for past injustices and in setting out the arguments
that can be deployed in support of this position Kukathas rehearses
a number of concerns similar to those examined by Jeremy Waldron,
which are discussed below. Kukathas next sets out objections to denying
the significance of the past and pays attention to the symbolic importance of demands to address past injustices, with specific reference to
Australian Aborigines. 'For many Aborigines, justice in contemporary
terms is inextricably linked with an acknowledgement of the past. And
doing justice now requires recognising and repudiating past injustice.'[31]
The third part of his argument articulates the case for collective responsibility and points out that in an example such as the Stolen Generations
mentioned above this requires bringing about a meeting of minds between the victims of injustice and the descendants of the perpetrators
of it. Fourth, he mounts a case against collective responsibility. Central
to this is the argument that collective responsibility presupposes that
Aboriginal and non-Aboriginal Australia are represented by two undifferentiated communities, but that it is difficult, if not impossible, to
establish that they are undifferentiated. There is no Aboriginal nation
as such but instead a mix of urban and rural Aboriginal peoples with
disparate interests and this is mirrored by non-Aboriginal communities.

---

[30] Ibid., p. 349.
[31] Chandran Kukathas, 'The Politics of Responsibility: How to Shift the Burden', unpublished paper (1999), p. 9.

Even if there were undifferentiated communities, the more important point, for Kukathas, is that

> there is no sense in which collectivities or communities can relate to one another, since communities themselves are not agents. Communities may relate to one another through agents – whether these be persons or institutions – but they cannot do so without them.
>
> Furthermore, if a community is to be held responsible there has to be some agent (or agents) who can be identified as responsible.[32]

The force of this argument, in Kukathas' reasoning, is that the collectivist approach 'does little to tell us who should be responsible and why', but more importantly that it shifts the burden on to society as a whole. Societies and communities, in his view, 'cannot act and, so, cannot act responsibly'.[33]

Later on, he argues that while communities and societies cannot be held responsible, associations with an authority structure can. 'Associations are groups which comprise individuals whose relations are ordered in such a way as to require them to take decisions on behalf of the group as a whole.'[34] Examples of associations are thus churches and the states, which have indeed been responsible for many past injustices. This leads him to state that responsibility does lie with institutions and not individuals, though 'individuals can be held responsible for not performing their institutional duties, or obstructing others from carrying out theirs'. At this point the argument has denied collective responsibility, accepted that associations can be responsible but denied that individuals other than those acting as agents of associations can be held 'directly responsible for the sins of the past or their consequences'.[35]

In the final part of his argument Kukathas asserts that responsibility is essential to a good society and repeats that responsibility must be located in agents. The burden of his argument now shifts to concern about the state as an agent. If it is the agent, then responsibility shifts to the state, but the state is an agent of society generally. This means the responsibility is shifted back to society, which is precisely what has been ruled out earlier in the argument. Laying responsibility at the feet of society would, he points out, reopen the individualist question of why citizens should be held responsible. Furthermore, as a liberal concerned with freedom and paring back the power of the state, Kukathas argues for 'denationalizing if not thoroughly privatizing responsibility'. Thus

---

[32] Ibid., p. 13.   [33] Ibid., p. 15.   [34] Ibid., p. 17.   [35] Ibid., p. 18.

a society in which responsibility is taken seriously has to be, in some way, a free society. For it must be a society in which responsibility – like power – is not concentrated but dispersed. It must not be a society in which it is easy for some [to] pass on responsibility to others, or for a few others to arrogate it to themselves. To some extent, to be able to take over responsibility is to be able to take power.[36]

The problem with this is that it is difficult, in the foreseeable future, to envisage a shift to individual responsibility that would result in the settlement of existing resentments and grievances arising from past injustices. To defer dealing with these until there are a sufficient number of individuals willing to identify themselves as responsible agents would be to do nothing. Locating the burden of responsibility in the manner preferred by Kukathas is essentially an ideal that may be unattainable.

Waldron's concern is not so much with whether there is collective responsibility for historic injustices as with whether there should be reparation for them, particularly with respect to the dispossession of land. 'People, or whole peoples, were attacked, defrauded, and expropriated; their lands stolen and their lives ruined',[37] but what, if any, reparation is owed? At the outset Waldron links the identity of individuals and communities alike to remembrance of past acts. Individuals establish a sense of themselves by reference to past acts. For communities this is even more important, for they outlast individuals and have a longer memory. 'To neglect the historical record is to do violence to this identity and thus the community that it sustains. And since communities help generate a deeper sense of identity for the individuals they comprise, neglecting or expunging the historical record is a way of undermining and insulating individuals as well.'[38] Waldron accepts that reparations are an important way of recognising that past injustices occurred, and are a way of apologising. Even if the form of reparation is symbolic it may be none the less important. 'Since identity is bound up with symbolism, a symbolic gesture may be as important to people as any material compensation.'[39] His purpose is to draw attention to the difficulties that may attend giving in to demands for reparations.

Waldron identifies and deals in turn with three different approaches that cast doubt on the wisdom of reparations: counterfactual reasoning about what might have happened if the injustices had not occurred; the possibility that injustices fade with time; and that over time the

---

[36] Ibid., p. 20. [37] Waldron, 'Superseding Historic Injustice', p. 4.
[38] Ibid., p. 6. [39] Ibid., p. 7.

circumstances that made an act unjust can change. The first of these concerns 'what would have happened if some event (which did occur) had not taken place'.[40] What, for example, would the tribal owners of land have done with it had it not been wrongfully appropriated? 'How would they have exercised their choice?' The purpose of such interrogation is to discover if the descendants of those who suffered injustice would now be better off than they are and the descendants of those who perpetrated the injustice worse off. 'The counter-factual approach [thus] aims to bring the present state of affairs as close to the state of affairs that would have obtained if some specifically identified injustice had not occurred.'[41] Waldron argues that this involves working through what he calls a 'contagion of injustice'. In other words, a chain of connected claims of justice that cannot be satisfied without a comprehensive redistribution of what is being contested. His conclusion is that in the final analysis it is probably impossible to reconstruct the past in a way that would be fair to those living at present.

The second of the approaches argues from the effects of the passage of time on entitlement to land. Here the starting point is the assumption that expropriation is a continuing injustice. Even though the original owners who were expropriated may be long dead it is argued that the tribes or groups to which they belonged live on and '[i]t is this enduring entity that has been dispossessed'. This also leads to difficulties, especially over whether entitlement survives and whether the passage of time diminishes the moral importance of rights to land. One argument concerning this is that after several generations 'certain wrongs' come to be seen 'as simply not worth correcting'. After a long period of time, it might be difficult to establish exactly who had what rights. Further, the use of land over time may establish the rights of claimants other than the 'original' occupants. In working through these arguments Waldron cites Locke's labour theory of property. We cannot, Waldron argues, 'dismiss out of hand the possibility that an expropriator may also in time replace the original embedded labor of the person she expropriated with something of her own'.[42] In closing his discussion of this approach he observes that '[h]istorical entitlements are most impressive when moral entitlement is conjoined with present possession',[43] and he draws attention to the extra credence accorded to claims involving sacred sites. Notwithstanding these exceptions his conclusion is that the passage of time does generally tend to diminish property rights.

---

[40] Ibid., p. 8.   [41] Ibid., p. 13.   [42] Ibid., p. 17.   [43] Ibid., p. 19.

Third, there is the proposition that what is an unjust act under one set of circumstances may under altered circumstances be just. Waldron uses the acquisition of land as an example. 'A scale of acquisition that might be appropriate in a plentiful environment with a small population may be quite inappropriate in the same environment with a large population, or with the same population once resources have become depleted. In a plentiful environment with a small population, an individual appropriation of land makes no one worse off.'[44] In support of this he cites Locke's argument, mentioned in Chapter 3:

> He that leaves as much as another man can make use of, does as good as take nothing at all. No Body could think himself injur'd by the drinking of another Man, though he took a good Draught, who had a whole River of the same Water left him to quench his thirst. And the case of Land and Water, where there is enough of both, is perfectly the same.[45]

To this Waldron adds that Locke himself recognised that 'the picture changed once the population increased to the point where scarcity was felt'.[46] He thus concludes that '[c]hanging circumstances can have an effect on ownership rights notwithstanding the moral legitimacy of the original appropriation'.[47] Claims about injustice he maintains, must, be responsive to changes of circumstance and if they are it seems likely that past injustices can be superseded.

There are at least four objections to Waldron's treatment of historic injustices. First, the example of land acquisition and the appeal to Locke just mentioned perpetuates another form of injustice by ignoring indigenous beliefs and subordinating them to Western political theory. Locke's argument did not take into account indigenous patterns of land use and belief systems that might have led to a different view concerning the justice or otherwise of appropriating native lands.

Second, the argument that altered circumstances can result in past injustices being superseded is too closely tied to the appropriation of land. It is not just a matter of land but also of destroyed or at least degraded cultures, and the loss, as Waldron himself recognises, of identity. With the loss of land came structures of oppression and domination that are not, if at all, easily superseded. Susan Dodds objects that Waldron's argument assumes land can be reduced to cash value but that there is no

---

[44] Ibid., p. 21.
[45] John Locke, *Two Treatises of Government*, ed. M. Goldie (London: Everyman, 1993), Book 2, Section 33, cited by Waldron, 'Superseding Historic Injustice', p. 21.
[46] Ibid., p. 21.   [47] Ibid., p. 24.

such commensurability. Indigenous peoples claim a spiritual relationship with land which suggests that it can be valued in different ways.
Not only that but

> rights over the same piece of land can be exercised simultaneously by
> holders of different land rights. Waldron's assumptions – that rights
> over land must be assigned wholly to one or another party and that
> all value in land is readily commensurable – oversimplify the value
> placed on land and the rights that can be held over land within a
> shared schema of land rights.[48]

As the aftermath of the Wik case in the High Court of Australia demonstrated, this is a controversial argument. The High Court determined
that native title could be held over land for which pastoral leases had
been issued. This prompted bitter debate and eventually legislation intended to codify the rights of pastoral and mining interests claimed that
the two were incompatible.

Third, Waldron's criteria for justice are not clearly spelt out but are
based on distribution. If different criteria, such as the oppression and
domination, as suggested by Iris Young,[49] were used, a different picture
might emerge. But in contemplating this it should be observed that the
logic of claims to self-determination suggest that emancipation from
structures of oppression and domination might depend on distributive
questions connected with land.

Fourth, Susan Dodds finds fault with Waldron's argument concerning
the example of New Zealand and the Treaty of Waitangi. Her objection
is that his argument '[s]lips between levels of debate: between responses
to injustice committed by one nation to another nation with which it has
a treaty and between citizens within a nation'.[50] The significance of this
is that the criteria for judging what is appropriate in the one situation
may not be at all appropriate in the other.

In the end we are left still needing to ask what can be done to resolve
the differences between communities that see themselves as the victims
of injustices and the descendants of those accused of having perpetrated
them. Where the injustices are to do with the appropriation of land, the
destruction of culture or genocide, there may be no way of correcting
them. The only possibility may be a frank admission that these things

---

[48] Susan Dodds, 'Justice, Indigenous Rights and Liberal Property Theory: Reflections on
Two Australian Cases', unpublished paper (1997), p. 11.
[49] Iris Marion Young, *Justice and the Politics of Difference* (Princeton University Press, 1990).
See discussion below.
[50] Dodds, 'Justice, Indigenous Rights', p. 11.

happened, coupled with an apology, not as the perpetrators of the injustices but as people who have benefited from them. This could be seen as engagement in a process of what Archbishop Desmond Tutu calls 'restorative justice', which he describes as the 'healing of breaches, the addressing of imbalances, the restoration of broken relationships . . . justice, restorative justice, is being served when efforts are being made to work for healing, for forgiveness and for reconciliation'.[51] This brings us back to Todorov and Nandy and the responsibility to engage in dialogue meant to understand others in their own terms as part of a search for common ground. Kukathas denies that this will solve past injustices: 'In part this is because dialogue in itself . . . will add little to the solution of a problem if the problem is the problem.' 'Endless discourse over an intractable problem', he observes, is unlikely to be productive.[52] This is too glib. The consequences of the failure to engage with others in the past is as much an historic injustice as those at the root of Waldron's concern with reparations. But an important difference is that the project suggested by Blaney and Inayatullah, building on Todorov and Nandy, is one that does not involve the complications that worry Waldron. It does not involve a redistribution of land or resources and so does not involve the issues of justice embedded in redistribution. This is not to say that there should not be redistributions or that they are not needed. Indeed, the dialogue suggested by Todorov's notion of collective responsibility is a necessary prelude to settling historic injustices that might involve redistribution issues.

The moral legitimacy of states and international society

The following discussion of moral legitimacy is framed only with reference to states containing minority indigenous populations. It should also be noted that the moral legitimacy of states is related to, but not coterminus with, political legitimacy. At the same time as the moral legitimacy of a particular state may be in question, the legitimacy of both its government and its international standing may be so widely accepted as to be beyond question. An example of this is Australia. Its moral legitimacy can be and is questioned because of both the way its Aboriginal peoples were dispossessed and its continued treatment of them; but neither

---

[51] Desmond Tutu, *No Future Without Forgiveness* (London: Rider, 1999), pp. 51–2.
[52] Kukathas, 'Politics of Responsibility', p. 14.

the political legitimacy of its government nor its place in international society have been an issue. In contrast, the moral legitimacy of a particular state may be so much at issue that the legitimacy of both its government and its international standing are either in jeopardy or not accepted. Of this an obvious example is South Africa before the end of apartheid. Its moral, political and international legitimacy were all rejected by black South Africans and a majority of other states. Standing on the continuum between these two examples might be China. Its treatment of Tibetans poses a serious question about its moral legitimacy. For some this is sufficient grounds to question its political and international legitimacy, but it is not in the situation that South Africa was prior to April 1994.

The sense of moral legitimacy that I am seeking to establish is suggested by the example of Australia just mentioned. When Britain occupied New South Wales it denied prior ownership of territory by the indigenous inhabitants, who are now known to have a history stretching at least as far back as 40,000 years. Following European occupation Aborigines were systematically dispossessed of their land, killed and deprived of their culture. The British claimed to be the first occupiers of Australia and this claim 'was the moral and legal foundation for settlement of the continent'.[53] To repeat Tim Rowse's words '"Australia" is morally illegitimate to the extent that it is founded on European denial of the continent's prior ownership by indigenous people.'[54] In the first instance then moral legitimacy refers to the circumstances under which a state had its origins. This need not be confined to the colonisation of non-Europeans by Europeans but may be extended also to cases such as the subjugation of the Scots and the Welsh by the English to create Great Britain or to the actions of non-Europeans against other non-Europeans.

In addition to the circumstances of the origin of particular states, the current treatment of indigenous peoples within states is a further dimension of moral legitimacy. The treatment of Tibetans within China has already been mentioned. Other examples include the genocide of Ache Indians in Paraguay[55] during the 1970s and the current situation of West Papuans. The future of indigenous West Papuans is threatened by Indonesia's transmigration policy and their human rights have been violated by actions against them involving Indonesian military forces and private security forces at the Freeport mine site. These and other

---

[53] Reynolds, *The Law of the Land*.   [54] Rowse, 'Mabo and Moral Anxiety'.
[55] See Richard Arens (ed.), *Genocide in Paraguay* (Philadelphia: Temple University Press, 1976).

cases all differ and it is useful to think of the variation as a spectrum of qualitative differences. Each case is different but involves, in common with the others, some degree or combination of subjugation, dispossession, and cultural or even physical genocide. The moral legitimacy of a state is thrown into question by the presence of one or more of these, either as part of a process of state formation resulting in a legacy of injustices towards disadvantaged and powerless indigenous groups or by ongoing state practices. It follows from this that a requirement of moral legitimacy is the absence of practices detrimental to indigenous peoples, conducted either as a policy of the state or with its knowledge in circumstances where it could act to prevent what is being done, but chooses not to do so.

A morally illegitimate state is one that either had its origins in the dispossession of indigenous peoples whose descendants continue to be dispossessed in important ways, and have unresolved claims against the settler state, or one in which there continue to be practices that discriminate against and threaten the survival of indigenous peoples within its borders. It is, in short, one that has harmed or continues to harm particular peoples and has yet to negotiate a mutually agreed reconciliation. To be regarded as morally legitimate a state needs to have done as much as it reasonably can to seek reconciliation with its indigenous peoples, to secure their rights and ensure the survival of indigenous cultures in accordance not only with the wishes of those that belong to them, but also international instruments such as the International Covenant on Civil and Political Rights.

I want to suggest that the achievement of moral legitimacy requires recognition and mutual agreement between indigenous peoples and the majority settler societies in which they are located. The failure to achieve this has been one of the major political problems arising from European conquest. I want to suggest also that moral legitimacy with regard to indigenous peoples depends on accepting difference, the recognition of cultural rights, and justice understood as the absence of domination and oppression. In order to pursue this line of inquiry the following discussion draws on the work of Iris Young,[56] Charles Taylor[57] and Will Kymlicka.[58]

[56] Young, *Justice and the Politics*.
[57] Charles Taylor, 'The Politics of Recognition', in Amy Gutman (ed.), *Multiculturalism: Examining the Politics of Recognition* (Princeton University Press, 1994).
[58] Will Kymlicka, *Liberalism, Community and Culture* (Oxford: Clarendon Press, 1989). See also Kymlicka's later *Multicultural Citizenship: A Liberal Theory of Minority Rights* (Oxford: Clarendon Press, 1995).

In her *Justice and the Politics of Difference*, Young rejects distribution as a criteria for justice and argues that domination and oppression should be 'the primary terms for conceptualising injustice' with regard to social groups. Her argument is 'that where different groups exist and some groups are privileged while others are oppressed, social justice requires explicitly acknowledging and attending to those group differences in order to undermine oppression'.[59] Young proposes that oppression may take one or more of five forms which she identifies as exploitation, marginalization, powerlessness, cultural imperialism and violence. She accepts that distributive issues are important but argues that 'other important aspects of justice include decision making procedures, the social division of labour, and culture'.[60] Distributive injustices, she argues 'may contribute to or result from these forms of oppression but none is reducible to distribution and all involve social structures and relations beyond distribution'. Consequently, for Young '[t]he concept of justice is coextensive with the political', and her definition of politics is Hannah Pitkin's: it is 'the activity through which relatively large and permanent groups determine what they will collectively do, settle how they will live together, and decide their future, to whatever extent this is within their power'.[61] According to this, justice demands that different groups are all able to represent their particular interests and participate in making the decisions that affect their future. The denial of difference means that particular needs and interests are not given due consideration and so contributes to oppression.

Participation in decision-making is crucial to Young's account of the politics of difference and justice. Social justice means 'the elimination of institutionalized domination and oppression'.[62] Domination 'consists in institutional conditions which inhibit or prevent people from participating in determining their actions or the conditions of their actions. Persons live within structures of domination if other persons or groups can determine without reciprocation the conditions of their action, either directly or by virtue of the structural consequences of their actions.'[63] The groups she has in mind are social groups defined by a sense of identity. A social group in this sense 'is collective of persons differentiated from at least one other group by cultural forms, practices, or way of life'.[64] Whether or not such a group is oppressed depends on whether it is subject to one or more of the five forms of oppression already mentioned. All of which fit, in some degree and at one time or

[59] Young, *Justice and the Politics*, p. 3.   [60] Ibid., p. 9.   [61] Ibid., p. 9.
[62] Ibid., p. 15.   [63] Ibid., p. 38.   [64] Ibid., p. 43.

another, indigenous peoples constituted as cultural groups – but cultural imperialism is particularly relevant. In Young's framework it is unjust because 'the oppressed group's own experience and interpretation of social life finds little expression that touches the dominant culture, while that same culture imposes on the oppressed group its experience and interpretation of social life'.[65]

In turning explicitly to the politics of difference, Young contrasts the assimilationist vision of the good society with one founded on the concept of 'democratic cultural pluralism'. The assimilationist vision is one that seeks to 'eliminate or transcend group difference' and denies 'either the reality or the desirability of social groups'. In the examples of Australia and Canada assimilationist policies are aimed at eliminating difference. By contrast, one vision of the good society is that it is one that defends democratic cultural pluralism, sustains 'equality among socially and culturally differentiated groups, who mutually respect one another and affirm one another in their differences'.[66] In this version of the good society difference is recognised and affirmed as something positive.

For Taylor the contrast is between the politics of universalism and of difference. The politics of universalism emphasises 'the equal dignity of all citizens, and the content of this politics has been the equalization of rights and entitlements'.[67] According to this notion of 'universal dignity' there should be no discrimination between citizens; all should be treated alike. The politics of difference seeks instead recognition of the unique identity of an individual or group and tolerates differential treatment. 'Where the politics of universal dignity fought for forms of non-discrimination that were quite "blind" to the ways in which citizens differ, the politics of difference often redefines non-discrimination as requiring that we make these distinctions the basis of differential treatment.' As an example Taylor cites giving Aboriginal groups rights not enjoyed by other citizens.[68] Where indigenous rights have been granted it has resulted in controversy fuelled by political movements such as One Nation in Australia, and in conflict between indigenous and human rights; as, for example, in the cases of *Canada* vs. *Lovelace*, *Sweden* vs. *Kitok*[69] and *Thomas* vs. *Norris*.[70]

---

[65] Ibid., p. 60.   [66] Ibid., p. 63.
[67] Taylor, 'Politics of Recognition', p. 37.   [68] Ibid., p. 39.
[69] Steiner and Alston (eds.), *Human Rights in Context*, pp. 1017–19, and Anaya, *Indigenous Peoples*, p. 101.
[70] Eisenberg, 'The Politics of Individual and Group Difference', p. 3.

Granting indigenous rights appears to entail abandoning the principle of equal dignity and the idea that all people should be treated alike. A justification for reverse or positive discrimination is that it is, as Taylor puts it, a necessary temporary measure to achieve a level playing field. But, as he goes on to point out, the politics of difference does not want a return to the 'difference blind' social space that would be the result of a level playing field. It wants instead 'to maintain and cherish distinctness, not just now but forever'.[71] Both the politics of equal dignity and the politics of difference are in his account based on the notion of equal respect but come into conflict over the 'underlying intuitions of value' embedded in each. In the logic of the politics of difference the judgement that one culture is less valuable than another is 'not only factually but also morally wrong'. 'Even to entertain [the] possibility [of one being less valuable] is to deny human equality.'[72] Taylor sums up his discussion of these opposing views with the observation that the politics of dignity reproaches the politics of difference for violating the principle of non-discrimination; the latter reproaches the former for 'negat[ing] identity by forcing people into a homogeneous mold that is untrue to them'. This, he continues

> would be bad enough if the mold were itself neutral – nobody's mold in particular. But the complaint generally goes further. The claim is that the supposedly neutral set of difference-blind principles of the politics of equal dignity is in fact a reflection of one hegemonic culture. As it turns out, then, only the minority or suppressed cultures are being forced to take alien form. Consequently, the supposed fair and difference-blind society is not only inhuman (because suppressing identities) but also in a subtle and unconscious way, itself highly discriminatory.[73]

The goal of 'universal dignity' is then one that contains the risk of, if not entails, the ascendancy of one cultural group over others. The effacement of difference is not a result of neutral and universal values but instead represents the perpetuation of cultural imperialism. To participate fully in social life minority groups must set aside those aspects of their culture that clash with the culture of mainstream society.

The idea that all people can be measured by a common standard is, Young points out, one that 'generates a logic of difference as hierarchical dichotomy . . .'. Whether it is the opposition of masculine and feminine or civilised and savage, the second term always denotes negative or

[71] Taylor, 'Politics of Recognition', p. 40.   [72] Ibid., p. 42.   [73] Ibid., p. 43.

inferior qualities. Consequently '[t]he marking of difference always implies a good/bad opposition; it is always a devaluation, the naming of an inferiority in relation to a superior standard of humanity'.[74] Against this the politics of difference asserts that cultural differences should not lead to exclusion, opposition or dominance, but to relationships based on the recognition and acceptance of those differences. It seeks to overturn the negative or 'oppressive' meaning that has generally been given to difference.

The concern with equal dignity does not end with the recognition of difference. It crops up again in connection with rights of cultural groups, and whether such groups should be given rights that are not available to other members of the society to which they belong. The democratic cultural pluralism advocated by Young would, she says, require 'a dual system of rights: a general system of rights which are the same for all, and a more specific system of group-conscious policies and rights'.[75] Special rights for groups need, however, to be justified. Liberals, in particular, are commonly represented as believing that any proposals that would limit individual rights in favour of group rights should be opposed. An important exception to this is Kymlicka, who maintains that cultural rights can be defended from a liberal standpoint. For him cultural membership is important not only for liberal theory but also, as for Young, justice. 'Considering the nature of cultural membership not only takes us down into the deepest reaches of a liberal theory of the self, but also outward to some of the most pressing questions of justice and injustice in the modern world.'[76] My concern with his argument is not so much his defence of liberalism as the case he makes for cultural or collective rights.

The kinds of group rights Kymlicka has in mind are those meant to preserve cultural identity and community. In Chapter 4, for example, it was shown how Aboriginal demands for land and self-determination are linked to the survival of Aboriginal cultural identity. Many liberals argue that measures such as the granting of land rights that are meant to protect communities are in fact unjust because they perpetuate 'ethnic or racial inequality',[77] and that in some cases they are rights gained at the expense of individual rights and so value the group over the individual.

---

[74] Young, *Justice and the Politics*, p. 170.   [75] Ibid., p. 175.
[76] Kymlicka, *Liberalism, Community and Culture*, p. 258, and see Amy Gutmann in Gutmann (ed.), *Multiculturalism: Examining the Politics of Recognition* (Princeton University Press, 1994).
[77] Kymlicka, *Liberalism, Community and Culture*, p. 150.

Kymlicka's solution is to defend the value of cultural membership as an essential source of individual worth.

An important step in the development of his argument is that political community is not necessarily coterminus with cultural community. Political communities may contain two or more cultural communities, and, as already mentioned in the preceding discussion of Young, one cultural group may dominate. If so there may be a case for giving the subordinate group, or groups, special rights; then this is at odds with both the notion of universal equality and the liberal emphasis on individual rights. Kymlicka thus argues that to defend minority rights within liberalism it is necessary to establish two things. First, that cultural membership has a more important status in liberal thought than is explicitly recognised. Second, that members of cultural minorities may be disadvantaged such that to rectify these disadvantages both justifies and requires minority rights. In other words, it is necessary 'to show that membership in a cultural community may be a relevant criterion for distributing benefits and burdens which are the concern of a liberal theory of justice'. His case for this is that the fate of cultural structures matters because it is only through them that individuals are able to fully gauge 'the options available to them, and intelligently examine their value'.[78] From this perspective cultural membership may be seen as a primary good that should be protected. 'Cultural membership is important in pursuing our essential interest in leading a good life, and so consideration of that membership is an important part of having equal consideration for the interests of each member of the community.'[79] Or, on the next page: 'Liberal values require both individual freedom of choice and a secure cultural context from which individuals can make their choices.'[80] Later still, cultural membership 'affects our very sense of personal identity and capacity'.[81] In this way he seeks to reconcile special measures to protect group rights with the individual choice that is at the core of the liberalism he chooses to defend.[82]

This concern with cultural membership and liberal values is extended in the more recent *Citizenship in Diverse Societies*, in which Kymlicka

---

[78] Ibid., p. 165.   [79] Ibid., p. 168.   [80] Ibid., p. 169.

[81] Ibid., p. 193. For a rebuttal of Kymlicka see Chandran Kukathas, 'Are There Any Cultural Rights?', *Political Theory*, 20: 1 (1992). The same issue contains a riposte from Kymlicka.

[82] A similar argument is mounted by Eisenberg who writes that 'A politics of group difference shares the goal of enhancing individual well-being, but does so while recognising that individual well-being is often dependent on the well-being of groups.' Eisenberg, 'The Politics of Individual and Group Difference, p. 12.

and Norman take up the question of 'how emerging theories of minority rights and multiculturalism affect the virtues of democratic citizenship'.[83] A core question in that book is 'whether there is a notion of citizenship for multi-ethnic states that fairly accommodates ethno-cultural differences, while still maintaining and promoting the sorts of virtues, practices, institutions, and solidarity needed for a flourishing democracy'.[84] This however takes us beyond the scope of the book.

My purpose in canvassing the issues raised by Young, Taylor and Kymlicka[85] has been to clarify what it means to talk about the moral legitimacy of states with indigenous people making claims against the governments and other citizens of those states. The argument is that the moral legitimacy of a state with a significant indigenous population depends in the first instance on the manner in which the state was founded. In the second instance, moral legitimacy is a matter of the current situation of the indigenous population. What I have tried to suggest is that moral legitimacy in this regard rests on the degree to which three conditions are being satisfied. First, that along with the elimination of oppression and domination coupled with participation in decision-making structures that affect them, there is a deliberate programme aimed at achieving justice for indigenous populations. Second, that there is a recognition of group difference in its positive sense and consequently a political system that supports rather than blocks a politics of group difference.[86] Third, that there is a recognition and legal expression of cultural and group rights in ways that leaves individuals free to live with the strictures of their cultural group or alternatively those of the wider community. Next to be considered is the assertion made earlier that the moral legitimacy of international society rests upon the moral legitimacy of the states that constitute it. To do that we must begin by asking what it means to talk about the morality of international society.

International morality in the framework of international society refers to actions that respect and uphold the norms of interstate behaviour meant to govern the mutual relations of states. These are the norms of sovereignty, equality and independence. They form part of the litany of any conventional introduction to international politics and scarcely

---

[83] Kymlicka and Norman (eds.), *Citizenship in Diverse Societies*, p. 1.   [84] Ibid., p. 17.
[85] See also the discussion of Young, Kymlicka and Tully in John Bern and Susan Dodds, 'On the Plurality of Interests: Aboriginal Self-Government and Land Rights', in Ivison, Patton and Sanders (eds.), *Political Theory and the Rights of Indigenous Peoples*, pp. 166–73.
[86] Concerning difference see also Young, *Inclusion and Democracy*, pp. 99–102.

need to be spelt out. Sovereignty refers in this connection to the principle that all states have, in theory, supreme authority over their own internal affairs. They are supposedly free to conduct their affairs as they choose without interference from other states, and governments seize on this to hide from international scrutiny. States accused of human rights violations typically claim that this is a domestic matter in which the international community should not interfere. Equality is the idea that all states, irrespective of their size and natural endowments, are, for the purposes of international law, equal. Independence follows from both of these. States that are sovereign and equal are said also to be independent and this is held to be inviolable. The corollary of all three is the principle of non-intervention, which is the primary norm of international relations. In support of the principle of sovereignty states have a duty set down in Article 2(1) of the Charter of the United Nations not to intervene in each other's affairs.[87]

The equality of states is of course a legal fiction; they are rarely equal in any way other than at law. Similarly, they do not have complete sovereignty and independence. In spite of their formal sovereign equality and independence, some states never have more than limited sovereignty. That is because they must take account of other states and in so doing may be constrained to make choices they would not otherwise make. Apart from this, sovereignty is increasingly questioned. In the contemporary world, states often have diminished and even no control over decisions that are crucial to their well-being. 'It is now more difficult to separate actions that solely affect a nation's affairs from those that have an impact on the internal affairs of other states, and hence to define the legitimate boundaries of sovereign authority.'[88] The effect of the increasing interdependence of states is that concepts such as territoriality,[89] independence and non-intervention are either losing their meaning or acquiring a new one. It is now increasingly argued that there are situations where the principle of non-intervention should, for humanitarian reasons, be over-ridden.[90]

---

[87] For an account of this view of international morality see Robert Jackson, *The Global Covenant: Human Conduct in a World of States* (Oxford University Press, 2000), pp. 178–82.
[88] Commission on Global Governance, *Our Global Neighbourhood: The Report of the Commission on Global Governance* (Oxford University Press, 1995), p. 70.
[89] See, for example, John Ruggie, 'Territoriality and Beyond: Problematising Modernity in International Relations', *International Organisation*, 47: 1 (1993).
[90] For arguments about this see Nicholas J. Wheeler, *Saving Strangers: Humanitarian Intervention in International Society* (Oxford University Press, 2000) and Donnelly 'Human Rights, 1–24.

A major purpose of international society is to maintain the degree of order between states necessary for the preservation of the states system. International order is consequently a primary concern for international society. Without international order, individual states and perhaps the states system itself are in jeopardy. This implies that states and the state system are worth preserving and hence that international society is to be valued for the role it has in achieving the goal of social coexistence. If indeed international society is able to maintain a degree of international order sufficient to avoid a catastrophic war; dissuade or prevent states from oppressing and taking the autonomy of the citizens of other states; or prevent the rise of an oppressive empire, that should be regarded as all to the good. In an earlier chapter it was suggested that the moral basis of international order extends beyond this and is to be valued to the extent that it delivers 'world order'. International society has a universal basis so long as it fosters the well-being of individuals everywhere. Essentially, international society is the means to international order which is in turn a means to promoting world order. In this scheme states have moral legitimacy to the extent that they promote the values of world order. To the extent that they do so, states are in and of themselves a good thing.

Here it is necessary to distinguish between the state as a form of political organisation and life within the state. The purpose of the state is contested but let us say that it is or should be to provide a framework within which citizens can pursue their own chosen vision of the good life. If that is what states do then we can say that they are good as a form of political organisation. The good state is then one that helps to reconcile competing claims concerning the good life, and assists in the realization of at least some of these claims. It is then also a state that is concerned with the pursuit of justice within its borders. In the context of international relations, however, the 'good state' takes on a different meaning. It refers not to the domestic arrangements within the state, but in a minimal sense to whether its actions in relation to other states conform to international morality. Beyond that minimal sense it may refer additionally to 'good international citizenship'[91] in the sense of being a state that has concern for the welfare of other states and peoples and contributes, as a matter of duty, to the maintenance of international order. A bad state, in each of these senses, would by contrast be one

[91] Andrew Linklater, 'What is a Good International Citizen?', in P. Keal (ed.), *Ethics and Foreign Policy* (Sydney: Allen & Unwin in association with the Department of International Relations, Australian National University, 1992).

that oppresses its citizens, prevents or inhibits them from pursuing a good life, habitually violates the norms of interstate relations, detracts from rather than contributes to international order, and is unconcerned by the welfare of other states or of particular groups within them. The good state is one that has concern for justice; leaving aside how we are to define this, both within its borders and in relations between states.

We are now in a position to consider more closely the claim that the moral legitimacy of international society is contingent upon the moral legitimacy of the individual states that comprise it. In Chapter 1 three of the claims made about international society were, first, that its expansion involved a process of subjugation, oppression and domination; second, that international society was a society of empires; and third, that it excluded particular peoples until they were able to cohere into or conform with European ideas of political organisation. It was in its inception not morally legitimate in relation to the way non-Europeans were treated. Our options for redressing the past are limited and what now counts is the continuing treatment of the descendants of peoples who were dispossessed. About this, the argument we are considering is that if a large number or even just a few key powerful states are morally illegitimate then the moral legitimacy of international society may be questioned. If through preserving the states system it protects morally illegitimate states while ignoring world order goals then its value should be doubted.

One way of dealing with this is to follow the strategy for dealing with cultural incommensurability once suggested by Chris Brown, which is discussed in Chapter 6. We could adopt the view that as long as order between states is maintained, domestic conditions within them do not matter and the moral legitimacy of international society as something that preserves the state systems is not affected. My response to this is that we should be concerned about a world in which a majority of states, a few states, or even just one, habitually torture, commit genocide, oppress, dominate or deprive minorities, or allow racist practices. Why should we want to preserve something that has as its purpose protecting political organisations that have the right to engage in such practices?

In the end, we must, I think, be concerned about justice in the sense defended by Young. Distribution is only part of the story and does not preclude injustices for which the criteria is oppression and domination. These criteria should, I think, be extended to international justice which is surely crucial to world order. If they were, and if it could be demonstrated that by preserving states international society was also supporting structures of oppression and domination – rather than combating and breaking them down – then it could be said that international society is, to that extent, morally illegitimate. It might then not be worth preserving unless the consequences of failing to do so would make matters worse.

It follows from what has been said so far that the more states there are that can be accepted as morally legitimate the stronger the claim that international society has moral legitimacy. Morally legitimate states in the sense spelt out in this chapter are also states that safeguard if not promote world order values. There are essentially two ways of maximising the number of morally legitimate states; either by other states using inducements, sanctions, force or other methods to encourage the practices that confer moral legitimacy, or by states voluntarily adopting such practices. If the latter requires that all states have shared values then a high degree of moral legitimacy in international society may be impossible to achieve.

6   Dealing with difference

The changing representations of indigenous peoples in international law discussed earlier reflect the evolution of European political theory. Prior to the establishment of a distinct positive international law, legal, political and moral reasoning were not separated into the distinct discourses they are more often than not assumed to be in contemporary theory and practice. As the example of Vattel writing Locke's ideas on property into international law showed, there was an important cross-fertilisation of ideas between political and legal writing. The two realms of thought were in many respects mutually constitutive, just as international law and international society have been. Preceding chapters have also shown that in European encounters with non-Europeans, difference and cultural incommensurability were important factors in shaping political and legal thought and in turn in denying the rights of indigenous peoples. Political and legal thought asserted the superiority of European culture and served to justify the dispossession of non-Europeans. As a whole, the study has been concerned to give indigenous peoples a more prominent place in the intellectual history of international society and this necessarily involves having to think about the impact cultural difference has on relationships both within states and across borders. This is not to say that culture has been neglected entirely by those concerned with understanding international society.

In an article that relates Martin Wight's three traditions of thought about international relations to understanding the nature of the European encounter with the 'first Australians', Timothy Dunne claims that 'certain thinkers . . . associated with the "English School" have not neglected questions of culture and identity'. This is, Dunne writes, especially true of Wight's lectures and he regards his own discussion of Wight as 'subversive of the recent claim that "culture and identity" are making a "dramatic comeback" in the post-Cold War period'.[1] Contrary to this, Dunne's view is that '[c]ivilisations, cultures, values, rules, encounters, meaning, and so on, have remained central to those working within the international society tradition (or "English School") from the early 1950s onwards'.[2] In support of this claim he singles out Wight's lecture on the 'Theory of Mankind: "Barbarians" '[3] as particularly significant, and claims: 'Arguably there is more attention to the question of cultural encounters in this one lecture than in the rest of mainstream International Relations thinking during the Cold War.'[4] Another way of putting this would be to say that while culture was not entirely neglected it has received only limited attention in international society scholarship.

As a scholar located in the English School, Dunne is concerned with the capacity of rationalism to comprehend the cultural pluralism of contemporary international society. He asks whether rationalism, as a vehicle for understanding international society, is 'a prisoner to its ethnocentric origins', and also whether it is able to empathise with the aspirations of indigenous peoples 'the world over'.[5] In the 'Theory of Mankind' lecture admired by Dunne, a fundamental question for Wight is: 'How far does international society extend?'[6] And in relation to this Wight makes the important point that rationalism in Europe began with the Spanish debate over the status of Amerindians that culminated in the 1550–51 disputation at Valladolid. In part this debate was precisely about the question of how far the international society of the time did and should extend. Dunne's assessment of Wight's lecture is that it 'reveals the moral ambiguities inherent in Rationalism: extending international law to encompass "barbarians" yet not granting them equal rights without calling into question the justice of the original possession of their lands; recognising the importance of protecting weaker "barbarian societies" only to segregate them in reserves'. In spite of this ambiguity Dunne clearly does think that rationalism can realise the potential immanent in it to reinvent itself, provided it can hold 'onto its progressive

---

[1] Dunne, 'Colonial Encounters in International Relations', p. 312. Dunne is referring to Yosef Lapid, 'Culture's Ship: Returns and Departures in International Relations Theory', in Lapid and F. Kratochwil (eds.), *The Return of Culture and Identity in IR Theory* (Boulder: Lynne Rienner, 1996).
[2] Dunne, 'Colonial Encounters', p. 312.
[3] Martin Wight, 'Theory of Mankind: "Barbarians" ', in Wight, Wight and Porter (eds.), *International Theory*.
[4] Dunne, 'Colonial Encounters', p. 310.   [5] Ibid., p. 310.
[6] Wight, 'Theory of Mankind', p. 49.

elements, such as its commitment to tolerating difference and its recognition of the existence of over-lapping rights and obligations in international society, while shedding its assumptions about racial superiority and the tendency in practice to accord primacy to the state as the "container" for community . . .'.[7]

Dunne's comments concerning the moral ambiguities of rationalism accord with the discussion, in Chapter 3, of the representation of non-Europeans in international law. The writings of Vitoria, Grotius and like-minded publicists support the view that the intellectual roots of rationalism tolerated both difference and the over-lapping rights and obligations entailed by including individuals in international society. These are elements that need to be recovered if the rationalist tradition is to provide a theoretical basis for the inclusion of indigenous peoples in the practices of international society. The acceptance of difference and the over-lapping rights and obligations attached to individuals were eroded as international society spread. Difference was progressively related to a hierarchy of stages of development, which justified the domination of less advanced peoples by Europeans. To reverse this, rationalism needs to borrow from disciplines beyond international relations and it might not be able to do that and at the same time remain distinct. Dunne is right in suggesting that rationalism needs to shed its tendency to regard the state as the 'container' of community, but this calls for being prepared to re-imagine community in ways that unravel the conception of international society presently enshrined in rationalist thought. One task of this chapter is to consider how political community might be re-imagined in ways that would extend the boundaries of moral community to allow for the cultural difference and self-determination of indigenous peoples.

The chapter first revisits the suggestions in Chapter 1 that international society is perhaps no more than an inner circle of states and that it has a moral basis to the extent that it delivers world order. It argues that world order must express more than merely the preferred values of the inner core if it is to avoid being part of a totalising project that suppresses difference. Next it argues that the classical theory in which rationalism is grounded codifies difference and serves to justify the imposition of Western values. Following that, it discusses how contemporary theory has sought to recognise and deal with difference in ways that seek to avoid the imposition of the values of one particular group over those

---

[7] Dunne, 'Colonial Encounters', p. 322.

of others. In the final part the focus shifts to frameworks available for rethinking community for the purpose of validating difference and extending the boundaries of moral community.

International society and world order

Like other kinds of society, contemporary international society is inevitably hierarchical. It has an inner core of states that set the criteria for membership and mutually recognise each other as full members. The criteria fixed by the inner circle of membership articulate rules of legitimacy and norms of behaviour. States that do not conform to these are relegated to an outer circle beyond the moral boundaries of the community comprising the inner circle. Since its inception international society has promulgated criteria for inclusion and exclusion and these change from one time to the next. In previous chapters we have seen how there was a progression from grounding these criteria in religion, to the capacity for reason, to the standard of civilisation – which projected European norms of social and political organisation on others – down to the present, in which there is increasing emphasis on the legitimacy of the internal constitution and practices of states. The differentiation between states, in this way, expresses standards of moral community that distinguish not only between states as being inside or outside international society, but also establish a hierarchy within it. Standards of moral community have more often than not involved low regard for the 'other'; and that is as true of internal as of external others.[8] Another way of putting this last point would be to say that even societies whose members appear to share a common culture have in their midst groups who are typed as different and may be marginalised.

Even so, to talk about an inner circle of states in the preceding manner is to suggest that members of that circle do have some fundamental values in common. Chris Brown suggests what these might be when he writes: 'Perhaps international society is a description that applies only to relations between states that are similarly constituted on broadly liberal lines, that is to say that it is only between such societies that normatively grounded relations are possible.'[9] Fred Halliday similarly

---

[8] See the discussion by Jacinta O'Hagan and Greg Fry, 'The Future of World Politics', in J. O'Hagan and G. Fry (eds.), *Contending Images of World Politics* (London: Macmillan, 2000), pp. 250–1.
[9] Chris Brown, 'Contractarian Thought and the Constitution of International Society', in T. Nardin and D. Mapel (eds.), *International Society: Diverse Ethical Perspectives* (Princeton University Press, 1998), p. 141.

depicts international society as being essentially limited to states that confer legitimacy on each other because of the similitude of their social and political make-up.[10] From this it follows that even though 'rightful' membership of it may be limited, there is nevertheless an international society of states. E. H. Carr, on the other hand, ventured that it is no more than something academics 'tried to conjure into existence'. In a letter to Stanley Hoffmann, he asserted: 'No international society exists, but an open club without substantive rules.'[11] Tim Dunne's interpretation of this interesting pronouncement is that Carr thought international society was a myth because of 'the structural inequality built into the system. Any society which accepts as "normal or permissible" discrimination between individuals, "on grounds of race, colour or natural allegiance", lacks the basic foundation for a moral order.'[12] This implies that if there is no such foundation there can be no actual international society.

In Chapter 1 it was suggested that a moral foundation for international society can be located in the concept of world order articulated by Hedley Bull, in which individuals are morally prior. Dunne argues that the moral universalism underpinning Bull's thought is evident in his 'insistence that individuals are the ultimate moral referent'. As mentioned earlier, Dunne's further suggestion is that, for Bull, international order 'is only to be valued to the extent which it delivers "world order"'.[13] Elsewhere I have argued that for international society to do that it would have to induce or enforce right conduct on the part of member states towards the people within their borders. It would mean international society deliberately acting in ways intended to curb actions that result in murder, torture, genocide, impoverishment and the denial of individual and collective rights.[14] And if international society does boil down to an inner circle of similarly constituted states, actions taken in its name would be ones agreed to or accepted by these few dominant states. For a culturally plural world in which there are cultural differences, both between states and within them, this is problematic. In the absence of agreement between all parties affected by actions intended to bolster world order, these actions might simply represent the imposition of the liberal or other values of core states. It is difficult to see how world order could in practice amount to more than the reproduction of the values of

---

[10] Halliday, *Rethinking International Relations*, ch. 5.
[11] Cited by Dunne, *Inventing International Society*, p. 35.
[12] Ibid., p. 35.   [13] Ibid., pp. 145–6.
[14] Paul Keal, 'An International Society?', in O'Hagan and Fry (eds.), *Contending Images*, p. 67.

dominant actors. In that case it would not be acceptable to those who hold different values and reject what they might justifiably regard as a totalising project enacted by the inner circle. The idea of a totalising project crops up later in connection with suggestions about extending the moral and political boundaries of community. The next section concerns the shortcomings of classical theory as a basis for conceptualising a more inclusive international society.

Omissions of classical theory

The principal theorists of international society and *ipso facto* of rationalism, have been people who self-consciously identify themselves with what Bull called the 'classical approach' to international relations theory. He defined this as one that employs the methods of history, law and philosophy.[15] More than just using the methods of these disciplines, the classical approach has also involved drawing on the ideas and findings contained in classic texts in a search for timeless truths that remain relevant to the present. Classic texts are often regarded as a source of wisdom that we ignore at our peril. In the words of Robert Jackson:

> the classical approach, certainly as understood by Wight and Bull, rests on a fundamental conviction: that there is more to be learned from the long history of speculation about international relations and from the many theorists who have contributed to that tradition than can be learned from any single generation alone – including the latest thought of the social science theorists of the past thirty years.[16]

In support of classical theory Jackson himself observes that contemporary international relations theory has lurched in the direction of attempting to interpret international relations in terms of the theories of other subjects. In so doing it has departed from attempting to work within, and extend the body of thought already developed within, the classical approach.

Various problems are inherent in a classical approach to thinking about European encounters with non-Europeans and cultural

---

[15] See Hedley Bull, 'International Theory: The Case for a Classical Approach', *World Politics*, 18: 3 (1966), and Hedley Bull, 'International Relations as an Academic Pursuit', in K. Alderson and A. Hurrell (eds.), *Hedley Bull on International Society* (London: Macmillan, 2000), ch. 9.
[16] Robert Jackson, 'Is There a Classical International Theory?', in S. Smith, K. Booth and M. Zalewski (eds.), *International Theory: Positivism and Beyond* (Cambridge University Press, 1996), p. 208. Also Jackson, *The Global Covenant*, p. 56.

difference. In the first place there is a danger, when using classical texts, of projecting the ideas of the present back into the past. In that case we may fail to see the world as people then did and apply to them the standards of our time. A further problem is that many canonical texts are, as Sanjay Seth argues about political theory, 'infused with orientalist assumptions and themes'. To study the Western tradition, to which they belong, 'is to study the history of Reason, as applied to politics; and it is to study and learn about the origins and premonitions of "our" (western) culture and thought'.[17]

In relation to this we saw, in earlier chapters, that in the early phases of the expansion of Europe key thinkers such as Vitoria regarded non-Europeans as fully human and entitled to the rights Europeans accorded to themselves. Non-Europeans were, however, progressively conceptualised by Europeans in ways that dehumanised them and represented their cultures or civilisations as inferior. The belief in their own superiority allowed Europeans to ignore the problem of mutual understanding between themselves and those who were 'different' or perceived as 'uncivilised'. By creating the concept of 'rational' and 'civilised' beings who were essentially European, and placing this above other conceptions of what it was to be fully human, Western theory not only denied cultural pluralism as a problem, it also imposed European (or Western) values as universal standards. The supposed superiority of European culture meant it was not considered necessary either to attempt to comprehend others in their own terms or to deal with them as equals. In essence, European political theory codified difference. Concern with the state and consolidation of structures of authority meant that 'uncivilised' non-Europeans were cited as negative examples to demonstrate the superiority of European forms of social and political organisation. The texts of classical political theory supported dispossession and help us to understand how and why 'less civilised' non-Europeans were excluded from the rights Europeans conferred upon themselves and conceded to each other. They are not helpful as a source for the development of an international political theory that would both situate indigenous peoples in international political theory and provide a normative framework for recapturing, extending and grounding their rights. To do this we may need to resort to the insights of disciplines other than those that have informed the classical approach. The next section canvasses examples of

---

[17] Sanjay Seth, 'A Critique of Disciplinary Reason: The Limits of Political Theory', *Alternatives*, 26: 1 (2001), 76.

how the insights of other disciplines have been applied to contemporary international relations theory dealing with difference.

The problem of cross-cultural understanding

In a 1988 special issue of *Millennium*, Chris Brown proposed that a pressing theoretical task was to formulate a coherent account of the moral underpinnings of North–South relations.[18] He argued that because of increasing levels of diversity, cultural pluralism had become more rather than less important with the passage of time, and that the existence of a set of cosmopolitan values, as a normative base for relations between these cultures, could not be assumed. Among other factors casting doubt on cosmopolitan values is the post-modernist and anti-foundationalist turn which has questioned and unsettled certainty about the Western values that issued from the Enlightenment. Brown proposed the idea of international society as one way, perhaps the most promising if not the only way, of accommodating cultural diversity. His premise for this was that the state, as a political form, was now 'divorced from its Western origins and part of the common property of mankind'.[19] Despite its origins as a 'western cultural export' it is now a universally accepted form. Thus international society founded on the morality of states can provide a framework for relations between states that represent diverse cultures. The logic of this is that the rules that constitute international society amount to a morality of states in which the ethic of coexistence is paramount. Essentially, Brown's argument, at that time, was that so long as states mutually agree to rules for the conduct of relations between them the differences in their cultural make-up do not matter. The engaging analogy drawn by John Vincent, with regard to this, was between international society and an egg-box. Just as the function of the egg-box is to separate the eggs, so the function of international society is to separate and cushion from each other, the states that are its members.[20]

As part of an assessment of the outlook for international society in a culturally plural world Richard Shapcott objects to both Vincent's

---

[18] Chris Brown, 'The Modern Requirement? Reflections on Normative International Theory in a Post-Western World', *Millennium*, 17: 2 (1988). See also the more recent discussion in Brown, 'Cultural diversity and international political theory', pp. 199–213.
[19] Brown, 'Cultural Diversity', p. 345.
[20] John Vincent, *Human Rights and International Relations* (Cambridge University Press, 1986), p. 123.

egg-box conception and Brown's suggestions concerning the morality of states. He argues that both authors effectively abandon the quest for dialogue between cultures. The ethics of coexistence builds upon Terry Nardin's notion of practical association and is merely another version of the egg-box view of international society. When conceived of in this way international society has the function of keeping apart the various purposive associations that are its constituents. It assumes that the constituents of international society are 'coherent, totally separate wholes' and overlooks the important ways in which their mutual relations form and reform their 'internal constitution and self-understanding'. As a practical association international society does not have the role of acting to bring about understanding and agreement about the differences between members. Instead, it eliminates difference by seeing culturally diverse states bound together by the rules of international society. It assumes that these rules, devised by the West, 'are equally applicable to the wider post-Western world'.[21] And it is for this reason that Shapcott objects to Brown's suggestion concerning the morality of states as a normative basis for North–South relations.

His argument is that for this to be a satisfactory basis for North–South relations the states of the South would all have 'to accept the authoritative status' of the rules and norms promulgated by the West. However, he doubts that there can be any universal agreement that is not, in the final analysis, simply 'an expression of the domination of one particular culture over another'.[22] For it to be anything else, it would have to be based on a genuine dialogue that resulted in cross-cultural understanding, one aimed at overcoming the incommensurability of cultures at least to the degree of achieving mutual acceptance of difference. The burden of Shapcott's argument is that the egg-box view should be abandoned in favour of reconceptualising international society 'as a means by which interactions between increasingly less distinct states, societies and civilisations, can be mediated'.[23]

As the means to achieving understanding between culturally different entities or what he describes as a 'fusion of horizons', Shapcott advocates Gadamer's proposal for a 'conversation' in hermaneutics. Bringing our horizon together with that of others, and so reaching a shared understanding, requires listening to what the other has to say

---

[21] Richard Shapcott, 'Conversation and Coexistence: Gadamer and the Interpretation of International Society', *Millennium*, 23: 1 (1994), 68. See also Shapcott, *Justice, Community and Dialogue*, pp. 44–5.
[22] Shapcott, 'Conversation and Coexistence', pp. 69–70.   [23] Ibid., pp. 80–1.

and accepting 'the presence of difference, the otherness of the other, without suspending their claim to truth'. We must be 'open to what an "other" horizon may have to say to us, and not merely it's [*sic*] self-understanding which we can never fully possess'.[24]

A similar route to achieving understanding between the representatives of different cultural standpoints is Andrew Linklater's application of Habermas' 'discourse ethics' to international relations.[25] Discourse ethics refers to the ground rules for dialogue between culturally different communities. It proceeds on the assumption that cultural difference is not a barrier to dialogue aimed at breaking down practices of exclusion and is concerned particularly with overcoming the exclusion of communities from debate about 'issues which affect their vital interests'. Discourse ethics

> argues that human beings need to be reflective about the ways in which they include and exclude others from dialogue. It argues the they should be willing to problematize bounded communities (indeed boundaries of all kinds) and that the legitimacy of practices is questionable if they have failed to take account of the interests of outsiders. – Discourse ethics argues that norms cannot be valid unless they can command the consent of everyone whose interests stand to be affected by them.[26]

To qualify as a true dialogue in conformity with the procedural rules of discourse ethics participants must 'suspend their own supposed truth claims [and] respect the claims of others'.

Crucial to discourse ethics is the idea that moral actors should think from the standpoint of others and recognise that their own beliefs are a reflection of their own experience and therefore partial. To reach a more impartial understanding it is necessary to attempt to think as others do. Dialogue based on thinking from the standpoint of others offers the prospect of identifying universal values, which all parties affected can accept and which are not open to the objection of being merely values imposed by dominant actors. Such an imposition has been common

---

[24] Ibid., p. 75 and Shapcott, *Justice*, pp. 142–50.
[25] Andrew Linklater, 'The Achievements of Critical Theory', in Smith, Booth and Zalewski (eds.), *International Theory*, and Linklater, *The Transformation of Political Community*, see especially chapter 3. For a critique of Linklater's account of discourse ethics see Richard Shapcott, 'Cosmopolitan Conversations: Justice, Dialogue and the Cosmopolitan Project', *Global Society*, 16: 3 (2002), 223–7.
[26] Linklater, 'Citizenship and Sovereignty, pp. 85–6.

in cross-cultural relations. In European encounters with indigenous non-Europeans the former tended to simply subsume the latter in their own ways of knowing. Little or no attempt was made to understand the standpoint of indigenous peoples. Consequently, we may ask whether the application of dialogic ethics would overcome this historic tendency. Is it possible that dialogue can overcome exclusion and the dominance of particular groups within borders or of dominant peoples in their relations across borders with other peoples?

Linklater himself acknowledges that 'the outcome of dialogue may be no more than an agreement to disagree'. Even this much progress would be sufficient reason to engage in dialogue but a major obstacle to achieving substantive agreement is that political interests may be too entrenched to allow the possibility of thinking from the standpoint of others. The perceived interests of the communities in dialogue may be so much at odds that there cannot be even an agreement to disagree. In the case of indigenous peoples the problem might be exacerbated by either intentional or unintentional racism. Particular individuals on both sides of a cultural and racial divide may well be open to each other but they may not necessarily be representative of, and supported by, the social and political groups to which they belong. Understanding others in their own terms may, sadly, be doomed from the outset. In the final analysis, discourse ethics may be politically naive if not curiously apolitical.

The aim of the dialogic ethics advocated by Linklater is that of 'facilitating the extension of moral and political community in international affairs'.[27] For Richard Devetak, this 'necessarily involves re-thinking the ideas of autonomy and community, and contending with the difficult practical issues of resolving the tension between identity and difference, the one and the many'.[28] He neither discusses the meaning of identity and difference nor the nature of the tension between them. My own understanding of these terms and of the tension between them is as follows: by identity I mean that which defines my self-image and certain of my values. It defines also the groups or categories with which I identify. Difference also defines me but in a negative sense. That which is different is that which I am not; it separates me from others. They are, as Anna Yeatman says, relational terms:

[27] Andrew Linklater, 'The Question of the Next Stage in International Relations Theory: A Critical-Theoretical Point of View', *Millennium*, 21: 1 (1992), 93.
[28] Richard Devetak, 'The Project of Modernity and International Relations Theory', *Millennium*, 24: 1 (1995), 40.

> A claim to identity necessarily involves the proposition that the subject concerned is sufficiently different from its relevant others as to have its own identity in relation to them. Identity claims always implicate an inherently linked dual operation: the construction of self is simultaneous with, the other side of the coin as, the construction of this self's others. Selfhood and otherness are relational terms.[29]

The friction between identity and difference is then that difference as a means to identity necessarily involves excluding those that are defined as different from belonging to the community to which my identity belongs. The two are, therefore, in opposition. It is, moreover, an opposition that has been compounded in European encounters with non-Europeans by the former seeing their difference as one that makes them superior to the latter. What would it require for them not to be in opposition? The nexus between identity and difference would have to be broken. Instead of what is different having the negative role of defining identity by defining what one is not, it would have to be valued for its own sake. Difference would have to be accepted as non-threatening and as valuable in and of itself.[30]

Linklater's project is grounded in, and intended to be a contribution to, critical theory, which is in many ways a continuation of Enlightenment themes. Enlightenment thinking celebrated reason, the autonomy of the individual and indeed the autonomy of reason. As Kant put it, Enlightenment depended on 'the freedom to make *public use* of one's reason in all matters'.[31] And, in earlier discussions, we saw how the supposed lack of reason was at one time a defining characteristic of otherness. Those lacking the capacity for reason were ignorant, and being ignoranant of ignorance marked out 'others' beyond the boundaries of the moral community to which 'civilised' Europeans belonged.[32] As well as reason the Enlightenment movement, especially as represented by Kant, was vitally concerned with the search for universal values attaching to the whole of humankind. Enlightenment thinking promoted the 'ideal of the unity of the species'.[33] In place of accepting the division

---

[29] Anna Yeatman, 'Justice and the Sovereign Self', in M. Wilson and A. Yeatman (eds.), *Justice and Identity: Antipodean Practices* (Wellington: Bridget Williams, 1995), p. 195.
[30] For further discussion of identity and difference see Young, *Inclusion and Democracy*, ch. 3 and William E. Connolly, 'Identity and Difference in Global Politics', in J. Der Derian and M. J. Shapiro (eds.), *International/Intertextual Relations: Postmodern Readings of World Politics* (Lexington, MA: Lexington Books, 1989), pp. 323–42.
[31] Hans Reiss (ed.), *Kant's Political Writings* (Cambridge University Press, 1970), p. 55.
[32] McGrane, *Beyond Anthropology*, p. 71.
[33] Andrew Linklater, *Beyond Realism and Marxism: Critical Theory and International Relations* (London: Macmillan, 1990), p. 59 cited by Devetak, 'Project of Modernity', p. 38.

of human beings into states, Enlightenment thinking called for conceptions of community in which the writ of such universal values could run. As the standard bearer of Enlightenment values critical international theory thus holds that 'freedom and universalism can no longer be confined to the limits of the state or nation. The realisation of the "good life" is not to be confined to these particularistic limits, but is to be universalised to humanity.'[34] This in turn implies expansion of the boundaries of moral community.

How the boundaries between those included in and excluded from moral communities are marked is a concern critical theory shares with post-structuralism. The two approaches are however in disagreement over the potential post-structural theorists see for the rational and cosmopolitan elements of critical theory to result in totalising discourses that privilege particular groups or states while devaluing others. Central to a post-structuralist approach to international relations theory is the application of de-construction, exemplified in the work of Jacques Derrida, as a method of critique.

Derrida drew attention to the hierarchical nature of 'conceptual oppositions' such as masculine/feminine or rational/emotional. These and similar oppositions are used in ways that do not acknowledge how one of the two terms is invariably given a higher status than the other. The one term governs the other with the 'privileged term supposedly signify[ing] a presence, propriety, or identity which the other lacks'.[35] Such oppositions result in discounting the relevance, importance or worth of what is designated by implication the lesser of the two. The significance of what it designates is relegated to either secondary importance, or, at the extreme, not assigned any importance at all. It is closed out of serious and equal consideration and subjected to the 'totalising discourse' attached to the dominant term. Oppositions result in closures and post-structuralism can be understood as 'a strategy of interpretation and criticism directed at theories and concepts which attempt closure against totalisation'.[36] Devetak explains that post-structuralism counters 'totalisation' or domination of discourse by undermining the status given to the privileged discourse or dominant social formation that it represents.

For Richard Ashley relations of domination prevent people from realizing autonomy understood as self-determination or the ability of people to make decisions about matters affecting their life without undue

---

[34] Devetak, 'Project of Modernity', p. 38.   [35] Ibid., p. 41.   [36] Ibid., p. 42.

interference. The states-system itself is a form of domination that restricts the autonomy of sub-state actors.[37] Given that emancipation calls for the abolition of unnecessary constraints on human freedom and the achievement of autonomy, this suggests a need to reconceptualise the nature of the state and the states-system in ways that de-centre state sovereignty. As a counter to totalisation, post-structuralism seeks to deploy a mode of unsettling or 'de-centering that leaves no privilege to any centre'. Consequently, questions concerning boundaries and closure are central to post-structuralist thought which, when applied to international relations theory, is concerned with 'resist[ing] the closure and totalisation associated with state sovereignty. Its main focus is to demonstrate the impossibility of establishing permanent boundaries around sovereign centres, showing that there are always competing sovereign claims which will frustrate sovereignty.'[38]

Earlier discussion re-counted Dianne Otto's argument that sovereignty needs to be uncoupled from the state if the authorship of aboriginality is to be fully restored to indigenous peoples. Her proposal would require us to re-conceptualise sovereignty in a way that resulted in de-centring it into one or more tiers. Over some matters the state would retain sovereignty, but indigenous peoples would gain sovereignty over certain matters of particular concern to them; especially, the reproduction of culture. In theory specific groups could have sovereignty over the reproduction of their culture within the constitutional structures of the territorially bounded states in which they are citizens. Changes of this kind would be resisted by those who regard sovereignty as indivisible. It would also attract objections from people opposed to group rights on the grounds that they are unfairly discriminatory. While it is important to recognise these objections they need not detain us here.

Of more immediate importance are the connections Otto makes between law, liberalism and sovereignty. Otto argues that liberalism and law have mutually constituted each other in ways that tie sovereignty to the state.[39] The liberal state places personal liberties and rights 'above religious, ethnic and other forms of communal consciousness'.[40] The liberal conception of sovereignty enshrined in law is thus an obstacle

---

[37] Richard K. Ashley, 'Three Modes of Economism', *International Studies Quarterly*, 27: 4 (1983), cited by Devetak, 'Project of Modernity', p. 37.
[38] Devetak, 'Project of Modernity', p. 43.
[39] Otto, 'A Question of Law or Politics?', 701–39.
[40] Parekh, *Rethinking Multiculturalism*, 183.

to re-defining sovereignty in ways that would enable it to be a foundation of indigenous cultural identity. Some liberals would respond to this by arguing that the liberal state allows cultural identity to flourish. However, the notion of Aboriginal sovereignty at the centre of Otto's proposal, and others like it, would require re-thinking sovereignty.

As part of his searching examination of the problems cultural diversity presents for political theory, Bhikhu Parekh also argues for the need to loosen the ties between sovereignty and the state. Whereas earlier political formations were tolerant of multiple identities, the modern state has tended towards being threatened by difference. Parekh observes that the modern state is 'a deeply homogenizing institution'. It evolved as a form of political organisation that expected its citizens 'to subscribe to an identical way of defining themselves and relating to each other and the state' and is consequently threatened 'by identities that can set-up "rival foci of loyalty"'.[41] As the recent history of Yugoslavia demonstrates only too well, such rival identities are a basis for both state-breaking and genocide. The presence of rival identities entails problems that cannot adequately be dealt with by the dominant theory of the state. 'In multi-ethnic and multinational societies whose constituent communities entertain different views on its nature, powers and goals, have different histories and needs, and cannot therefore be treated in an identical manner, the modern state can easily become an instrument of injustice and oppression and even precipitate the very instability and secession it seeks to prevent.'[42] Parekh concludes that, 'Since we can neither write off the modern state nor continue with its current form, we need to reconceptualise its nature and role. This involves loosening the traditionally close ties between territory, sovereignty and culture and re-examining the assumptions lying at the basis of the dominant theory of the state.'[43]

Though from very different standpoints, both Parekh and Otto are urging us to reconsider the requirements for states to be able to accommodate cultural plurality without perpetuating the injustice and oppression that has been experienced by subordinate cultures and peoples. They both call for a close consideration and re-thinking of the nature of political community in order to identify the conditions needed to establish culturally diverse communities. What follows canvasses a variety of approaches to political community with particular reference to how they deal with difference. It is not in any way intended to be a

---

[41] Ibid., p. 184.   [42] Ibid., p. 185.   [43] Ibid., p. 194.

comprehensive discussion of this but instead to be indicative of some of the difficulties associated with conceptualising political communities that would attend to difference.

Political community and difference

Proposals concerning political community represent a variety of purposes and take different forms. Some concern arrangements within states while others focus on reforming relations between states and other actors in international relations. The discussion that follows assumes that there are crucial connections between domestic and international levels so includes ideas framed with regard to the basis of relations within states as well as between them. Linking all of the ideas discussed is the question of whether any of them is able to deal with difference in ways that do not involve subordination to the totalising project of a dominant cultural community.

Multiculturalism within the state

Parekh distinguishes between proceduralist, assimilationist, civic assimilationist and millet models of political integration as different modes of dealing with the competing 'demands of unity and diversity'. He places the proceduralist and assimilationist models at the opposite ends of a continuum with the civic assimilationist model in the middle. Proceduralists accept diversity but believe 'the deep moral and cultural differences to be found in multicultural societies cannot be rationally resolved, and our sole concern should be to ensure peace and stability'. From this perspective the role of the state is to lay 'down the minimally necessary general rules of conduct, subject to which citizens remain free to lead their self-chosen lives'.[44] Assimilationists are more or less unconcerned with the claims of diversity and disagree with people leading self-chosen lives based on cultural difference. The assimilationist view is that the citizens of a state should share one comprehensive culture that covers all areas of life. Assimilationists seek to deny if not obliterate difference. Occupying the middle ground, civic assimilationists stress the importance of a shared political culture. This provides the framework for meaningful dialogue, the resolution of differences and the pursuit of common goals by culturally diverse groups within the state. In this model cultural differences are relegated to the private realm thus

---

[44] Ibid., p. 199.

reinforcing the dichotomy between the public and private realms found in other aspects of politics. Finally, the millet model alludes to the practice in the Ottoman Empire and other political formations, of allowing enclaves of difference in their midst.[45] The Ottomans allowed Christians to pursue their own beliefs and culture surrounded by the wider and different Islamic culture. In part the standard of civilisation reflected the need to protect the integrity of these enclaves and, apart from them being subject to interference, the millet system did not resolve the tension between the demands of unity and diversity. It did not provide for the common social and political bonds necessary to political community and the members of millets were never more than second-class citizens.

Parekh finds all four of these models to be problematic. 'The assimilationist theory more or less ignores the claims of diversity, and the millet theory those of unity. The proceduralist and civic assimilationist theories respect both, but fail to appreciate their dialectical interplay and strike a right balance between them.'[46] As an alternative, Parekh suggests the need to foster a multicultural society that 'meets certain conditions. These include a consensually grounded structure of authority, a collectively acceptable set of constitutional rights, a just and impartial state, a multiculturally constituted common culture and multicultural education, and a plural and inclusive view of national identity.'[47] By meeting these conditions a multicultural society that is 'stable, cohesive, vibrant and at ease with itself' can be created and sustained.

Parekh's defence of multicultural societies and the conditions he suggests matter in the context of this book in at least three respects. First, in relation to international society, intolerance of cultural diversity within states has been a cause of conflict and civil wars.[48] Cultural recognition supported by appropriate constitutional political processes can help prevent violent struggle of the kind that has in the past spilt over borders and become an international problem. To the extent that multicultural policies contribute to stable states they may be seen as also contributing to order between states. Second, it is argued that multicultural policies are necessary to justice and the elimination of domination by one group of other groups within states.[49] In that case multiculturalism may be seen as promoting world order and ought, for that reason, to be

---

[45] See Jason Goodwin, *Lords of the Horizons: A History of the Ottoman Empire* (London: Vintage, 1999).
[46] Parekh, *Rethinking Multiculturalism*, p. 206.   [47] Ibid., p. 236.
[48] Tully, *Strange Multiplicity*, p. 140.
[49] Kymlicka and Norman (eds.), *Citizenship in Diverse Societies*.

endorsed by international society. Third, while indigenous peoples are likely to be beneficiaries of multicultural policies, multiculturalism does not deal with self-determination, which we have argued is the central right sought by indigenous peoples. For indigenous peoples multiculturalism is much less relevant than the idea of multination states. In part this is because indigenous peoples have a relationship with the state that is different from that of other minorities. As the original inhabitants and traditional owners of lands occupied by forebears of the dominant society, they have claims against the state that other culturally defined groups do not.

Multinational states

Canada is a prime example of a multinational state,[50] and it is consequently not surprising that Canadian scholars have led discussion of the concept. Among them is Peter Russell, who explains that while Canada is certainly a multicultural state it is more than just this:

> Functioning as a multinational political community means something much more difficult and problematic than multi-culturalism. It means, in the Canadian case, acknowledging that two groups, French Canadians and Indigenous peoples are not just cultural minorities but political societies with the special rights of homeland peoples to maintain political jurisdictions in which they can ensure their survival as distinct peoples.[51]

The political societies to which he refers are ones that regard themselves as nations and hence 'claim the same right of self-determination as other colonised or conquered nations around the world'. For Canadians the intellectual and political problem about this has been 'how to reconcile competing nationalisms within a single state'.[52]

Debate over this focuses on federalism and the constitutional arrangements most likely to support a 'system for dividing and sharing power so as to make meaningful self-government possible'.[53] In *Finding Our Way*, Kymlicka distinguishes between territorial and multination federalism. Territorial federalism is represented by most federations in which

---

[50] Other examples include the United Kingdom, Belgium, and Spain.

[51] Peter H. Russell, 'Constitutional Politics in Multi-National Canada', *Arena Journal*, 14 (1999/2000), 77.

[52] Will Kymlicka, *Finding Our Way: Rethinking Ethnocultural Relations in Canada* (Ontario: Oxford University Press, 1998), p. 127.

[53] Ibid., p. 135.

the aim has been 'to protect the equal rights of individuals within a common national coummunity, not to recognise the rights of national minorities to self-government'. By contrast, in a genuinely multinational federal system, 'federalism would have to be seen not just as a means by which a single national community can divide and diffuse power, but as a means of accommodating the desire of national minorities for self-government'.[54] Later in the same book he observes that 'the pursuit of self-government by national minorities reflects a desire to weaken the bonds with the larger political community, and in fact to question its very nature, authority, and permanence',[55] which is an enterprise he endorses.

James Tully, who prefers the term 'diverse federalism' to multination federalism, has been particularly concerned with constitutionalism in relation to cultural diversity and multinational democracy. In *Strange Multiplicity* he argues that 'the basic law and institutions of modern societies, and their authoritative traditions of interpretation, are *unjust* in so far as they thwart the forms of self-government appropriate to the recognition of cultural diversity'.[56] Consequently, he gives an account of constitutionalism in which a constitution is a form of activity:

> A contemporary constitution can recognise cultural diversity if it is reconceived as what might be called a 'form of accommodation' of cultural diversity. A constitution should be seen as a form of activity, an intercultural dialogue in which the culturally diverse sovereign citizens of contemporary societies negotiate agreements on their forms of association over time in accordance with the three conventions of mutual recognition, consent and cultural continuity.[57]

Mutual recognition refers to the requirement that a just form of consititution must 'give recognition to the legitimate demands of diverse cultures in a manner that renders everyone their due'.[58] In relation to this, '[d]iverse federalism is a means of conciliation because it enables peoples mutually to recognise and reach agreement on how to assemble or federate the legal and political differences they wish to continue into the association'.[59] Consent refers to the principle that a constitution should be an expression of popular sovereignty. Last, cultural continuity requires respect for the continuity of cultures of self-rule.[60]

In his introduction to a later work Tully focuses on 'multinational democracy', which he describes as a 'new and distinctive type of political

---

[54] Ibid., p. 138. [55] Ibid., p. 170. [56] Tully, *Strange Muliplicity*, p. 5.
[57] Ibid., p. 30. [58] Ibid., p. 6. [59] Ibid., p. 140. [60] Ibid., ch. 5.

association that is coming into prominence at the dawn of the Twenty First Century'. 'Multinational democracies', he writes, 'are contemporary societies composed not only of many cultures (multicultural) but also two or more nations (multinational)', or peoples.[61] They are associations that share four defining characteristics. First, '[t]he members of the nations are, or aspire to be, recognised as self-governing peoples with the right of self-determination as this is understood in international law and democratic theory'.[62] Second, however, they are not independent nation states and 'participate in the political institutions of their self-governing nations and the larger, self-governing multi-nation'. Third, 'the nations and the composite multination are constitutional democracies', and fourth, 'multinational democracies are also multicultural'.[63]

In elaborating his theory of multinational democracies, Tully explains the fundamental importance of what he calls 'the activity of mutual disclosure and acknowledgement'. By this he means the 'inter-subjective activity of competing over recognition (separate from the end-state of recognition at which it aims) . . .'. A crucial question related to this is which form of democracy is most conducive to 'the politics of recognition to be played freely from generation to generation, with as little domination as possible'. And this leads to the proposition that freedom is the primary question for multinational democracies. In particular, the question of whether 'the members of an open society [have the freedom] to change the constitutional rules of mutual recognition and association from time to time as their identities change'. This freedom is, to Tully's mind, 'an aspect of the freedom of self-determination of peoples'.[64] What he proceeds to say bears quoting in full:

> A multinational society will be free and self-determining just insofar as the constitutional rules of recognition and association are open to challenge and amendment by the members. If they are not open, they constitute a structure of domination, the members are not self-determining, and the society is unfree. Freedom *versus* domination is thus the emerging focus of politics in multinational societies at the dawn of the new millennium.[65]

Iris Marion Young similarly argues for understanding freedom as the absence of domination and links non-domination to self-determination.[66]

---

[61] James Tully, 'Introduction' in J. Tully and A.-G. Gagnon (eds.), *Multinational Democracies* (Cambridge University Press, 2001), p. 1.
[62] Ibid., p. 20.   [63] Ibid., p. 3.
[64] Ibid., p. 5. All quotations in this paragraph are drawn from p. 5.   [65] Ibid., p. 6.
[66] Young, *Inclusion and Democracy*, p. 259.

The universal community of mankind

Cosmopolitanism views individuals everywhere as belonging to a universal human community in which there are shared rights and obligations. Membership of this community transcends citizenship and state boundaries and requires us to be sensitive to harm being done to 'others' beyond our borders. As well as embracing the ideal of a universal human community, cosmopolitanism embraces the search for universal moral principles. In relation to ethics, cosmopolitanism, to paraphrase John Vincent, has us all out of the egg-box, out of the eggs it separated and scrambled in the frying pan. However, its universal elements do not mean that it is a doctrine of world government. Kant, who is celebrated as a foundational cosmopolitan thinker, conceived of the community of mankind and universal moral principles as being compatible with states as the primary unit of political organisation. In his essay on perpetual peace, Kant imagined a world federation of democratic states in which cosmopolitan right is confined to the right of 'hospitality' – meaning that strangers and foreigners should be welcomed and treated with respect.

Contemporary writers use cosmopolitanism in broader senses. Among them is Mary Kaldor who adopts it as a foil against the politics of identity she sees at the root of contemporary intra-state wars or 'new wars'. These are conflicts that use ethnic, racial or religious identity as the basis of political power. They involve the establishment of particularist political communities that exclude those who are different. And the inexorable way such communities are established is through 'ethnic cleansing', achieved by either forcing those who are different to move or otherwise killing them. For Kaldor, cosmopolitanism holds the promise of undermining this particularism. She thus cites Anthony Appiah's observation that cosmopolitanism takes pleasure 'from the presence of difference [and] celebrates the fact that there are *different* local human ways of being'. She herself uses the term 'to refer both to a positive political vision, embracing tolerance, multiculturalism, civility and democracy, and to a more legalistic respect for certain overriding universal principles which guide political communities at various levels, including the global political level'.[67] In common with other writers discussed in this chapter, she calls for a reconstruction of legitimacy and, like David Held, for a cosmopolitan law which she defines as a combination of humanitarian law and human rights.

[67] Mary Kaldor, *New and Old Wars: Organised Violence in a Global Era* (Cambridge: Polity Press, 1999), p. 88.

Held's *Democracy and the Global Order* explicitly calls for a cosmopolitan order supported by a reconception of law and democracy. Integral to his aim of devising a theory of democracy that is responsive to the effects of globalisation is the necessity of finding new ways of conceptualising domestic and international legitimacy. For Held, domestic politics can no longer be considered apart from global processes and his specific concern is with the 'place of the state and democracy within the international order'.[68] Hitherto the modern state has provided a framework for government intended to be both limited and fair and for that reason is encased in procedural rules. At the core of democracy, on the other hand, is the principle of self-determination, understood as the principle that the citizens of states should be free to determine the conditions affecting their lives. These choices confer legitimacy on state policies and actions if they are respected.

Self-determination in this sense and the stipulation that democratic government is limited government are essential elements of the *Principle of Autonomy*, which is crucial to his reformulation of democracy. It states:

> persons should enjoy equal rights and accordingly, equal obligations in the specification of the political framework which generates and limits the opportunities available to them; that is, they should be free and equal in the determination of the conditions of their own lives, so long as they do not deploy this framework to negate the rights of others.[69]

In order to specify the conditions under which autonomy is possible, Held proposes a test of impartiality and the absence of what he calls 'nautonomy'. The test of impartiality is a variation of the requirement underpinning discourse ethics that decisions and actions must be acceptable to all people affected by them. In Held's words, impartiality means a 'willingness . . . to reason from the point of view of others'; and the test of impartiality is to arrive at a 'political position which no party "could reasonably reject" '.[70] The concept of nautonomy refers to situations in which 'relations of power systematically generate asymmetries of life-chances'. These he defines as 'the chances a person has of sharing the socially generated economic, cultural or political goods, rewards and opportunities typically found in his or her community'.[71] And this resonates clearly with the shorter life expectancy, higher rates

---

[68] David Held, *Democracy and the Global Order: From the Modern State to Cosmopolitan Governance* (Cambridge: Polity Press, 1995), p. 36.
[69] Ibid., p. 147.   [70] Ibid., p. 164.   [71] Ibid., p. 171.

of incarceration and lower levels of health and education experienced by indigenous peoples.

Nautonomic structures undermine the Principle of Autonomy and Held identifies seven sites of power that generate such structures: physical and emotional well-being, welfare, culture, civic associations, the economy, the organisation of violence and coercive relations, and the sphere of regulatory and legal institutions. As a means of preventing or at least restricting the capacity of these sites to generate nautonomic outcomes Held proposes that they need to be regulated by rights codified in democratic public law. In accordance with the test of impartiality these rights would safeguard the ability of people to participate in determining the conditions that affect their lives. Held explains that cosmopolitan democratic law would be different in kind from current domestic and international law. It would transcend 'the particular claims of nations and states and [extend] to all in the "universal community"'.[72]

In turning to the international dimensions of his argument Held reiterates the need for autonomy to be underpinned by democratic public law embodying the seven clusters of rights meant to safeguard against nautonomic outcomes. At the same time he asks whether these rights are citizenship rights, human rights or some other kind of right. He reasons that they are neither citizenship rights nor human rights. If they were the former that would leave them attached to the state, which in some cases will be implicated in the denial of autonomy. Human rights find expression in both regional and international instruments that often cut across the claims of states. Partly because of this it is assumed that they are universal. However many states and sub-state groups see these supposedly universal values as having issued from a mainly Western culture that is in conflict with the values of their own culture. Consequently there is 'tension between the claims of national identity, religious affiliation, state sovereignty and international law' that may be difficult if not impossible to resolve.[73]

Held's argument culminates in a radical re-visioning of the nature of political community in which the Principle of Autonomy entails a duty to establish a cosmopolitan community of 'democratic states and societies committed to upholding democratic public law both within and across their own boundaries'.[74] As a result, states would no longer be 'the sole centres of legitimate power within their own borders'. The meaning

---

[72] Ibid., p. 228.   [73] Ibid., p. 223.   [74] Ibid., p. 229.

and limits of sovereign authority would be specified by cosmopolitan democratic law, with sovereignty uncoupled from state borders. In addition to this task, the new law would shape and delimit 'a system of diverse and overlapping power centres' with sovereignty apportioned between them.

Held's vision is richly suggestive and while it is not framed with reference to indigenous peoples, it contains concepts that can be applied to thinking about them. The concept of nautonomy is applicable to the situation of many indigenous peoples whose life chances can be restricted by the asymmetries generated by the sites of power that affect them. In this respect their situation is no different from that of many other people, whether indigenous or not. Nevertheless, the concept of nautonomy stands as one that is intrinsically useful in the way it focuses attention on the role structures of power have in creating inequalities. In relation to indigenous peoples it has the particular virtue of including culture as a source of asymmetries of power. And as a negative condition it helps illuminate the preferable value of autonomy.

The Principle of Autonomy has direct relevance to the relationship between indigenous peoples and the settler societies in which they are embedded. Generally, indigenous peoples have not had the free and equal say in determining the conditions of their own lives that this principle would require. A necessary condition for indigenous peoples to achieve this may be self-government of their historic homelands. It might be only in areas under their own control that indigenous peoples could be fully free to determine the conditions of their lives. In Held's model of global order the right to self-government would be safeguarded by cosmopolitan democratic law with the Principle of Autonomy at its jurisprudential core. Denial of the right to self-government would be felt community wide as an affront to the values of cosmopolitan order. In this way, his scheme can be seen as one that would ensure that global standards were established for relations with all indigenous peoples precisely because they would now be included in a cosmopolitan global community of humankind. These standards would have legal expression, establish criteria of legitimacy, and set out the obligations of the global community.

Held's proposals offer a vision and a sense of direction but are ultimately utopian and fraught with difficulties. It is difficult to see how his vision could be realized. In the first place, the stipulation in the Principle of Autonomy that people 'should be free and equal in the determination of their own lives' expresses an aspiration of many indigenous peoples.

The only way the majority of indigenous peoples can hope to obtain self-determination in this sense is within the constitutional structure of the states in which they are encased. Most states, however, seek to deny meaningful self-determination to indigenous peoples, and they are unlikely to adopt the Principal of Autonomy that would require them to modify their policies and practices. In the foreseeable future states are unlikely to accept that self-determination can be satisfactorily uncoupled from state sovereignty. As long as states remain the primary form of political organisation this is a considerable obstacle to indigenous peoples determining the conditions of their own existence.

Second, the idea of a test of impartiality that would limit the conditions of autonomy to those defensible on the grounds of being 'in principle equally acceptable to all parties or social groups' is inherently problematic. Key aims of indigenous peoples that would have to be met for them to have autonomy have been fiercely contested. It may in the end be impossible to secure agreement on matters that would meet the conditions of the principle of autonomy. It calls for people to be able to determine the conditions of their lives 'so long as they do not deploy this framework to negate the rights of others'. The ability to determine the conditions of their lives may mean privileging indigenous peoples in ways that are seen as creating unfair inequalities between other groups. Satisfying some indigenous claims may involve negating the rights of other non-indigenous and indigenous groups alike. An example of this might be the preclusion of mining rights on indigenous lands or closing off the right to pastoral leases on tribal lands. In still other cases it could result in a clash between group rights and human rights, requiring a defence of cultural rights. The test of impartiality may be difficult if not impossible to achieve in the realm of cultural relations. A constant theme through this study has been the incommensurability of cultures, that in the final analysis may defeat attempts to satisfy the test of impartiality.

Third, Held rejects citizenship rights as the ones needed to safeguard the Principle of Autonomy, because they are embodied in states that may be either in decline under the pressure of globalisation, or else irretrievably implicated in limiting autonomy. This implies that the Principle of Autonomy would stand above states and put the rights that constitute it beyond the reach of states. It is difficult to imagine the circumstances in which states would willingly consent to such a loss of authority.

Fourth, the idea of a cosmopolitan democratic law is appealing but once again it is difficult to see how such a law would be agreed upon, adopted and implemented. Realizing the ideal of cosmopolitan democratic law would require states to cooperate in relinquishing aspects of their sovereignty and authority that are currently regarded as central to statehood and this they are unlikely to do. The political objections of particular states to the establishment of the International Criminal Court suggests there are probably no promising precedents. Apart from that, the expectations about what a recasting of law could achieve are reminiscent of the hope invested in the rule of law after World War I and subsequent schemes for world peace through law. The rule of law is a laudable goal but one ultimately subject to politics.

Fifth, it has to be asked whether radical changes are needed to secure the rights of indigenous peoples. It can be argued that the best way of safeguarding and extending the rights of indigenous peoples is through the adoption by the UN General Assembly of the 1994 Draft Declaration on Indigenous Rights with the right of self-determination stipulated in Article 3. Further, this would have a much better prospect of success than attempts to redesign the political and legal arrangements of the world. Against this, it can be objected that significant groups of indigenous peoples remain encased in and subject to the settler societies that dispossessed them and need the protection of rules and organisations that stand above states and are not currently available. This is not to say that all indigenous peoples are still in the situation of having their rights denied. The Inuit and Cree peoples of Canada and the Māori of Aoteora New Zealand are examples of peoples who substantially have achieved self-determination over the conditions of their lives.

Finally, Held's theory is a validation of democracy and we need to ask why we should adopt democracy as a value. In response to this it can be argued that indigenous peoples' rights are much more likely to be achieved in a democracy that stands or falls on whether or not it has regard for rights and the rule of law fairly administered. Governments and international regimes that do not have regard for democratic norms are much less likely to be either concerned with or constrained by the rights of citizens or cultural groups. Nevertheless, the promotion of democracy may in the end simply reflect a reproduction of the existing order preferred by the inner circle of states, and for many presently subordinated or excluded people be no more than the latest form of totalising project visited upon the dominant Western culture of that inner circle, particularly because of the majority principle so often at the centre of democratic practice.

Undoing the Westphalian state

For Andrew Linklater, 'the deepest moral question in international re-lations' is 'the relationship between obligations to the state and the rest of humanity'.[75] And in conjunction with this, 'transforming political community is the primary objective of International Relations theory'.[76] The political community in need of transformation is the Westphalian state system in which states stand between the individual and the uni-versal community of mankind, with citizens owing their primary moral obligations to the state and to their fellow citizens in front of others be-yond their borders. Of particular concern to Linklater is that '[w]hether within states, or in the relations between them, the same issue arises: how to give public expression to cultural differences without encourag-ing or unleashing particularism'.[77] Communities tend to result in clo-sure that excludes the other within and beyond its borders from its moral community.

Linklater is engaged in the search for a form of ethical universalism that does not repeat the concern of the Enlightenment project to define and promulgate an Archimedian moral standpoint embodying 'univer-salisable' conceptions of the good life that do not suit everybody. Such conceptions impose a single identity in which those who are different are subordinated to a dominant culture. The notion of ethical universalism promoted by Linklater is the ideal of a dialogic community, founded on respect for difference and sensitivity to the 'needs of victims of the total-izing project', in which they are subjected to single conceptions. Arising from this, a central issue is the extent to which the right of communal self-determination can be over-ridden by principles of cosmopolitan morality, of which a dialogic ethic would be part. Reimagining polit-ical community is consequently necessary to the accommodation of a universal ethic.

Linklater supports a post-Westphalian community in which 'more complex associations of universality and difference can be developed by breaking the nexus between sovereignty, territoriality, and citizen-ship and by promoting wider communities of discourse'.[78] As evidence that there may be a nascent community of this kind already, he refers to the evolution of the European Community. Linklater regards a pluralist society of states, a solidarist society of states, and a post-Westphalian states system as the 'ideal-typical frameworks of action ... available to

[75] Linklater, *The Transformation*, pp. 60–61.
[76] Ibid., p. 45.   [77] Ibid., p. 27.   [78] Ibid., p. 60.

states which are committed to enlarging the boundaries of moral and political community and to cooperating with others to eradicate unjust modes of exclusion'.[79] The first two of these correspond respectively with Nardin's practical and purposive associations. Whereas a pluralist society is one in which states representing different cultures adopt 'principles of association' that enable them to coexist, relations in a solidarist community 'are based on agreement about a range of moral principles'. By contrast, states in post-Westphalian arrangements

> do not only break with the traditional habits associated with state sovereignty but also relinquish many of their sovereign powers entirely. The principles of international governance which are integral to this framework of action no longer presuppose the commitment to sovereignty, territoriality, nationality and citizenship which differentiates the modern form of political community from all previous forms of human organisation.[80]

The loosening of sovereignty Linklater calls for is ultimately concerned with the problem of how to include others, without ignoring difference, by imposing supposedly universal standards that are in fact the ideas of one particular dominant culture. One difficulty with this is that his post-Westphalian model is informed by developments in the European Union. Arguably it is fundamentally Eurocentric and would be difficult to realize on a global scale. To extend it beyond Europe would require many states to accept standards of human rights and government they presently reject as being part of the very Western totalising project from which Linklater seeks to escape.

It should be clear enough that Linklater's proposals about the transformation of political community are inseparable from his concern with the ethical foundations of global politics. The importance he places on the community of mankind and on the universality of dialogic ethics locates him on the perimeters of cosmopolitanism.

A recurring suggestion in this study has been that international society is, in essence, an inner circle or club of rich, liberal states that determine the conditions and status of membership. Among these conditions is the requirement of meeting certain standards of internal legitimacy. The inner circle is in this way the arbiter of international legitimacy. From its inception, in Europe, the modern states system has applied criteria of its own making to the treatment of other peoples and political entities. 'Others' have been assigned to various levels of status and treatment

---

[79] Ibid., p. 166.   [80] Ibid., p. 167.

according to how closely they conform to the mores and principles of the inner circle. Practices of inclusion and exclusion are fundamental to the constitution of international society but its members have been insensitive to the full effects of them. The criteria and norms laid down by the small number of dominant states at its core is seen by those subject to them and critics alike, as the imposition of 'totalising discourse'. It is a discourse that represents the domination of one culture over others, and for many scholars and practitioners the elimination of this practice is a core problem for international society. This, however, involves underestimating the extent to which the relationship between cultures is not, to reiterate an earlier point, a one-way process. Contact between cultures results in mutual transformations. It follows that extending the boundaries of the moral community of international society involves not simply drawing more people into conformity with its rules but indeed devising ways to accommodate diversity and safeguard the rights of those who are different. And it is for this reason that the question of the need to reimagine domestic and international political community has become important.

This chapter has canvassed a seemingly disparate literature, which nevertheless contains recurring themes and similarities. First has been a cluster of issues concerning self-determination, sovereignty and autonomy. A second theme is the need for dialogue in aid of cross-cultural understanding, tolerance and the achievement of new political arrangements within states.

Several of the authors discussed argue that there is need to uncouple self-determination and sovereignty from the state. In the case of Linklater, this is extended to breaking the 'nexus between sovereignty, territoriality and citizenship'. The need for this stems from the desire to eliminate domination, and give autonomy to groups that have hitherto had their freedom restricted or even denied. Self-determination, as mentioned in previous chapters, is understood in this discussion as giving peoples the freedom to determine the conditions affecting their lives. This in turn involves recognising that states are, in the main, multinational or multipeople. Tim Dunne's observations concerning the portrayal, in rationalist writings, of the state as a container of community, point to the need to break away from the identification of nation and state. States can and do contain much more than a single community or 'peoples' engaged in a struggle for autonomy. The aim of most indigenous peoples is not secession but autonomy or self-determination within the constitutional structures of the state; hence the importance of the concept of multinational democracies. This requires new understandings of self-determination and sovereignty and a departure from conventional conceptions of the state being the container of a single community. The same applies to Linklater's representation of the post-Westphalian state as one that relinquishes many of its sovereign powers.

Self-determination is fundamental as well to Held's account of autonomy and the reformulation of democracy, which, in his theory, are to be safeguarded by cosmopolitan democratic law. He conceives of this as a law that would transcend the particular claims of nations and states and extend to all in a 'universal community'. It follows from this that it would be law requiring a reinterpretation of self-determination in ways that uncoupled it from the state. Less clear is exactly how the groups that are fundamental to indigenous rights would be integrated into a cosmopolitan law that would *prima facie* be a law in which individuals are the paramount subjects.

An author not so far discussed in this chapter but important for understanding self-determination as freedom from domination is Iris Marion Young. In *Inclusion and Democracy* she argues that self-determination should be understood as 'non-domination' and not, as it has been in international relations, as 'non-interference' in the internal affairs of other states. Indeed in some cases non-interference may be inconsistent with the requirements of global justice.[81] Young rejects the idea of a singular nation as one that does not do justice to the social complexities of the world and argues for the recognition of distinct peoples. In her view, essentialist nationalism represses 'differences within and forge[s] a bounded unity of national membership'.[82] Consequently, '[m]any peoples suffer at the hands of nation-building efforts to suppress or assimilate culturally distinct peoples', and so indigenous peoples 'claim rights of self-determination against the states that assert authority over them'.[83] For Young, 'self-determination of peoples involves regulating international relations to prevent domination of peoples. Such international regulation must be inclusively democratic, however, which means that all those whose actions are regulated must participate together in the process of formulating regulatory institutions and procedures'. Young is explicit that her defence of self-determination for distinct peoples 'does not mean that each people has a right to sole governance of a single, bounded, contiguous territory inhabited only by members of

---

[81] Young, *Inclusion and Democracy*, p. 237.
[82] Ibid., p. 252.   [83] Ibid., p. 255.

their own group'.[84] On the contrary, '[u]nderstood as non-domination, self-determination must be detached from territory'.[85] Young's account thus clearly resonates with and supports the suggestion throughout this chapter that self-determination and sovereignty do need to be rethought in ways that uncouple them from the territorial nation-state.

A final point concerning the theme of self-determination concerns the discussion of rationalism with which the chapter began and subsequent comments about classical theory. The reassessment of self-determination and sovereignty which would uncouple these concepts from the state and allow them to be exercised as a right of sub-state groups is not part of the conceptual framework or lexicon of either rationalism or classical theory. Consequently, for rationalism to be able to, in Timothy Dunne's words, 'empathize with indigenous peoples "the world over"', it would need to accommodate a more complex world of multiple actors and overlapping sovereignties. The discussion in this chapter suggests that it does not have the intellectual foundations to do so.

The second theme mentioned above was the need for an ethical dialogue aimed at thinking from the standpoint of others. Shapcott's concern with bridging cultural divides by bringing horizons together, Linklater's account of discourse ethics in aid of inclusion, Parekh's plea for tolerance and understanding, Held's test of impartiality, and Tully's mutual recognition as the underpinning of diverse federalism illustrated by the *Spirit of the Haida Gwaii*,[86] are all premised on a willingness to comprehend difference and engage in what Tully calls a 'politics of recognition'. In spite of the scepticism expressed earlier regarding discourse ethics, some form of it underpins much of the discussion of relations between different groups referred to in this chapter.

In conclusion, I wish to return to the suggestion in the Introduction to the book and repeated earlier in this chapter, that the moral basis of international society ought to be an obligation to promote and safeguard the value of world order. For international society to promote world order, the states that constitute it would have to be willing to encourage right conduct by states towards peoples within their borders. In extreme cases it would mean responsible member states intervening to stop or prevent actions that result in murder, torture, genocide, impoverishment

[84] Ibid., p. 260.   [85] Ibid., p. 260.
[86] The *Spirit of the Haida Gwaii* refers to a sculpture by the Haida artist Bill Read. It is of a canoe in which diverse mythic creatures jostle for a place and somehow find one as the vessel proceeds. For Tully the sculpture is a metaphor for diverse federalism.

and the denial of individual and collective rights, and so on. This would clearly be an anti-pluralist international society in the sense that it would have to take actions over which there was no agreement between all the parties involved, and that might be regarded as intolerant of plural conceptions of the good. Such a society would need to be one with the capacity and will to intervene, under certain circumstances, in the domestic affairs of states, which may or may not belong to it, in the name of world order. It would, in other words, resemble what Nicholas Wheeler calls a solidarist international society.[87]

At least two difficulties would follow from this. In the first place, actions deliberately taken to defend or produce world order could have the potential to disrupt international order. Consequently, there is bound to be some inconsistency and even incoherence in attaching the moral basis of international society to world order. The second problem relates to the suggestion noted more than once previously that, as a moral agent, international society may be no more than an inner circle of rich liberal states. In that case, the world order it constructs is likely to involve the imposition of the liberal values of the dominant actors. Resistance to this by states and peoples who do not share those values is already a source of disruption to international order.

---

[87] Nicholas J. Wheeler, *Saving Strangers: Humanitarian Intervention in International Society* (Oxford University Press, 2000).

Conclusion

A leading theme in this book has been the significance of the historic and continuing treatment of indigenous peoples for the moral legitimacy of international society. It was argued that if the moral legitimacy of states that constitute international society can be questioned then so also should that of international society, which has, as one of its purposes, the survival of those states. In order to coexist, the states that comprise international society articulate and agree to rules and norms for the conduct of their mutual relations. Increasingly they also agree to rules and norms, such as those expressed in the international human rights regime, which set standards for the internal conduct of states. The moral legitimacy of international society with regard to indigenous peoples is a question that could be substantially settled were it to adopt norms and rules that set standards for the conduct of states with indigenous populations. This could be achieved especially if the rules and norms adopted were ones that helped to fully establish indigenous peoples as subjects of constitutional and international law.

The inquiry in this book has led me to adopt the position that indigenous peoples should be recognised, by states and international society alike, as 'peoples' with the right to self-determination, both within constitutional law and international or emerging global law. There are several interconnected reasons for reaching this conclusion. First, the subjugation and domination of indigenous peoples by European settlers resulted in the destruction of cultures and indigenous identities. The vital link between land and culture meant that when dispossessed of the lands they had traditionally occupied many indigenous peoples were cut off from the well-spring of their culture and identity. Not only this, European settlers typically dealt with indigenous peoples either by attempting to eliminate them or by seeking to assimilate them into

Western value systems and ways of life. Indigenous peoples were rarely regarded, to recall Todorov's words, as both different and equal. The elimination of people who are different is clearly unacceptable and so is assimilation, unless it is the free choice of the individual or people being assimilated. Difference should be valued, not only for its own sake but also because to do otherwise would be to privilege one understanding of what it is to be human over others. For indigenous peoples this would represent a continuation of domination.

Second, recognition of indigenous peoples is a crucial step towards reconciliation based on sharing political and territorial space. Dominant settler societies are not going to go away and if there are to be just relations between settler societies and indigenous peoples there must be mutual agreement about the conditions for sharing that space. The only alternatives to sharing are the denial of rights or the removal of indigenous peoples. Neither of these are acceptable moral alternatives at the beginning of the twenty-first century. A just reconciliation between indigenous peoples and settler societies requires self-determination with peoples, indigenous and non-indigenous, negotiating with each other in a respectful manner on a nation-to-nation basis. It is not a question of carving out territory but of jurisdictions coexisting within state boundaries.

All 'peoples', and indeed individuals, both indigenous and non-indigenous, should enjoy freedom from domination. In the case of indigenous peoples this is all the more pressing because they have had to deal with a disproportionate share of domination. I agree with Iris Marion Young and David Held that freedom from domination entails the right to determine the conditions of one's own existence; in other words, self-determination. Self-determination is a core right for indigenous peoples. For peoples constituted as a state it is an accepted right written into the norms of international society. Indigenous peoples do not seek statehood but instead the right and the power to control the reproduction of distinct cultures and to enjoy what is distinctive in those cultures, including language, attachment to place and kinship links. The self-determination sought by indigenous peoples leaves individuals free to choose to live as members of the dominant culture. The right to uphold cultural traditions and values is one that all people, indigenous and non-indigenous alike, expect, and it is enshrined, as previously mentioned, in Article 27 of the International Covenant on Civil and Political Rights.

Recognition of indigenous peoples as 'peoples' with the right to self-determination in law necessarily involves, as was argued in Chapter 4, moving away from the identification of self-determination with state-hood and the myth of the unitary identity of peoples contained within the boundaries of former colonies. Self-determination should now be understood in a way that uncouples it from the state and allows for the self-determination of two or more peoples within the territorial bound-aries of the state. In chapter 6 multinational states and Tully's concept of diverse federalism were mentioned as modes of political organisation that would accommodate an association of different peoples. Diverse federalism is underpinned by a form of constitutionalism in which a constitution is not a static document but an activity that takes the form of 'an intercultural dialogue in which the culturally diverse sovereign citizens of contemporary societies negotiate agreements on their forms of association over time'.[1] The form of constitutionalism advocated by Tully relies on a politics of mutual recognition in which there is respect-ful dialogue. It embraces 'Not one national narrative, but a diversity of criss-crossing and contested narratives through which citizens partici-pate in and identify with in their association.'[2] I support this vision of political community and believe it has relevance to many states that are willing to seek just arrangements of governance for the peoples collected within their borders.

Primary among the reasons for recognising peoples with the right of self-determination within constitutional law is that this would safe-guard the position of indigenous peoples as distinct cultural groups, especially when accompanied by land rights. Since indigenous peoples or nations do not constitute states and cannot hope therefore to bring cases before the International Court of Justice, they need recourse to national courts as 'peoples'. As well as facilitating this, recognition in constitutional law would also confer legitimacy on states that take that step. It would, at the same time, indicate that those states are secure enough not to fear fragmentation, which is not the intention of the ma-jority of indigenous peoples who seek their self-determination within the constitutional structures of the state. Recognition, however, would require liberal legal cultures more open to the ways and language of others. There is a further reason for recognition in constitutional law: states which have in the past dispossessed and mistreated their indige-nous population owe it to the peoples that constitute that population to incorporate their cultural and property rights, their right to be different, in the legal systems of the state. This may involve some problems in

---

[1] Tully, *Strange Multiplicity*, p. 30.   [2] Ibid., p. 183.

reconciling indigenous law with the laws of the state, but there is no reason why, with goodwill, there cannot be agreement.

In practice, the apprehension states have about self-determination for sub-state groups may mean that recognition in constitutional law follows the lead of standards set by international law. Inscribing self-determination for indigenous peoples into international law would decisively make them, as peoples possessing group rights, subjects rather than objects of international law. They would have clear means of appeal against the states in which they are located. One route to this, discussed previously, would be through adoption by the General Assembly of the Draft Declaration on Indigenous Rights. It was noted in Chapter 4 that the General Assembly is a vital source of norms for indigenous peoples. While Declarations are not binding on states and are not considered primary sources of international law, they do influence states, and over time and with usage can become accepted as an international law norm and representative of customary international law.[3] By supporting adoption of the Draft Declaration, the core members of international society would, through the General Assembly, contribute to world order and hence also to their own moral standing.

With the exception of the international human rights regime centred on individuals, the subjects of international law are states. Global democratic law of the kind suggested by David Held would have the advantage of widening the scope of law to include other actors, such as groups of indigenous peoples that are currently not adequately comprehended. It would be a law in which sovereignty and self-determination are uncoupled from the state. Recognition of indigenous peoples as peoples with the right of self-determination would require international law to embrace new entities and concepts. This should not be rejected out of hand but seen instead as a chance to make a positive contribution to the inevitable evolution of law in response to global political and social change. International law does in any case already represent evolving global social norms.[4]

Without in any way wanting to retract from endorsing the recognition of indigenous peoples as 'peoples' with the right of self-determination, it must be acknowledged that this is complicated by the relationship between indigenous and human rights. Indigenous rights complement

[3] Venne, *Our Elders*, p. 135.
[4] Matthew S. R. Palmer, 'International Law/Intercultural Relations', *Chicago Journal of International* Law, 1 (Spring 2000), p. 165.

and are an extension of human rights. They give expression to distinctive conceptions of political and social relations and allow for the value of preserving distinct groups. Yet when discussing the relationship between the two in Chapter 4 it was pointed out that because 'the unit of human discourse is the human being'[5] there is an inherent and inescapable tension between human and indigenous rights. The fact that indigenous rights are group rights means that they might undermine the nature of human rights in cases where particular individuals do not wish to be subjected to the will of the group. I agree with Anna Yeatman that the individual is the fundamental unit of human rights discourse, but I do not accept that this is a sufficient reason to reject giving recognition of the right to indigenous self-determination. Clearly it does mean that in some cases there will be a conflict between group and individual rights, but to reject one set of rights in favour of the other in perpetuity would not be just. The tension between the two is one that has to be lived with and resolved as the need arises.

In concluding Chapter 6 I suggested that setting international standards for human and indigenous rights can be seen as anti-pluralist. So also can linking the legitimacy of states to whether they promote indigenous rights as international norms. Simply put, pluralism is the view that states need not be concerned with each other's domestic affairs if these do not impinge on their relations with one another. 'Pluralism is . . . an expression of the constitutional freedom of sovereign states and the wide variety of domestic values accommodated by those same states.'[6] A pluralist international society is one in which states deal with cultural and other differences through mutual recognition of each other's right to exist, respect for each other's dignity and freedom, and by not treating values as absolute. States and the people within them have sovereignty over deciding which values are best for them. Consequently, it can be argued that to recommend international standards to be followed by states in the treatment of their indigenous peoples, particularly when this includes the right of self-determination, is to undermine the sovereign independence of states, which is a fundamental norm of international society. Indeed this is a major reason why states, which do not want their sovereignty eroded, have resisted and will continue to resist adopting the 1994 Draft Declaration.

---

[5] Yeatman, 'Who Is the Subject of Human Rights?', in Meredyth and Minson (eds.), *Citizenship and Cultural Policy*, p. 113.
[6] Jackson, *The Global Covenant*, p. 179.

A further and related argument is that the standards embodied in indigenous rights would simply result in an imposition of the liberal values of the states that have so far been the main sponsors of indigenous rights. Just as human rights are supposedly universal so the principles contained in the Draft Declaration are intended to apply universally to all indigenous peoples. Both human and indigenous rights can be seen as expressions of liberal values that are not in fact universal, and consequently as anti-plural. Chris Brown is not alone in arguing that there are no universal human rights. For him, 'The contemporary human rights regime is, in general, and, for the most part, in detail, simply a contemporary, internationalised and universalised, version of the liberal position on rights.'[7] It can be seen as a denial of plural conceptions of the good. Extended to indigenous rights, which are not Brown's concern, this can be read as the suggestion that they would result in the imposition of uniformity. Not only that, it can be imagined that indigenous peoples might be given the right of self-determination only to find that the states of which they are citizens oblige them to conform to liberal principles of governance.

The first point to make about this is that the rights embodied in the Draft Declaration emerged from a process in which there was widespread indigenous participation. It is consequently difficult to see the principles written into the Draft Declaration as simply ones that would be imposed on indigenous peoples. Second, setting standards for the conduct of states is not so much a matter of denying plural conceptions of the good but of setting limits to them. Diversity is all very well, but, as Brown himself once pointed out, if 'diversity entails that states have the right to mistreat populations, then it is difficult to see why such diversity is valued'.[8] International society should, I believe, have a role in setting these limits. Third, rather than indigenous rights being inimical to diversity and therefore anti-pluralist, it can be argued that to be an anti-pluralist is, paradoxically, actually to be a pluralist. The right to self-determination within the structures of existing states supports the right to be different. Indigenous rights are about upholding plurality within states and, by extension, diversity in the world as a whole. It may well be that the discourse of rights, whether human or indigenous, is mired in liberalism. Diversity may be limited by this, but

---

[7] Brown, 'Universal Human Rights: A Critique', in Dunne and Wheeler (eds.), *Human Rights in Global Politics*, p. 105.
[8] Chris Brown, *International Relations Theory: New Normative Approaches* (New York: Columbia University Press, 1992), p. 125.

liberal regimes are the ones most likely to establish and defend rights.[9] Liberalism might actually encourage indigenous rights.

At the beginning of this inquiry it was suggested that a measure of the worth of international society ought to be the extent to which it supports and advances world order understood as order in human society as a whole. Order in this sense does not refer to discipline and hierarchy, but to just relationships between humans founded on the right to be different, the inclusion of those who are different, and to freedom from domination. The inquiry of the book has shown that the expansion of international society involved the domination and subordination of indigenous peoples with political theory and international law serving to justify dispossession and colonisation. In particular, indigenous peoples became objects rather subjects of international law. This would be decisively reversed by the recognition of indigenous peoples as 'peoples' with the right of self-determination. The adoption of indigenous rights, including self-determination, would provide a set of standards supporting indigenous peoples in their claims against dominant peoples, redress the role of international society in their dispossession, and contribute to world order. Indigenous rights firmly grounded in law have the potential to positively affect the lives of between 250 and 300 million inhabitants of the globe. International society does set standards and there needs to be more attention given to the ways in which it is a moral agent able to promote just relations in human society as a whole.

The distinctive contribution of this book lies, I hope, in what it has suggested about the potential for international society to act as a standard setter and moral agent. I have wanted to suggest in particular that international society can help redress the legacy of its historic expansion by acting as a standard bearer. Were it to be adopted, the Draft Declaration on the Rights of Indigenous Peoples would be an important set of norms against which to measure the moral legitimacy of individual states. And by providing this measure, international society, acting through the institutions of the United Nations, would contribute to its own legitimacy. Of course the norms set out in the Declaration might be observed in the breach, but there would be political costs in ignoring them. These costs may eventually encourage states with outstanding reconciliation issues to resolve them. By so doing, they would contribute, even if only in a small way, to world order understood as the welfare and rights of individuals everywhere.

[9] Russell, 'My People's Courts', p. 52.

Appendix: Draft United Nations Declaration on the Rights of Indigenous Peoples

As agreed upon by the members of the UN Working Group on Indigenous Populations at its Eleventh Session, Geneva, July 1993. Adopted by the UX Sub-commission on Prevention of Discrimination and Protection of Minorities by its resolution 1994/45, August 26, 1994. UN Doc. E/CNA/1995/2, E/CNA/Sub.2/1994/56, at 105 (1994).

Affirming that indigenous peoples are equal in dignity and rights to all other peoples, while recognising the right of all peoples to be different, to consider themselves different, and to be respected as such,

Affirming also that all peoples contribute to the diversity and richness of civilisations and cultures, which constitute the common heritage of humankind,

Affirming further that all doctrines, policies and practices based on or advocating superiority of peoples or individuals on the basis of national origin, racial, religious, ethnic or cultural differences are racist, scientifically false, legally invalid, morally condemnable, and socially unjust,

Reaffirming also that indigenous peoples, in the exercise of their rights, should be free from discrimination of any kind,

Concerned that indigenous peoples have been deprived of their human rights and fundamental freedoms, resulting, *inter alia,* in their colonisation and dispossession of their lands, territories and resources, thus preventing them from exercising, in particular, their right to development in accordance with their own needs and interests,

Recognising the urgent need to respect and promote the inherent rights and characteristics of indigenous peoples, especially their rights to their lands, territories and resources, which derive from their political, economic and social structures and from their cultures, spiritual traditions, histories and philosophies,

Welcoming the fact that indigenous peoples are organising themselves for political, economic, social and cultural enhancement and in order to bring an end to all forms of discrimination and oppression wherever they occur,

Convinced that control by indigenous peoples over developments affecting them and their lands, territories and resources will enable them to maintain and strengthen their institutions, cultures and traditions, and to promote their development in accordance with their aspirations and needs,

Recognising also that respect for indigenous knowledge, cultures and traditional practices contributes to sustainable and equitable development and proper management of the environment,

Emphasising the need for demilitarisation of the lands and territories of indigenous peoples, which will contribute to peace, economic and social progress and development, understanding and friendly relations among nations and peoples of the world,

Recognising in particular the right of indigenous families and communities to retain shared responsibility for the upbringing, training, education and well-being of their children,

Recognising also, that indigenous peoples have the right freely to determine their relationships with States in a spirit of coexistence, mutual benefit and full respect,

Considering that treaties, agreements and other arrangements between States and indigenous peoples are properly matters of international concern and responsibility,

Acknowledging that the Charter of the United Nations, the International Covenant on Economic, Social and Cultural Rights and the International Covenant on Civil and Political Rights affirm the fundamental importance of the right of self-determination of all peoples, by virtue of which they freely determine their political status and freely pursue their economic, social and cultural development,

Bearing in mind that nothing in this Declaration may be used to deny any peoples their right of Self-determination,

Encouraging States to comply with and effectively implement all international instruments, in particular those related to human rights, as they apply to indigenous peoples, in consultation and cooperation with the peoples concerned,

Emphasising that the United Nations has an important and continuing role to play in promoting and protecting the rights of indigenous peoples,

Believing that this Declaration is a further important step forward for the recognition, promotion and protection of the rights and freedoms of indigenous peoples and in the development of relevant activities of the United Nations system in this field,

Solemnly proclaims the following United Nations Declaration on the Rights of Indigenous Peoples:

Part I

Article 1

Indigenous peoples have the right to the full and effective enjoyment of all human rights and fundamental freedoms recognised in the Charter of the United Nations, the Universal Declaration of Human Rights and international human rights law.

Article 2

Indigenous individuals and peoples are free and equal to all other individuals and peoples in dignity and rights, and have the right to be free from any kind of adverse discrimination, in particular that based on their indigenous origin or identity.

Article 3

Indigenous peoples have the right of self-determination. By virtue of that right they freely determine their political status and freely pursue their economic, social and cultural development.

Article 4

Indigenous peoples have the right to maintain and strengthen their distinct political, economic, social and cultural characteristics, as well as their legal systems, while retaining their rights to participate fully, if they so choose, in the political, economic, social and cultural life of the State.

Article 5

Every indigenous individual has the right to a nationality.

Part II

Article 6

Indigenous peoples have the collective right to live in freedom, peace and security as distinct peoples and to full guarantees against genocide or any other act of violence, including the removal of indigenous children from their families and communities under any pretext.

In addition, they have the individual rights to life, physical and mental integrity, liberty, and security of person.

Article 7

Indigenous peoples have the collective and individual right not to be subjected to ethnocide and cultural genocide, including prevention of and redress for:

(a) Any action which has the aim or effect of depriving them of their integrity as distinct peoples, or of their cultural values or ethnic identities;

(b) Any action which has the aim or effect of dispossessing them of their lands, territories or resources;

(c) Any form of population transfer which has the aim or effect of violating or undermining any of their rights;

(d) Any form of assimilation or integration by other cultures or ways of life imposed on them by legislative, administrative or other measures;

(e) Any form of propaganda directed against them.

Article 8

Indigenous peoples have the collective and individual right to maintain and develop their distinct identities and characteristics, including the right to identify themselves as indigenous and to be recognised as such.

Article 9

Indigenous peoples and individuals have the right to belong to an indigenous community or nation, in accordance with the traditions and customs of the community or nation concerned. No disadvantage of any kind may arise from the exercise of such a right.

Article 10

Indigenous peoples shall not be forcibly removed from their lands or territories. No relocation shall take place without the free and informed consent of the indigenous peoples concerned and after agreement on just and fair compensation and, where possible, with the option of return.

Article 11

Indigenous peoples have the right to special protection and security in periods of armed conflict.

States shall observe international standards, in particular the Fourth Geneva Convention of 1949, for the protection of civilian populations in circumstances of emergency and armed conflict, and shall not:

(a) Recruit indigenous individuals against their will into the armed forces and, in particular, for use against other indigenous peoples;

(b) Recruit indigenous children into the armed forces under any circumstances;

(c) Force indigenous individuals to abandon their lands, territories or means of subsistence, or relocate them in special centres for military purposes;

(d) Force indigenous individuals to work for military purposes under any discriminatory conditions.

Part III

Article 12

Indigenous *peoples* have the right to practise and revitalise their cultural traditions and customs. This includes the right to maintain, protect and develop the past, present and future manifestations of their cultures, such as archaeological and historical sites, artifacts, designs, ceremonies, technologies and visual and performing arts and literature, as well as the right to restitution of cultural, intellectual, religious and spiritual property taken without their free and informed consent or in violation of their laws, traditions and customs.

Article 13

Indigenous peoples have the right to manifest, practise, develop and teach their spiritual and religious traditions, customs and ceremonies; the right to maintain, protect, and have access in privacy to their religious and cultural sites; the right to the use and control of ceremonial objects; and the right to the repatriation of human remains.

States shall take effective measures, in conjunction with the indigenous peoples concerned, to ensure that indigenous sacred places, including burial sites, be preserved, respected and protected.

Article 14

Indigenous peoples have the right to revitalise, use, develop and transmit to future generations their histories, languages, oral traditions, philosophies, writing systems and literatures, and to designate and retain their own names for communities, places and persons.

States shall take effective measures, whenever any right of indigenous peoples may be threatened, to ensure this right is protected and also to ensure that they can understand and be understood in political, legal and administrative proceedings, where necessary through the provision of interpretation or by other appropriate means.

Part IV

Article 15

Indigenous children have the right to all levels and forms of education of the State. All indigenous peoples also have this right and the right to establish and control their educational systems and institutions providing education in their own languages, in a manner appropriate to their cultural methods of teaching and learning.

Indigenous children living outside their communities have the right to be provided access to education in their own culture and language.

States shall take effective measures to provide appropriate resources for these purposes.

Article 16

Indigenous peoples have the right to have the dignity and diversity of their cultures, traditions, histories and aspirations appropriately reflected in all forms of education and public information.

States shall take effective measures, in consultation with the indigenous peoples concerned, to eliminate prejudice and discrimination and to promote tolerance, understanding and good relations among indigenous peoples and all segments of society.

Article 17

Indigenous peoples have the right to establish their own media in their own languages. They also have the right to equal access to all forms of non-indigenous media.

States shall take effective measures to ensure that State-owned media duly reflect indigenous cultural diversity.

Article 18

Indigenous peoples have the right to enjoy fully all rights established under international labour law and national labour legislation.

Indigenous individuals have the right not to be subjected to any discriminatory conditions of labour, employment or salary.

Part V

Article 19

Indigenous peoples have the right to participate fully, if they so choose, at all levels of decision-making in matters which may affect their rights, lives and destinies through representatives chosen by themselves in accordance with their own procedures, as well as to maintain and develop their own indigenous decision-making institutions.

Article 20

Indigenous peoples have the right to participate fully, if they so choose, through procedures determined by them, in devising legislative or administrative measures that may affect them.

States shall obtain the free and informed consent of the peoples concerned before adopting and implementing such measures.

Article 21

Indigenous peoples have the right to maintain and develop their political, economic and social systems, to be secure in the enjoyment of their own means of subsistence and development, and to engage freely in all their traditional and other economic activities. Indigenous peoples who have been deprived of their means of subsistence and development are entitled to just and fair compensation.

Article 22

Indigenous peoples have the right to special measures for the immediate, effective and continuing improvement of their economic and social conditions, including in the areas of employment, vocational training and retraining, housing, sanitation, health and social security. Particular attention shall be paid to the rights and special needs of indigenous elders, women, youth, children and disabled persons.

Article 23

Indigenous peoples have the right to determine and develop priorities and strategies for exercising their right to development. In particular, indigenous peoples have the right to determine and develop all health, housing and other economic and social programmes affecting them and, as far as possible, to administer such programmes through their own institutions.

Article 24

Indigenous peoples have the right to their traditional medicines and health practices, including the right to the protection of vital medicinal plants, animals and minerals.

They also have the right to access, without any discrimination, to all medical institutions, health services and medical care.

Part VI

Article 25

Indigenous peoples have the right to maintain and strengthen their distinctive spiritual and material relationship with the lands, territories, waters and coastal seas and other resources which they have traditionally owned or otherwise occupied or used, and to uphold their responsibilities to future generations in this regard.

Article 26

Indigenous peoples have the right to own, develop, control and use the lands and territories, including the total environment of the lands, air, waters, coastal seas, sea-ice, flora and fauna and other resources which they have traditionally owned or otherwise occupied or used. This includes the right to the full recognition of their laws, traditions and customs, land-tenure systems and institutions for the development and management of resources, and the right to effective measures by States to prevent any interference with, alienation of or encroachment upon these rights.

Article 27

Indigenous peoples have the right to the restitution of the lands, territories and resources which they have traditionally owned or otherwise occupied or used, and which have been confiscated, occupied, used or damaged without their free and informed consent. Where this is not possible, they have the right to just and fair compensation. Unless otherwise freely agreed upon by the peoples concerned, compensation shall take the form of lands, territories and resources equal in quality, size and legal status.

Article 28

Indigenous peoples have the right to the conservation, restoration and protection of the total environment and the productive capacity of their lands, territories and resources, as well as to assistance for this purpose from States and through international cooperation. Military activities shall not take place in the lands and territories of indigenous peoples, unless otherwise freely agreed upon by the peoples concerned.

States shall take effective measures to ensure that no storage or disposal of hazardous materials shall take place in the lands and territories of indigenous peoples.

States shall also take effective measures to ensure, as needed, that programmes for monitoring, maintaining and restoring the health of indigenous peoples, as developed and implemented by the peoples affected by such materials, are duly implemented.

Article 29

Indigenous peoples are entitled to the recognition of the full ownership, control and protection of their cultural and intellectual property.

They have the right to special measures to control, develop and protect their sciences, technologies and cultural manifestations, including human and other genetic resources, seeds, medicines, knowledge of the properties of fauna and flora, oral traditions, literatures, designs and visual and performing arts.

Article 30

Indigenous peoples have the right to determine and develop priorities and strategies for the development or use of their lands, territories and other resources, including the right to require that States obtain their free and informed consent prior to the approval of any project affecting their lands, territories and other resources, particularly in connection with the development, utilisation or exploitation of mineral, water or other resources. Pursuant to agreement with the indigenous peoples concerned, just and fair compensation shall be provided for any such activities and measures taken to mitigate adverse environmental, economic, social, cultural or spiritual impact.

Part VII
Article 31
Indigenous peoples, as a specific form of exercising their right to self-determination, have the right to autonomy or self-government in matters relating to their internal and local affairs, including culture, religion, education, information, media, health, housing, employment, social welfare, economic activities, land and resources management, environment and entry by non-members, as well as ways and means for financing these autonomous functions.

Article 32
Indigenous peoples have the collective right to determine their own citizenship in accordance with their customs and traditions. Indigenous citizenship does not impair the right of indigenous individuals to obtain citizenship of the States in which they live.
Indigenous peoples have the right to determine the structures and to select the membership of their institutions in accordance with their own procedures.

Article 33
Indigenous peoples have the right to promote, develop and maintain their institutional structures and their distinctive juridical customs, traditions, procedures and practices, in accordance with internationally recognised human rights standards.

Article 34
Indigenous peoples have the collective right to determine the responsibilities of individuals to their communities.

Article 35
Indigenous peoples, in particular those divided by international borders, have the right to maintain and develop contacts, relations

and cooperation, including activities for spiritual, cultural, political, economic and social purposes, with other peoples across borders.

States shall take effective measures to ensure the exercise and implementation of this right.

Article 36

Indigenous peoples have the right to the recognition, observance and enforcement of treaties, including the right to agreements and other constructive arrangements concluded with States or their successors, approval of any project according to their original spirit and intent, and to have States honour and respect such treaties, agreements and other constructive arrangements. Conflicts and disputes which cannot otherwise be settled should be submitted to competent international bodies agreed to by all parties concerned.

Part VIII

Article 37

States shall take effective and appropriate measures, in consultation with the indigenous peoples concerned, to give full effect to the provisions of this Declaration. The rights recognised herein shall be adopted and included in national legislation in such a manner that indigenous peoples can avail themselves of such rights in practice.

Article 38

Indigenous peoples have the right to have access to adequate financial and technical assistance, from States and through international cooperation, to pursue freely their political, economic, social, cultural and spiritual development and for the enjoyment of the rights and freedoms recognised in this Declaration.

Article 39

Indigenous peoples have the right to have access to and prompt decision through mutually acceptable and fair procedures for the resolution of conflicts and disputes with States, as well as to effective remedies for all infringements of their individual and collective rights. Such a decision shall take into consideration the customs, traditions, rules and legal systems of the indigenous peoples concerned.

Article 40

The organs and specialised agencies of the United Nations system and other intergovernmental organisations shall contribute to the full realisation of the provisions of this Declaration through the mobilization, *inter alia,* of financial cooperation and technical assistance. Ways and means of ensuring participation of indigenous peoples on issues affecting them shall be established.

Article 41

The United Nations shall take the necessary steps to ensure the implementation of this Declaration including the creation of a body at the highest level with special competence in this field and with the direct participation of indigenous peoples. All United Nations bodies shall promote respect for and full application of the provisions of this Declaration.

Part IX

Article 42

The rights recognised herein constitute the minimum standards for the survival, dignity and well-being of the indigenous peoples of the world.

Article 43

All the rights and freedoms recognised herein are equally guaranteed to male and female indigenous individuals.

Article 44

Nothing in this Declaration may be construed as diminishing or extinguishing existing or future rights indigenous peoples may have or acquire.

Article 45

Nothing in this Declaration may be interpreted as implying for any State, group or person any right to engage in any activity or to perform any act contrary to the Charter of the United Nations.

Select bibliography

Aboriginal and Torres Strait Islander Social Justice Commission. *First Report 1993*. Australian Parliamentary Paper 261. Canberra: Australian Government Printing Service, 1993.

Alderson, Kai and Hurrell, Andrew (eds.). *Hedley Bull on International Society*, London: Macmillan, 2000.

Alexandrowicz, C. H. *The European–African Confrontation: A Study in Treaty Making*, Leiden: Sijthoff, 1973.

Alfred, Taiaiake. *Peace, Power, Righteousness: An Indigenous Manifesto*, Ontario: Oxford University Press, 1999.

Anaya, S. James. *Indigenous Peoples in International Law*, New York: Oxford University Press, 1996.
  'Indigenous Peoples And International Law Issues', *American Society of International Law Proceedings*, 92 (April 1998), 96–99.

Arens, Richard (ed.). *Genocide in Paraguay*, Philadelphia: Temple University Press, 1976.

Arneil, Barbara. *John Locke and America: The Defence of English Colonialism*, Oxford: Clarendon Press, 1996.

Asch, Michael (ed.). *Aboriginal and Treaty Rights in Canada: Essays on Law, Equity, and Respect for Difference*, Vancouver: University of British Columbia Press, 1987.

Ashley, Richard K. 'Three Modes of Economism', *International Studies Quarterly*, 27: 4 (1983), 463–96.

Attwood, Bain and Markus, Andrew. 'The Fight for Aboriginal Rights', in R. Manne (ed.), *The Australian Century: Political Struggle in the Building of a Nation*, Melbourne: Text Publishing, 1999, 264–92.

Balandier, Georges. *The Sociology of Black Africa: Social Dynamics in Central Africa*, London: Deutsch, 1970 [1955].

Barsh, Russell. 'Indigenous Peoples in the 1990s: From Object to Subject of International Law?', *Harvard Human Rights Journal*, 7 (Spring 1994), 33–86.
  'Indigenous Peoples and the Idea of Individual Human Rights', *Native Studies Review*, 10: 2 (1995), 35–55.

Bern, John and Dodds, Susan. 'On the Plurality of Interests: Aboriginal Self-Government and Land Rights', in D. Ivison, P. Patton and W. Sanders (eds.), *Political Theory and the Rights of Indigenous Peoples*, Cambridge University Press, 2000, 163–79.

Bernard, F. M. *Herder's Social and Political Thought from Enlightenment to Nationalism*, Oxford: Clarendon Press, 1965.

Bernheimer, R. *Wild Men in the Middle Ages: A Study in Art, Sentiment and Demonology*, Cambridge, MA: Harvard University Press, 1952.

Bird, John, Land, Lorraine and Macadam, Murray (eds.). *Nation to Nation: Aboriginal Sovereignty and the Future of Canada*, Toronto: Irwin Publishing, 2002.

Birrell, Bob and Hirst, John. 'In 2002, Just Who Is an Aborigine?', *Sydney Morning Herald*, 15 August 2002.

Blackstone, William. *Commentaries on the Laws of England, Vol. II, Of the Rights of Things (1766)*, Intr. H. W. Brian Simpson, Chicago: University of Chicago Press, 1979.

Blaney, David L. and Inayatullah, Nameen. 'Prelude to a Conversation of Cultures in International Society?, Todorov and Nandy on the Possibility of Dialogue', *Alternatives*, 19 (1994), 23–51.

Bokor-Szego, Hanna. *The Role of the United Nations in International Legislation* (New York: North Holland Publishing Company, 1978).

Borrows, John. 'Wampum at Niagara: The Royal Proclamation, Canadian Legal History, and Self-Government', in M. Asch (ed.), *Aboriginal and Treaty Rights in Canada: Essays on Law, Equity, and Respect for Difference*, Vancouver: University of British Columbia Press, 1987, 155–72.

'With or Without You: First Nations Law (In Canada)', *McGill Law Journal*, 41 (June 1996), 629–65.

' "Landed" Citizenship: Narratives of Aboriginal Political Participation', in W. Kymlicka and W. Norman (eds.), *Citizenship in Diverse Societies*, Oxford University Press, 2000, 326–42.

Brennan, F. *One Land One Nation: Mabo–Towards 2001*, St Lucia: University of Queensland Press, 1995.

Brown, Chris. 'The Modern Requirement? Reflections on Normative International Theory in a Post-Western World', *Millennium*, 17: 2 (Summer 1988), 339–48.

International Relations Theory: New Normative Approaches, New York: Columbia University Press, 1992.

'International Theory and International Society: The Viability of the Middle Way', *Review of International Studies*, 21: 2 (1995), 183–96.

'Contractarian Thought and the Constitution of International Society', in T. Nardin and D. Mapel (eds.), *International Society: Diverse Ethical Perspectives*, Princeton University Press, 1998, 132–43.

'Universal Human Rights: A Critique' in T. Dunne and N. J. Wheeler (eds.), *Human Rights in Global Politics*, Cambridge University Press, 1999, 103–27.

'Cultural Diversity and International Political Theory', *Review of International Studies*, 26: 2 (April 2000), 199–213.

'Moral Agency and International Society', *Ethics and International Affairs*, 15: 2 (2001), 87–98.

Brysk, Alison. 'Turning Weakness into Strength: The Internationalization of Indian Rights', *Latin American Perspectives*, 23: 2 (Spring 1996), 38–57.

From Tribal Village to Global Village: Indian Rights and International Relations in Latin America, Stanford University Press, 2000.

Bull, Hedley. 'The Grotian Conception of International Society, in M. Wight and H. Butterfield (eds.), *Diplomatic Investigations*, London: Allen & Unwin, 1966, 51–73.

'International Theory: The Case for a Classical Approach', *World Politics*, 18: 3 (April 1966), 361–77.

'International Relations as an Academic Pursuit', in K. Alderson and H. Hurrell (eds.), *Hedley Bull on International Society*, London: Macmillan, 2000, 246–64.

The Anarchical Society, 2nd edn, London: Macmillan, 1995.

'The Third World and International Society', *Yearbook of World Affairs* (1979), 15–31.

Justice in International Relations, The Hagey Lectures, Waterloo Ont.: Waterloo University, 1984. Reproduced in K. Alderson and A., Hurrell (eds.), *Hedley Bull On International Society*, London: Macmillan, 2000, 206–45.

'The Revolt Against the West', in H. Bull and A. Watson (eds.), *The Expansion of International Society*, Oxford University Press, 1985, 217–28.

'European States and African Political Communities', in H. Bull and A. Watson (eds.), *The Expansion of International Society*, Oxford: Oxford University Press, 1985, 96–116.

'The Importance of Grotius in International Relations', in H. Bull, B. Kingsbury and A. Roberts (eds.), *Hugo Grotius and International Relations*, Oxford: Clarendon Press, 1992, 65–93.

Bull, Hedley and Watson, Adam (eds.). *The Expansion of International Society*, Oxford: Oxford University Press, 1985.

Bull, H. B., B. Kingsbury and A. Roberts (eds.), *Hugo Grotius and International Relations*, Oxford: Clarendon Press, 1992.

Burger, Julian. *The GAIA Atlas of First Peoples: A Future for the Indigenous World*, Harmondsworth: Penguin, 1990.

Butt, Peter and Eagleson, Robert. *Mabo, Wik and Native Title*, 3rd edn, Sydney: Federation Press, 1988.

Carr, E. H. *The Future of Nations: Independence or Interdependence?*, London: Kegan Paul, 1941.

Cass, D. 'Re-Thinking Self-Determination: A Critical Analysis of Current International Law Theories', *Syracuse Journal of International Law and Commerce*, 18 (Spring 1992), 22–31.

Chartrand, Paul L. A. H. 'Self-Determination without a Discrete Territorial Base?' in D. Clark and R. Williamson (eds.), *Self-Determination: International Perspectives*, London: Macmillan, 1996, 302–12.

Clark, Donald. and Williamson, Robert (eds.). *Self-Determination: International Perspectives*, London: Macmillan, 1996.

Clifford, James. *The Predicament of Culture: Twentieth-Century Ethnography, Literature, and Art*, Cambridge, MA: Harvard University Press, 1988.

Cobban, Alfred. *The Nation-State and National Self-Determination*, London: Collins, 1969.

Cobo, José Martinez. Study of the Problem Against Indigenous Populations, vol. v, Conclusions, Proposals and Recommendations, UN DOC E/CN 4/Sub 2 1986/7, Add 4, para 379 and 381.

Cohen, Benjamin. *The Question of Imperialism: The Political Economy of Dominance and Dependence*, London: Macmillan, 1974.

Commission on Global Governance. *Our Global Neighbourhood: The Report of the Commission on Global Governance*, Oxford University Press, 1995.

Connolly, William E. 'Identity and Difference in Global Politics', in J. Der Derian and M. J. Shapiro (eds.), *International/Intertextual Relations: Postmodern Readings of World Politics*, Lexington, MA: Lexington Books, 1989, 323–42.

Cottingham, John. *Rationalism*, London: Paladin, 1984.

Crawford, James. *The Creation of States in International Law*, Oxford: Clarendon Press, 1979.

Crawford, James (ed.), *The Rights of Peoples*, Oxford: Clarendon Press, 1988.

Cutler, A. Claire. 'The "Grotian tradition" in International Relations', *Review of International Studies*, 17: 1 (January 1991), 41–65.

Daes, Erica-Irene A. 'The Right of Indigenous Peoples to "Self-Determination" in the Contemporary World Order', in D. Clark and R. Williamson (eds.), *Self-Determination: International Perspectives*, London: Macmillan, 1996, 47–57.

Delgamuukw v. British Columbia (Macfarlane J.A.). *Dominion Law Reports*, 104 (4th), 1993, 470–548.

D'Entreves, A. P. *Natural Law: An Introduction to Legal Philosophy*, London: Hutchinson University Library, 1972.

Devetak, R. 'The Project of Modernity and International Relations Theory', *Millennium*, 24: 1 (1995), 27–51.

Diaz-Polanco, Hector. 'Indian Communities and the Quincentenary' Trans. John F. Uggen, *Latin American Perspectives*, 19: 3 (Summer 1992), 6–24.

Diderot, Denis. *Political Writings*, ed. J. H. Mason and R. Wokler, Cambridge University Press, 1992.

Dodds, S. 'Justice, Indigenous Rights and Liberal Property: Reflections on Two Australian Cases', Unpublished paper, 1997.

Dodson, Michael. 'Land Rights and Social Justice' in Y. Galarrwuy (ed.), *Our Land is Our Life: Land Rights – Past, Present and Future*, St Lucia: University of Queensland Press, 1997, 39–51.

Donnelly, Jack. 'Human Rights: A New Standard of Civilization?' *International Affairs*, 74: 1 (1998), 1–24.

Doyle, Michael. *Empires*, Ithaca: Cornell University Press, 1986.

Duffié, Mary Kay. 'Goals for Fourth World Peoples and Sovereignty Initiatives in the United States and New Zealand', *American Indian Culture and Research Journal*, 22: 1 (1998), 183–212.

Dunne, Timothy, 'Colonial Encounters in International Relations: Reading Wight, Writing Australia', *Australian Journal of International Affairs*, 51: 3 (November 1997), 309–23.

Inventing International Society: A History of the English School, London: Macmillan, 1998.

Durie, Mason. *Te Mana, Te Kāwanatanga: The Politics of Māori Self-Determination*, Auckland: Oxford University Press, 1998.

Eisenberg, Avigail. 'The Politics of Individual and Group Difference in Canadian Jurisprudence', *Canadian Journal of Political Science*, 27: 1 (March 1994), 3–21.

Elliott, J. H. *The Old World and the New 1492–1650*, Cambridge University Press, 1992.

Falk, Richard. 'The Rights of Peoples (In Particular Indigenous Peoples)', in J. Crawford (ed.), *Rights of Peoples*, Oxford: Clarendon Press, 1988, 17–37.

Human Rights Horizons: The Pursuit of Justice in a Globalizing World, London: Routledge, 2000.

Fleras, Augie. 'Politicising Indigeneity: Ethno-politics in White Settler Dominions', in P. Haverman (ed.), *Indigenous Peoples' Rights in Australia, Canada, and New Zealand*, Auckland: Oxford University Press, 1999, 187–234.

Foster, Hamar. 'Canada: "Indian Administration" from the Royal Proclamation of 1763 to Constitutionally Entrenched Rights', in P. Haverman (ed.), *Indigenous Peoples' Rights in Australia, Canada, and New Zealand*, Auckland: Oxford University Press, 1999, 351–77.

Francis, Mark. 'The Cultural Identity of Indigenous Peoples and the Failure of Canadian Political Theory'. Unpublished paper delivered to the Annual Conference of the Australasian Political Science Association, Brisbane 2001.

Franck, Thomas. M. 'The Emerging Right to Democratic Governance', *The American Journal of International Law*, 86: 1 (1992), 46–75.

Fry, Greg. 'Framing the Islands: Knowledge and Power in Changing Australian Images of 'The South Pacific', *The Contemporary Pacific*, 9: 7 (Fall 1997), 305–44.

Gagnon, Alain-G. and Tully, James (eds.). *Multinational Democracies*, Cambridge University Press, 2001.

Ghai, Yash. 'Ethnicity and Autonomy: A Framework for Analysis', in Y. Ghai (ed.), *Autonomy and Ethnicity: Negotiating Competing Claims in Multi-ethnic States*, Cambridge University Press, 2000, 1–26.

Gibson, C. *Spain in America*, New York: Harper-Torch Books, 1966.

Gilpin, Robert. *War and Change in World Politics*, Cambridge University Press, 1981.

Goodwin, Jason. *Lords of the Horizons: A History of the Ottoman Empire*, London: Vintage, 1999.

Gong, G. W. *The Standard of 'Civilization' in International Society*. Oxford: Clarendon Press, 1984.

Gray, Andrew. 'The Indigenous Movement in Asia', in R. H. Barnes, A. Gray and B. Kingsbury (eds.), *Indigenous Peoples of Asia*, Ann Arbor, MI: Association for Asian Studies, 1995, pp. 35–58.

Grotius, Hugo. *The Law of War and Peace*, trans. F. W. Kelsey, Classics of International Law Series, Oxford: Clarendon Press, 1925.

Gutmann, Amy (ed.). *Multiculturalism: Examining the Politics of Recognition*, Princeton University Press, 1994.

Halliday, Fred. *Rethinking International Relations*, Basingstoke: Macmillan, 1994.

Hamilton, Bernice. *Political Thought in Sixteenth-Century Spain: A Study of the political ideas of Vitoria, De Soto, Suárez, and Molina*, Oxford: Clarendon Press, 1963.

Hanke, L. *The Spanish Struggle for Justice in the Conquest of America*, Boston: Little-Brown, 1965.

Hannum, Hurst. 'Self-Determination in the Post-Colonial Era', in D. Clark and R. Williamson (eds.), *Self-Determination: International Perspectives*, London: Macmillan, 1996, 12–43.

Haverman, Paul (ed.). *Indigenous Peoples' Rights in Australia, Canada, and New Zealand*, Auckland: Oxford University Press, 1999.

Hechter, Michael. *Internal Colonialism: The Celtic Fringe in British National Development 1536–1966*, Berkeley: University of California Press, 1975.

Held, David. *Democracy and the Global Order: From the Modern State to Cosmopolitan Governance*, Cambridge: Polity Press, 1995.

Hinsley, F. H. *Sovereignty*, 2nd edn, Cambridge University Press, 1986.

Hobbes, Thomas. *Leviathan*, ed. C. B. Macpherson, Harmondsworth: Penguin, 1968.

Hobson, J. A. *Imperialism: A Study*, Ann Arbor: University of Michigan Press, 1972 [1902].

Human Rights and Equal Opportunity Commission. *Bringing Them Home: Report of the National Inquiry into the Separation of Aboriginal and Torres Strait Islander Children from Their Families*, Canberra: Australian Government Printing Service, April 1997.

Husband, T. *The Wild Man: Medieval Myth and Symbolism*, New York: Metropolitan Museum of Art, 1980.

Huxley, G. L. 'Aristotle, Las Casas and the American Indians', *Proceedings of the Royal Irish Academy*, 80 (1980), 57–68.

Iorns, Catherine J. 'Indigenous Peoples and Self Determination: Challenging State Sovereignty', *Case Western Reserve Journal of International Law*, 24: 2 (Spring 1992), 199–348.

Irons Magallanes, Catherine J. 'International Human Rights and their Impact on Domestic Law on Indigenous Peoples' Rights in Australia, Canada, and New Zealand', in P. Haverman (ed.), *Indigenous Peoples' Rights in Australia, Canada, and New Zealand*, Auckland: Oxford University Press, 1999, 235–76.

Iveson, Duncan, Patton, Paul and Sanders, Will (eds.). *Political Theory and the Rights of Indigenous Peoples*, Cambridge University Press, 2000.

Jackson, Robert. 'Is There a Classical International Theory?', in S. Smith K. Booth and M. Zalewski (eds.), *International Theory: Positivism and Beyond*, Cambridge University Press, 1996, 203–18.

The Global Covenant: Human Conduct in a World of States, Oxford University Press, 2000.

Janis, M. W. 'American Versions of the International Law of Christendom: Kent, Wheaton and the Grotian Tradition', *Netherlands International Law Review*, 39 (1992), 37–61.

Kaldor, Mary. *New and Old Wars: Organized Violence in a Global Era*, Cambridge: Polity Press, 1999.

Keal, Paul. *Unspoken Rules and Superpower Dominance*, London: Macmillan, 1983.

' "Just Backward Children": International Law and the Conquest of Non-European Peoples', *Australian Journal of International Affairs*, 49: 2 (November 1995), 191–206.

'An International Society?', in J. O'Hagen and G. Fry (eds.), *Contending Images of World Politics*, London: Macmillan, 2000, 61–75.

Keohane, R. 'International Institutions: Two Approaches', in R. Keohane, *International Institutions and State Power*, Boulder: Westview Press, 1989, 158–179.

Kingsbury, Benedict. 'Claims by Non-State Groups in International Law', *Cornell International Law Journal*, 25: 3 (1992), 481–513.

' "Indigenous Peoples" as an International Legal Concept', in R. H. Barnes, A. Gray and B. Kingsbury (eds.), *Indigenous Peoples of Asia*, Michigan: The Association for Asian Studies, 1995, 13–34.

' "Indigenous Peoples" In International Law: A Constructivist Approach to the Asian Controversy', *The American Journal of International Law*, 92 (1998), 414–57.

'The Applicability of the International Legal Concept of "Indigenous Peoples" in Asia', in J. R. Bauer, and D. A. Bell (eds.), *The East Asian Challenge For Human Rights*, Cambridge University Press, 1999, 336–77.

Kukathas, Chandran. 'Are There Any Cultural Rights?', *Political Theory*, 20: 1 (February 1992), 105–39.

'The Politics of Responsibility: How to Shift the Burden', Unpublished paper, 1999.

Kymlicka, Will. *Liberalism, Community and Culture*, Oxford: Clarendon Press, 1989.

'A Reply to Chandran Kukathas', *Political Theory*, 20: 1 (February 1992), 140–46.

Multicultural Citizenship: A Liberal Theory of Minority Rights, Oxford: Clarendon Press, 1995.

Finding Our Way: Rethinking Ethnocultural Relations in Canada, London: Oxford University Press, 1998.

'Theorizing Indigenous Rights', *University of Toronto Law Journal*, 49 (Spring 1999), 281–293.

Kymlicka, Will and Norman, Wayne (eds.). *Citizenship in Diverse Societies*, Oxford University Press, 2000.

Lanyon, Anna. *Malinche's Conquest*, Sydney: Allen & Unwin, 1999.

Lapid, Yosef and Kratochwil, Friedrich (eds.). *The Return of Culture and Identity in IR Theory*, Boulder: Lynne Rienner, 1996.

Lauterpacht, H. *International Law, The Collected Papers*, Vols. 1 and 2, ed. E. Lauterpacht, Cambridge University Press, 1970, 1975.

Lebvre, L. 'Civilisation: Evolution of a Word and a Group of Ideas', in P. A. Bourke (ed.), *A New Kind of History: The Writings of Lucien Lebvre*, London: 1973, 219–57.

Lindley, M. F. *The Acquisition and Government of Backward Territory in International Law: Being a Treatise on the Law and Practice Relating to Colonial Expansion*, New York: Negro Universities Press, 1969 [1926].

Linklater, Andrew. *Beyond Realism and Marxism: Critical Theory and International Relations*, London: Macmillan, 1990.

Men and Citizens in the Theory of International Relations, 2nd edn, London: Macmillan, 1990.

'The Question of the Next Stage in International Relations Theory: A Critical-Theoretical Point of View', *Millennium*, 21: 1 (1992), 77–98.

'What Is a Good International Citizen?', in P. Keal (ed.), *Ethics and Foreign Policy*, Sydney: Allen & Unwin in association with the Australian National University, 1992, 21–43.

'Rationalism', in S. Burchill and A. Linklater *et al.*, *Theories of International Relations*, Basingstoke: Macmillan, 1994, 93–118.

'The Achievements of Critical Theory', in S. Smith, K. Booth and M. Zalewski (eds.), *International Theory: Positivism and Beyond*, Cambridge University Press, 1996, 279–98.

'Citizenship and Sovereignty in the Post-Westphalian State', *European Journal of International Relations*, 2: 1 (1996), 77–103.

The Transformation of Political Community: Ethical Foundations of the Post-Westphalian Community, Cambridge: Polity Press, 1998.

Locke, John. *Two Treatises of Government*, ed. M. Goldie, London: Everyman, 1993.

Lovejoy, Arthur O. *The Great Chain of Being. The History of an Idea*, Cambridge, MA: Harvard University Press, 1948.

Lynch, Owen. 'The Sacred and the Profane', *St. Thomas Law Review*, 9 (Fall 1996), 93–102.

Maaka, Roger and Fleras, Augie. 'Engaging with Indigeneity: Tino Rangati-ratanga in Aotearoa', in D. Iveson, P. Patton and W. Sanders (eds.), *Political Theory and the Rights of Indigenous Peoples*, Cambridge University Press, 2000, 89–109.

Mabo v. Queensland. The Australian Law Journal, 66: 7 (July 1992), 408–99.

Mamdani, Mahmood. 'Beyond Settler and Native as Political Identities: Overcoming the Political Legacy of Colonialism', *Society for Comparative Study of Society and History* (2001), 651–64.

Manne, Robert. 'The Stolen Generation', *Quadrant*, 42 (January–February 1988), 53–63.

Marks, Greg. C. 'Indigenous Peoples in International Law: The Significance of Francisco De Vitoria and Bartolomé De Las Casas', *The Australian Yearbook of International Law*, 13 (1992), 1–51.

Marshall, P. J. and Williams, Glyndwr. *The Great Map of Mankind: British Perceptions of the World in the Age of Enlightenment*, London: Dent, 1982.

Mason, Andrew. 'Political Community, Liberal-nationalisms, and the Ethics of Assimilation', *Ethics*, 109: 2 (January 1999), 261–86.

McGrane, Bernard. *Beyond Anthropology: Society and the Other*, New York: Columbia University Press, 1989.

McNeil, Kent. 'The Meaning of Aboriginal Title', in M. Asch (ed.), *Aboriginal and Treaty Rights in Canada: Essays on Law, Equity, and Respect for Difference*, Vancouver: University of British Columbia Press, 1987, 135–153.

Macpherson, C. B. *The Political Theory of Possessive Individualism: Hobbes to Locke*, New York: Oxford University Press, 1964.

Meek, Ronald. L. *Social Science and the Ignoble Savage*, Cambridge University Press, 1976.

Melbourne, Hineani. *Māori Sovereignty: The Māori Perspective*, Auckland: Hodder Moa Beckett, 1995.

Mikaere, Ani, Milroy, Stephanie. 'Review: Treaty of Waitangi and Maori Land Law', *New Zealand Law Review*, 3 (2001), 379–99.

Millett, Michael, 'Identity Fight Delays Poll', *Sydney Morning Herald*, 14 August 2002.

Montaigne, Michel de. *The Complete Essays*, trans. M. A. Screech, Harmondsworth: Penguin, 1991.

Montesquieu. *The Spirit of the Laws*, trans. and ed. A. M. Cohler, B. C. Miller and H. S. Stone, Cambridge University Press, 1989.

Muldoon, James. *The Americas in the Spanish World Order: The Justification for the Conquest in the Seventeenth Century*, Philadelphia: University of Pennsylvania Press, 1994.

Nardin, Terry. *Law, Morality and Relations of States*, Princeton University Press, 1983.

Nardin, Terry and Mapel, David (eds.). *International Society: Diverse Ethical Perspectives*, Princeton University Press, 1998.

Traditions of International Ethics, Cambridge University Press, 1992.

Nash, June. 'The Reassertion of Indigenous Identity: Mayan Responses to State Intervention in Chiapas', *Latin American Research Review*, 30: 3 (1995), 7–41.

Neumann, Ivar B. 'Self and Other in International Relations', *European Journal of International Relations*, 2: 2 (1996), 139–74.

Neumann, Ivar B. and Walsh, Janet M. 'The Other in European Self-definition: An Addendum to the Literature on International Society', *Review of International Studies*, 17 (1991), 327–48.

Nunes, Keith D. ' "We Can Do Better": Rights of Singular Peoples and the United Nations Draft Declaration on the "Rights Of Indigenous Peoples" ', *St. Thomas Law Review*, 7 (Summer 1995), 521–55.

Nussbaum, A. *A Concise History of the Law of Nations*, rev edn, New York: 1954.
O'Hagen, Jacinta and Fry, Greg (eds.). *Contending Images of World Politics*, London: Macmillan 2000.
Oppenheim, L. *International Law: A Treatise*, vol. I, 8th edn, ed. H. Lauterpacht, London: Longmans, 1967.
Orange, Claudia. *The Story of a Treaty*, Auckland: Bridget Williams, 2001.
Ortiz, Roxanne Dunbar. 'Indigenous Rights and Regional Autonomy in Revolutionary Nicaragua', *Latin American Perspectives*, 14: 1 (Winter 1987), 43–66.
Otto, Dianne. 'A Question of Law or Politics? Indigenous Claims to Sovereignty in Australia', *Syracuse Journal of International Law and Commerce*, 21 (1995), 701–39.
'Subalternity and International Law: The Problems of Global Community and the Incommensurability Of Difference', *Social and Legal Studies*, 5: 3 (1996), 337–64.
Outram, Dorinda. *The Enlightenment*, Cambridge University Press, 1996.
Pagden, Anthony. 'The "School of Salamanca" and the "Affairs of the Indies"', *History of Universities*, 1 (1981), 71–112.
The Fall of Natural Man: The American Indian and the Origins of Comparative Ethnology, Cambridge University Press, 1982.
European Encounters with the New World: From Renaissance to Romanticism, New Haven: Yale University Press, 1993.
Lords of All the World: Ideologies of Empire in Spain, Britain and France c.1500–c.1800, New Haven: Yale University Press, 1995.
Pagden, Anthony (ed.). *The Languages of Political Theory in Early-Modern Europe*, Cambridge University Press, 1987.
Palmer, Matthew S. R. 'International Law/Intercultural Relations', *Chicago Journal of International Law*, 1 (Spring 2000), 159–65.
Parekh, Bikhu. *Rethinking Multiculturalism: Cultural Diversity and Political Theory*, London: Macmillan, 2000.
Pearson, Noel. 'From Remnant Title to Social Justice', *Australian Journal of Anthropology*, 6: 1 (1995), 95–100.
'The Concept of Native Title at Common Law', in Y. Galarrwuy (ed.), *Our Land is Our Life: Land Rights – Past, Present and Future*, St Lucia: University of Queensland Press, 1997, 150–62.
'Principles of Communal Native Title', *Indigenous Law Bulletin*, 5: 3 (October 2000), 4–7.
'Reconciliation: To Be or Not To Be – Separate Aboriginal Nationhood or Aboriginal Self-determination and Self-government within the Australian nation?', *Aboriginal Law Bulletin*, 3: 16 (April 1993), 14–17.
Penrose, Boies. *Travel and Discovery in the Renaissance, 1420–1620*, Cambridge, MA: Harvard University Press, 1952.
Perkins, Steven C. 'Researching Indigenous Peoples Rights Under International Law 1' (1999), http://www.rci.rutgers.edu/~sperkins/ipr2.html accessed 31/07/2002.
Pettman, Ralph. *International Politics*, Melbourne: Longman Cheshire, 1991.

Pocock, J. G. A. 'Law, Sovereignty and History in a Divided Culture: The Case of New Zealand and the Treaty of Waitangi', *McGill Law Journal*, 43 (October 1998).

Pocock, John. 'Waitangi as Mystery of State: Consequences of the Ascription of Federative Capacity to the Maori', in D. Ivison, P. Patton and W. Sanders (eds.), *Political Theory and the Rights of Indigenous Peoples* (Cambridge: Cambridge University Press, 2000).

Pritchard, Sarah (ed.). *Indigenous Peoples, the United Nations and Human Rights*, Sydney: Zed Books, 1998.

'The United Nations and the Making of a Declaration on Indigenous Rights', *Indigenous Law Bulletin.* http://www.austlii.au/au/special/rsproject/rslibrary/ilb/vol3/no89/1.html accessed 21/02/2002.

Pufendorf, S. *On the Duty of Man and Citizen According to Natural Law*, ed. James Tully, trans. M. Silverthorne, Cambridge University Press, 1991.

Raby, Peter. *Bright Paradise: Victorian Scientific Travellers*, London: Pimlico, 1996.

Reiss, Hans (ed.). *Kant's Political Writings*, Cambridge University Press, 1970.

Remec, P. *The Position of the Individual in International Law According to Grotius and Vattel*, The Hague: Nijhoff, 1960.

Reus-Smit, Christian. 'Introduction', in C. Reus-Smit (ed.), *The Politics of International Law*, Unpublished manuscript.

Reynolds, Henry. *The Law of the Land*, Melbourne: Penguin, 1992.
Aboriginal Sovereignty: Three Nations, One Australia?, Sydney: Allen & Unwin, 1996.

Rousseau, J. J. 'Discourse on Inequality', in *Political Writings*, ed. A. Ritter and J. C. Bondanella, New York: Norton, 1988.

Rowse, Tim. 'Mabo and Moral Anxiety', *Meanjin*, 2 (Winter 1993), 229–52.
Indigenous Futures: Choice and Development for Aboriginal and Islander Australia, Sydney: University of New South Wales Press, 2002.

Rubin, A. P. 'International Law in the Age of Columbus', *Netherlands International Law Review*, 39 (1992), 6–35.

Ruddy, F. S. *International Law in the Enlightment: The Background of Emerich de Vattel's 'Le Droit des Gens'*, Dobbs Ferry, NY: 1975.

Ruggie, John. G. 'Territoriality and Beyond: Problematizing Modernity in International Relations', *International Organization*, 47: 1 (Winter 1993), 139–74.

Russell, Peter. 'Constitutional Politics in Multi-National Canada', *Arena Journal*, 14 (1999/2000), 75–82.
'Corroboree 2000 – A Nation Defining Event', *Arena Journal*, 15 (2000), 25–38.
'My People's Courts as Agents of Indigenous Decolonisation?', *Law in Context*, 18: 1 (2001), 50–61.

Said, Edward. *Orientalism*, Harmondsworth: Penguin, 1985.

Schwartz, Stuart B. (ed.). *Implicit Understandings: Observing, Reporting, and Reflecting on the Encounters Between Europeans and Other Peoples in the Early Modern Era*, Cambridge University Press, 1994.

Scott, J. B. *The Spanish Origin of International Law*, Oxford University Press, 1934.

Seth, Sanjay. 'A Critique of Disciplinary Reason: The Limits of Political Theory', *Alternatives*, 26: 1 (2001), 73–92.

Shapcott, Richard. 'Conversation and Coexistence: Gadamer and the Interpretation of International Society, *Millennium*, 23: 1 (1994), 57–83.

Justice, Community and Dialogue in International Relations, Cambridge University Press, 2001.

'Cosmopolitan Conversations: Justice, Dialogue and the Cosmopolitan Project', *Global Society*, 16: 3 (2002), 221–43.

Sharp, Andrew. *Justice and the Māori: The Philosophy and Practice of Māori Claims in New Zealand Since the 1970s*, 2nd edn, Auckland: Oxford University Press, 1997.

Shaw, Karena. 'Indigeneity and the International', *Millennium*, 31: 1 (2000), 55–81.

Shaw, M. 'The Western Sahara Case', *The British Yearbook of International Law*, 49 (1978).

International Law, 2nd edn, Cambridge: Grotius Publications, 1986.

Global Society and International Relations, Cambridge: Polity Press, 1994.

Shklar, Judith K. *Montesquieu*, Oxford University Press, 1987.

Silverblatt, Irene. 'Becoming Indian in the Central Andes of Seventeenth-Century Peru', in Gyan Prakash (ed.), *After Colonialism: Imperial Histories and Postcolonial Displacements*, Princeton University Press, 1995, 279–98.

Simon, Herbert. 'Human Nature in Politics: The Dialogue with Political Science', *American Political Science Review*, 79: 2 (1985), 293–304.

Simpson, Gerry J. 'The Diffusion of Sovereignty: Self-Determination in the Post-Colonial Age', *Stanford Journal of International Law*, 32: 2 (1996), 255–86.

Smith, Anthony. *National Identity*, Reno: University of Nevada Press, 1991.

Smith, Bernard. *European Vision and the South Pacific*, Melbourne University Press, 1989.

Imagining the Pacific: In the Wake of the Cook Voyages, Melbourne University Press, 1992.

Smith, Steve, Booth, Ken and Zalewski, Marysia (eds.). *International Theory: Positivism and Beyond*, Cambridge University Press, 1996.

Sparrow, Rob. 'History and Collective Responsibility', *Australasian Journal of Philosophy*, 78: 3 (September 2000), 346–59.

Spinner-Halev, Jeff. 'Land, Culture and Justice: A Framework for Group Rights and Recognition', *The Journal of Political Philosophy*, 8: 3 (2000), 319–42.

Stannard, David. *American Holocaust*, New York: Oxford University Press, 1992.

Steiner, Henry J. and Alston, Philip (eds.). *International Human Rights in Context: Law, Politics, Morals*, Oxford: Clarendon Press, 1996.

Stephenson, M. A. and Ratnapala, Suri (eds.). *Mabo: A Judicial Revolution: The Aboriginal Land Rights Decision and its Impact on Australian Law*, St Lucia: University of Queensland Press, 1993.

Sterba, James P. 'Understanding Evil: American Slavery, the Holocaust, and the Conquest of the American Indians', *Ethics*, 106: 2 (January 1996), 424–48.

Select bibliography

Stone, Julius. 'Approaches to the Notion of International Justice', Jerusalem: Truman Center Publications No. 4, Hebrew University of Jerusalem, 1970.

Stonich, Susan (ed.). *Endangered Peoples' of Latin America: Struggles to Survive and Thrive*, Westport, CT: Greenwood Press, 2001.

Strelein, Lisa Mary. 'Indigenous Self-Determination Claims and the Common Law in Australia', Ph.D. thesis, The Australian National University, April 1998.

Taylor, Charles. 'The Politics of Recognition', in Amy Gutmann (ed.), *Multiculturalism: Examining the Politics of Recognition*, Princeton University Press, 1994, 25–73.

Tennant, Chris. 'Indigenous Peoples, International Institutions, and the International Legal Literature from 1945–1993', *Human Rights Quarterly*, 16 (1994), 1–57.

Thomas, Nicholas. *Colonialism's Culture: Anthropology, Travel and Government*, Cambridge: Polity Press, 1994.

Thompson, Ruth (ed.). *The Rights of Indigenous Peoples in International Law: Selected Essays on Self-Determination*, Saskatchewan: University of Saskatchewan, Native Law Centre, 1987.

Thornbury, Patrick. 'Some Implications of the UN Declaration on Minorities for Indigenous Peoples', in Eyassu Gayim and Kristian Myntti (eds.), *Indigenous and Tribal Peoples' Rights – 993 and After* (Rovaniemi: University of Lapland, 1955).

Todorov, Tzvetan. *The Conquest of America: The Question of the Other*, New York: Harper Torch, 1992.

On Human Diversity: Nationalism, Racism, and Exoticism in French Thought, Harvard University Press, 1993.

Tomasi, John. 'Kymlicka, Liberalism, and Respect for Cultural Minorities', *Ethics*, 105 (April 1995), 580–605.

Tuck, Richard. *Natural Rights Theories: Their Origin and Development*, Cambridge University Press, 1979.

Hobbes. Oxford: Oxford University Press, 1989.

The Rights of War and Peace: Political Thought and the International Order from Grotius to Kant, Oxford University Press, 1999.

Tully, James. *A Discourse on Property: John Locke and his Adversaries*, Cambridge University Press, 1980.

An Approach to Political Philosophy: Locke in Contexts, Cambridge University Press, 1993.

'Aboriginal Property and Western Theory: Recovering a Middle Ground', *Social Philosophy and Policy*, 11: 2 (Summer 1994), 153–80.

Strange Multiplicity: Constitutionalism in an Age of Diversity, Cambridge University Press, 1995.

'The Struggles of Indigenous Peoples for and of Freedom', in D. Iveson, P. Patton and W. Sanders (eds.), *Political Theory and the Rights of Indigenous Peoples*, Cambridge University Press, 2000, 36–59.

'Introduction', in A.-G. Gagnon and J. Tully (eds.), *Multinational Democracies*, Cambridge University Press, 2001, 1–33.

Turner, Dale. 'This Is Not a Peace Pipe: Towards an Understanding of Aboriginal Sovereignty', Ph.D. thesis, McGill University, 1979.

'Vision: Towards an Understanding of Aboriginal Sovereignty', in W. Norman and R. Beiner (eds.), *Contemporary Canadian Political Philosophy*, Oxford University Press, 2001.

Tutu, Desmond. *No Future Without Forgiveness*, London: Rider, 1999.

Vattel, Emmerich De. *The Law of Nations*. Philadelphia: Johnson and Co., 1863 (reprinted New York: AMS Press, 1982).

Venne, Sharon. 'Understanding Treaty 6: An Indigenous Perspective', in M. Asch (ed.), *Aboriginal and Treaty Rights in Canada: Essays on Law, Equity, and Respect for Difference*, Vancouver: University of British Columbia Press, 1987, 173–207.

'Self-Determination Issues in Canada: A First Person's Overview', in D. Clark and R. Williamson (eds.), *Self-Determination: International Perspectives*. London: Macmillan, 1996, 291–301.

Our Elders Understand Our Rights: Evolving International Law Regarding Indigenous Rights, Penticon, BC: Theytus Books, 1998.

Vincent, R. John. *Human Rights and International Relations*, Cambridge University Press, 1986.

Vitoria, Francisco de. *Political Writings*, ed., A. Pagden and J. Lawrence, Cambridge University Press, 1991.

Waldron, Jeremy. 'Superseding Historic Injustice', *Ethics*, 103: 1 (October 1992), 4–28.

Walker, Ranginui, 'Māori Sovereignty, Colonial and Post-Colonial Discourses', in P. Haverman (ed.), *Indigenous Peoples Rights in Australia, Canada, and New Zealand*, Auckland: Oxford University Press, 1999, 108–22.

Watts, Ronald L. 'Federalism and Diversity in Canada', in Y. Ghai (ed.), *Autonomy and Ethnicity: Negotiating Competing Claims in Multi-ethnic States*, Cambridge University Press, 2000, 29–52.

Wendt, Alexander E. 'The Agent–Structure Problem in International Relations Theory', *International Organization*, 41: 3 (Summer 1987), 335–70.

Westlake, John. *The Collected Papers of John Westlake on Public International Law*, ed. L. Oppenheim, Cambridge University Press, 1914.

Wheaton, Henry. *Elements of International Law*, New York: Da Capo Press, 1972 [1836].

White, Hayden. 'The Forms of Wildness: Archaeology of an Idea', in E. Dudley and Maximillian E. Novak (eds.), *The Wild Man Within: An Image in Western Thought from the Renaissance to Romanticism*, University of Pittsburgh Press, 1972.

Wick, Raidza Torres, 'Revisiting the Emerging International Norm on Indigenous Rights: Autonomy as an Option', *Yale Journal of International Law*, 16 (Summer 2000), 291–99.

Wight, Martin. 'Western Values in International Relations', in H. Butterfield and M. Wight (eds.), *Diplomatic Investigations: Essays in the Theory of International Politics*, London: Allen & Unwin, 1966, 89–131.

Systems of States, Leicester: Leicester University Press, 1977.

Wight, Martin, Gabriele Wight and Brian Porter (eds.). *International Theory: The Three Traditions*, Leicester: Leicester University Press, 1991.

Wilkins, Kerry. 'But We Need the Eggs: The Royal Commission, the Charter of Rights and the Inherent Right of Aboriginal Self-Government', *University of Toronto Law Journal*, 49 (Winter 1999), 53–121.

Williams, Robert A. *The American Indian in Western Legal Thought: The Discourses of Conflict*, New York: Oxford University Press, 1990.

'Encounters on the Frontiers of International Human Rights Law: Redefining the Terms of Indigenous Peoples' Survival in the World', *Duke Law Journal*, 4 (September 1990), 660–704.

Wilmer, Franke. *The Indigenous Voice in World Politics: Since Time Immemorial*, London: Sage, 1993.

Wokler, Robert. 'Perfectable Apes in Decadent Cultures: Rousseau's Anthropology Revisited', *Daedalus*, 107 (1978), 107–14.

Rousseau, Oxford University Press, 1995.

Yeatman, Anna. 'Justice and the Sovereign Self', in M. Wilson and A. Yeatman (eds.), *Justice and Identity: Antipodean Practices*, Wellington: Bridget Williams, 1995, 195–211.

'Who Is the Subject of Human Rights?', in D. Meredyth and J. Minson (eds.), *Citizenship and Cultural Policy*, London: Sage Publications, 2001, 104–19.

Young, Iris Marion. *Justice and the Politics of Difference*, Princeton University Press, 1990.

Inclusion and Democracy, New York: Oxford University Press, 2000.

Young, Robert J. C. *Postcolonialism: An Historical Introduction*, Oxford: Blackwell, 2001.

Yunupingu, Galarrwuy (ed.). *Our Land is Our Life: Land Rights – Past, Present and Future*, St Lucia: University of Queensland Press, 1997.

Index

Index

'otherness' 21, 22, 86, 111–112, 196
Otto, Dianne 142, 146–147, 151, 152–153, 154, 198–199
Ottoman Empire 36, 42, 85, 201
Oviedo, Gonzalo Fernandez de 63

Pacific islanders 158–160
Pagden, Anthony 6, 19, 57, 61–64, 65, 70, 81, 93, 157
Paraguay 173
Parekh, Bhikhu 199, 200, 201, 215
particularism 205, 211
Pearce, Darryl 145
Pearson, Noel 151
'peoples' 53–55, 136, 141–142, 217–223
Peru 75, 100, 107
Phillimore, R. 97
pluralism 81, 163, 176–178, 186, 191–192, 221–223
plurality 47, 53, 64, 199, 222
Pocock, J. G. A. 149, 151
political organisation 31, 37, 182–183, 191, 199, 205 see also civil society
and Amerindians 76–77, 82, 98–99
and civilisation 52, 73, 104
political society 41, 51, 52, 77, 104, 111, 112
Indian 82, 85, 98, 100, 101
political theory 80, 83, 170, 185, 191, 199, 223
Portugal 42, 162
positivists 109
post-structuralism 197–198
principle of attachment 62, 63, 64
property 50, 51, 75–76, 95, 99 see also land
Locke on 6, 21, 76–80, 95, 97–100, 169–170
Pufendorf on 80, 96
Smith on 75
Vattel on 101, 111
Waldron on 169
property rights 20, 38, 75–79, 83, 93–98, 123, 169
Pufendorf, Samuel von 5, 74, 77, 80, 87, 88, 96–98

race 20, 47
racism 45, 47–48, 88, 165, 187, 195
scientific 66, 73
rationalism 4–5, 20, 23, 25–26, 81–82, 186–187, 190, 215
realism 3, 4, 81
recognition 23, 30–31, 145, 174, 201, 203–204, 215, 218–223
reconciliation 23, 172, 174, 218, 223
Remec, P. 109, 110

Renaissance 65, 68, 111
reparations 168–170, 172
revolutionism 4
rights 1, 3, 18, 33–34, 50, 53, 160
and cultural pluralism 176–177, 178–180, 202–210, 213, 214, 221–223
and international law 87–107, 108, 113, 153–154
and IR theory 23, 186, 187, 191
and self-determination 11–12, 126–136, 141–147, 151–152, 214, 218–220
and self-identification 13, 14
and sovereignty 152–153, 198
and states 11, 53–54
and the UN 14, 22
European attitudes to 19, 21, 35, 66, 71, 76, 111, 185
from indigenous perspective 138, 147–151
Rights of War and Peace, The 6, 87, 102
Roosevelt, Franklin D. 127
Rousseau, Jean-Jacques 75, 76–77
Rowse, Tim 1–2, 140–141, 173
rules 3–4, 112
and culture 192, 193, 213
and states 2, 27–28, 33, 81, 188, 200, 206, 217
Russia 38–39

Sahagún, Bernardino de 61
Said, Edward 158–159
savages 61–62, 64, 67, 72–74, 76, 158, 160
and 'state of nature' 76–77, 111
noble and ignoble 72, 74–76
scholasticism 87–88, 89, 94
self-determination 11–12, 18, 22, 23, 113, 126–136, 171, 211
and cultural membership 13, 178, 218, 222
and decolonisation 43, 113
and democracy 206, 214
and domination 197, 214–215
and law 54, 151–155, 217–223
and multiculturalism 202–204
and states 4, 114, 125, 152–153, 209, 213–215, 218–221
and the UN 114, 115, 119, 121–122, 210
indigenous perspectives of 147–151
obstacles to 136–147
self-identification 7, 12–13, 14, 49–50
self-preservation 79, 87, 109
Sepulveda, Juan Gines de 71, 89, 91–92, 108
Shapcott, Richard 5, 192–194, 215
slavery 34, 67, 70–71, 83, 87, 93

CAMBRIDGE STUDIES IN INTERNATIONAL RELATIONS